Working with **S**corporations

2nd Edition

A Practitioner's Guide To Estate, Business and Compensation Planning for S Corporations

Dennis C. Reardon J.D., LL.M., CLU, ChFC

NATIONAL UNDERWRITER®

The National Underwriter Co. • 505 Gest St. • Cincinnati, OH 45203-1716

Library of Congress Catalog Card Number: 96-69429

ISBN 0-87218-163-4

A publication of the Advanced Sales Reference
Department of The National Underwriter Company

Copyright © 1992, 1996
The National Underwriter Company

Second Edition

Printed in the United States of America

DEDICATION

To Lenore.

ACKNOWLEDGEMENTS

A note of appreciation to my clients, for giving me the opportunity to assist them in meeting their estate and business planning objectives, with or without S corporation complications.

I would like to express my gratitude to Rick Taylor, CPA, of Destree, DeYoung & Guldan, of Green Bay, Wisconsin, for his assistance with respect to Chapters 5, 6, and 7 in the first edition. Furthermore, his innovative work in regard to Grantor Retained Annuity Trusts (GRATs) was a significant reference in the new material on that topic that appears in Chapter 6.

I also express my appreciation to Darlene K. Chandler and Kimberely J. Adams of The National Underwriter Company for their editorial assistance.

My secretaries, Denise M. Carey and Geraldine Vecchiolli, deserve special thanks for their help in typing and organizing the second edition of this book.

I have dedicated the second edition of this book to my wife, Lenore, who, with our children, Elise and Daniel, has provided love and joy in my life.

ABOUT THE AUTHOR

Dennis C. Reardon is an attorney in Wayne, Pennsylvania. He specializes in tax matters related to estate, business, retirement and compensation planning. He is also an adjunct professor at The American College and a consultant to other professionals in regard to life insurance planning matters. He has previously held positions on the staff of the American Society of CLU and ChFC, Provident Mutual Life Insurance Company of Philadelphia, and The Hartford Insurance Group.

Mr. Reardon has spoken on tax and insurance planning topics at meetings of The American Institute of Certified Public Accountants (AICPA) Employee Benefits Conference; the Million Dollar Round Table (1986, 1988, 1990); the Association for Advanced Life Underwriting (AALU); the LIMRA Advanced Sales Forum; the Washington State Bar Association and Seattle Estate Planning Council; the New York City Estate Planning Council; the Philadelphia Association of Life Underwriters; CLU Institutes, the National Video Teleconference, and the Annual Meeting and Forum of the American Society of CLU and ChFC; Golden Key Society Seminars of the American College; the Mid-Atlantic Regional Conference of the IAFP; CLU chapters in Philadelphia, Baltimore, St. Louis, Dallas, Atlanta, Phoenix and many other sites; and groups of leading agents for numerous life insurance companies, as well as other professional groups.

In addition to writing on tax and benefit planning subjects for American Society of CLU and ChFC publications, his articles have appeared in the *Estates, Gifts and Trusts Journal*; *Estate and Financial Planners Quarterly*; *Financial Strategies*; and other industry publications. He is the editor of a chapter on life insurance and annuities in *Income Taxation of Individuals*, a publication of Matthew Bender Company. He has also developed the course materials and has been an instructor since 1987 for the Insurance Concepts course that is part of the Tax Management Seminars offered by KPMG Peat Marwick for continuing education of its professional staff.

Mr. Reardon is a graduate of the University of Connecticut (B.A.); Western New England College, School of Law (J.D.); Temple University (LL.M, Taxation); and has earned the designations of Chartered Life Underwriter (CLU) and Chartered Financial Consultant (ChFC) from the American College. He is a member of the bars of Pennsylvania and Massachusetts; the Pennsylvania and American Bar Associations; the Philadelphia Bar Association, along with its Taxation Section, and its Probate and Trust Law Section; and the Philadelphia Chapter of the American Society of CLU and ChFC. He is a past President of the Delaware County Estate Planning Council and is also a member of the Estate Planning Council of both Philadelphia and Chester Counties.

PREFACE

The second edition of this book preserves major portions of the same text contained in the first edition. However, it covers various developments that have occurred in the tax law during the nearly five-year period between the first and second editions.

Immediately prior to publication of this book, the Small Business Job Protection Bill of 1996 was signed into law. It amended several sections of the Internal Revenue Code that pertain to S corporation taxation. For instance, the maximum number of shareholders permitted to own stock in an S corporation has been increased from 35 to 75; qualified pension and profit-sharing plans and certain charitable organizations are now permitted to own S corporation stock; and the requirements of the election of a short taxable year have been revised. Perhaps the change of greatest interest to the readers of this book is the introduction of the "electing small business trust," which is designed to permit more flexibility in estate planning. The changes brought about by the Small Business Protection Bill of 1996 are incorporated throughout the text and appendices of this book.

In addition, individual income tax rates have changed; various final regulations pertaining to the Code sections governing S corporations have been issued; and other changes in the broader tax law have also occurred. Certain planning techniques have gained additional prominence, such as Grantor Retained Annuity Trusts (GRATs) and Intentionally Defective Irrevocable Trusts (IDITs). The merits of these techniques in conjunction with transfers of S corporation stock are discussed in Chapter 6 as a major addition to the book. Other subjects are also covered that are not necessarily peculiar to S corporations, but nonetheless affect life insurance planning for S corporation shareholder-employees, such as the position expressed by the IRS in regard to equity split dollar plans (see reference to TAM 9604001 in Chapter 4).

The purpose of this book is to concentrate on the estate, business and compensation planning areas that affect shareholders and employees of S corporations. More particularly, the book is focused on the life insurance funding applications that are a central part of a variety of planning techniques. This book has been written with the expectation that it will be read by those who are regularly involved in the estate, business and compensation planning for S corporation owners: life underwriters, attorneys and accountants. With that in mind, it does not purport to be a comprehensive reference on all aspects of S corporation planning. Much of the discussion contained in the text assumes the existence of an S corporation, and, in some instances, also assumes the reader's familiarity with a C corporation. In that regard, many of the situations described compare and contrast the tax planning result that would occur for either an S or a C corporation.

Chapter 1 offers a summary of the basic S corporation requirements and an overview of the tax rules concerning income, basis and distributions to shareholders. Chapter 1 is organized to provide a base of information that serves as a springboard for the discussion and analysis of particular S corporation planning techniques and treatment of life insurance policies that are contained in the rest of the book. The objective of Chapters 2, 3, and 4 is to describe how the operation of the S corporation tax rules influence three typical forms of life insurance policy ownership. Chapter 2 describes the planning applications in which "bonus plans" may be used for personally owned life insurance policies. Chapter 3 concentrates on how the S corporation tax rules affect premiums, cash values, dividends, and death proceeds of corporate owned life insurance. Particular attention is paid to how the S corporation shareholder's basis in stock is affected by the ongoing ownership of corporate owned life insurance. Chapter 4 deals with split dollar plans: it compares and contrasts how various types of split dollar plans may be designed and utilized for both C and S corporations.

Chapters 5 through 7 describe how a variety of estate, business and compensation planning techniques may be used by S corporation owners on behalf of themselves, their families and their employees. Chapter 5 covers alternative methods of structuring business continuation plans, focusing on the design and funding of buy-sell agreements and, once again, comparing and contrasting how such planning may be done for both S and C corporations. Chapter 6 contains an analysis of the ownership eligibility rules that govern trusts holding S corporation stock. It also considers the operation of those rules within a range of frequently encountered estate planning scenarios. Chapter 7 discusses compensation planning generally and benefit planning, in particular. It describes the tax treatment accorded to certain benefits provided for two percent shareholder-employees of S corporations, certain aspects of qualified and nonqualified deferred compensation plans and a few thoughts on other forms of compensation planning for S corporation owners and employees.

The chapters are followed by two appendices that contain supplementary material, including sections of the Internal Revenue Code and selected rulings and other pronouncements of the IRS pertaining to S corporations.

D.C.R.

September, 1996.

TABLE OF CONTENTS

Chapter 1

OVERVIEW OF THE S CORPORATION

INTRODUCTION

Subchapter S was added to the Internal Revenue Code by the Technical Amendments Act of 1958.[1] Its enactment was the eventual result of an earlier budget message recommendation by President Eisenhower that was aimed at avoiding the influence of federal income tax laws on the selection of the form of organization adopted by small businesses. Following a fizzled attempt to create a new law in 1954, Congress came up with a different approach in its creation of Subchapter S corporations in 1958. Part of its purpose was to eliminate the double taxation of corporate income. If a small business elected to be a Subchapter S corporation, its income would be taxed to its shareholders, and no corporate level tax would apply. The shareholders were taxed regardless of whether they actually *received* the income. Conversely, if an S corporation incurred a net operating loss, its shareholders enjoyed the tax benefit of deducting their respective shares of the loss against income reported on their individual returns. Until the widespread proliferation of S corporations that occurred after individual income tax rates were reduced by the Tax Reform Act of 1986, the ability to carry losses over to the shareholder's individual tax return frequently motivated S corporation elections. In many instances, S corporation status was elected for new businesses that anticipated operating losses before reaching profitability. For example, the owner of a more established business might set up a new operation as an S corporation. The S corporation election permitted losses to be carried over to an individual return while allowing the new business to enjoy the nontax advantages of incorporation.

In the ensuing years after the statutory creation of S corporations, the various sections of the Internal Revenue Code ("Code") controlling the taxation of S corporation shareholders have been amended as part of broader tax legislation. The next major chapter in the S corporation story occurred in 1982, when the Subchapter S Revision Act of 1982 (the

"Revision Act") was enacted.[2] The Revision Act introduced the term "S corporation," rather than the former designation of "Subchapter S corporation." More significantly, the Revision Act streamlined and simplified the tax treatment accorded businesses and their shareholders who had elected S corporation status. In general, the S corporation was treated as a flow through entity that would be taxed in a manner more similar to a partnership than had previously been the case. Generally, the Revision Act substituted Code sections 1361-1379 in place of the sections that had pertained before its enactment. Subject to certain exceptions, the Revision Act became effective for taxable years beginning after December 31, 1982.

The Tax Reform Act of 1986 (TRA '86) offers the next major development in S corporation history.[3] TRA '86, of course, was the most significant tax law revision of the past several decades. The 1986 Act redesignated the Code as the Internal Revenue Code of 1986. The sweeping new tax legislation was introduced by Congress, without a hint of irony, under the banner of "fairness, simplicity and efficiency." The so-called "blue book," formally known as *The General Explanation of the Tax Reform Act of 1986*," offers the following comments with respect to each of the broad legislative goals:[4]

1.   *Fairness*: "A primary objective of Congress was to provide a tax system that ensures that individuals with similar incomes pay similar amounts of tax ... With the adoption of these restrictions, the elimination of other preferences, and other base-broadening provisions, the Act sharply reduces the top individual tax rate from 50% to 28%, while leaving the tax burden of the highest income groups essentially unchanged."

2.   *Efficiency*: "The Act's most important measures in promoting the efficiency of the economy and in reducing the interference of the tax system in labor, investment, and consumption decisions are the dramatic reductions in personal and corporate tax rates. Lower marginal tax rates stimulate work effort and saving by leaving more of each additional dollar of wage and investment income in the hands of the taxpayer. Further, lower tax rates reduce the value of tax deductions, leading investment and consumption decisions to be made more on the basis of their economic merits and less on the value of tax benefits."

3.   *Simplicity*: "The Act reduces the complexity of the tax code for many Americans. The Act provides just two individual tax brackets ... The changes made by this Act represent a historic reform of the federal income tax structure. By providing sharply lower tax rates to individuals and corporations, the need for special tax preferences is greatly diminished."

When the smoke cleared, the highest effective *individual* tax rate was 28% and the highest effective *corporate* tax rate was 34%. (In addition, both the individual and the corporate tax systems imposed a five percent surtax that results in a marginal rate of 33% for individuals and 39% for corporations at certain levels of income.)

Prior to TRA '86, the highest marginal tax rates were 50% for individuals and 46% for corporations. A closely held corporation might have retained a portion of its earnings (and be subject to the corporate tax at a 15% rate, for example), rather than distribute its earnings to an owner who would have been taxed at progressively higher rates up to 50%. After TRA '86, apart from the effect of the five percent surtax, even the highest income earners were subject to an effective tax rate of only 28%. Consequently, many tax advisers had recommended S corporation status so that all of the income received by a shareholder-employee would be taxed at the 28% individual rate because an S corporation is generally not subject to the corporate income tax.

In addition, while TRA '86 eliminated preferential treatment of capital gains, it did not alter the tax rate applicable to dividend income. Owners of closely held corporations have traditionally dealt with the prospect of "double taxation" when earnings are accumulated within a business and subsequently withdrawn. As a result, most closely held C corporations avoid paying dividends. Shareholders active in the business prefer to receive the highest amount of "reasonable compensation" possible rather than a dividend that is nondeductible to the corporation. In contrast, the owner of an S corporation is taxed on any money received as compensation or as a distribution of earnings without any concern about whether the business is subject to taxation.

Since the enactment of TRA '86, a tremendous number of new and existing businesses have elected to become S corporations. While other factors may have played a part,[5] it is fair to say that reduced individual income tax rates were the principal motivation that inspired many S corporation elections.

The Revenue Act of 1987 also played a role in the growth of S corporation elections. The 1987 Act eliminated graduated income tax rates for "qualified personal service corporations" (QPSC).[6] A QPSC is specifically defined in Code section 448(d)(2). In general, it is a professional corporation, that is, an incorporated practice or business owned by doctors, lawyers, accountants, etc. The eradication of graduated income tax rates for these corporations means that the first dollar of taxable income realized by a QPSC that is a C corporation is taxed at a 34% rate. Professionals who decide to remain incorporated can choose one of two fundamental income tax planning strategies:

(1)   make sure that all of the corporation's income is paid out in the form of compensation, benefits and other expenses while maintaining C corporation status, or

(2)   elect S corporation status.

A growing number of professional corporations have elected to become S corporations, thereby permitting their owners to be taxed at individual income tax rates, with no intervening layer of corporate taxation.

INDIVIDUAL TAX RATES RISE AGAIN

The historically low individual income tax rates introduced by TRA '86 fell victim to the revenue needs of the government. The Revenue Reconciliation Act of 1990 created a 31% income tax bracket.[7] Individual tax rates nearly came full circle to their former levels (pre-TRA '86) when the Revenue Reconciliation Act of 1993 was signed into law. That Act added marginal rates of 36% and 39.6% above certain levels of income. As a result, the highest individual income tax rates are higher than the highest corporate tax rates — a reversal of the rate alignment that originally sparked the widespread adoption of S corporations several years ago.

Does the rise in individual income tax rates portend a lesser popularity for S corporations? It should not, and, in the author's experience, it has not, produced that effect. After all, an individual who draws substantial compensation from a C corporation is subject to the same income taxation as one who is a well-paid shareholder-employee of an S corporation. Furthermore, money left in a C corporation will be subject to a corporate tax rate that leads to double taxation for the shareholder-employee if a shareholder distribution is subsequently made.

EXAMPLE. Big Kath is the owner of The Okemo Spa, Inc. ("Spa"), a C Corporation. Big Kath files a joint income tax return with her husband, Big Ed. Big Kath and Big Ed draw combined annual salaries in excess of $250,000 and they usually also receive an additional bonus of 10% to 20% of their salaries. The Spa has had an exceptionally good year and Big Kath has the opportunity to pay herself a bonus of $100,000. After conferring with her financial advisers, Big Kath decides to take $50,000 as a bonus in the current year and leave the other $50,000 in the business because she wishes to avoid being taxed at a higher individual tax rate.

If the Spa were an S corporation, Big Kath would be taxed on the entire $100,000, whether she withdraws the money as a bonus or is taxed as a shareholder. However, because the Spa is a C corporation, if Big Kath takes a bonus of $50,000, the Spa would be taxed on the other $50,000 of corporate income. Even if the money left in the corporation can be paid out to Big Kath as compensation in a future year at a lesser individual rate than the maximum rate applicable in the current year if an S election were in effect, the difference in individual rates is not as significant as the added corporate tax that the Spa must pay as a C corporation. Specifically:

If the Spa is a C corporation:

	Additional Income to Big Kath	Additional Tax to Big Kath
Year 1	$ 50,000	$20,000
Year 2	$ 50,000	$20,000
Total	$100,000	$40,000

If the Spa is an S corporation:

	Additional Income to Big Kath	Additional Tax to Big Kath
Year 1	$100,000	$45,000
Year 2	0	0

Corporate taxation:

	C Corp Income	C Corp Tax	S Corp Income	S Corp Tax
Year 1	$50,000	$10,000	0	0
Year 2	0^8	0^8	0	0

In this example, it is assumed that Big Kath will be taxed at a 40% rate if the Spa is a C corporation and she will be taxed at a 45% rate if the Spa is an S corporation. The 40% and 45% rates represent the combined federal and state marginal income tax rate applicable to Big Kath and Big Ed after all deductions and credits are taken into account. Similarly, the 20% corporate income tax rate shown above assumes a combined federal and state income tax rate. Naturally, in a given state, local income tax rates applicable to individuals and corporations may vary significantly.

Even if the Spa is taxed at the lowest corporate tax rate, the overall cost to the corporation, and to Big Kath as a shareholder-employee, is greater if the Spa is a C corporation than if it were an S corporation. Unless significant tax legislation affecting corporate and individual rates emerges in the future, it is likely that those corporations currently operating as S corporations or C corporations will retain their status. Newly formed corporations are apt to elect S status unless individual business traits or particular financial circumstances of their owners direct otherwise.

S CORPORATION REQUIREMENTS

Code section 1361 defines an S corporation as a "small business corporation" for which an election under Section 1362(a) is in effect for a taxable year. In other words, without taking action otherwise, a business that incorporates is automatically a C corporation. As such, it is subject to the rules of the Code which impose a tax on the corporation's income. The S corporation rules offer an alternative system of taxation to a business owner.[9] The most important feature of the system is that the shareholders, rather than the corporation, are subject to income taxation. In addition, a number of particular requirements and limitations are imposed by the S corporation rules on its shareholders. And, there are other aspects of corporate taxation that still apply to S corporations because their operation is unchanged by the election to be an S corporation.[10]

The complete text of the relevant sections of the Internal Revenue Code pertaining to S corporations, including amendments made by the Small Business Job Protection Act of 1996, is reproduced in Appendix A. Our purpose in this chapter is to focus on those requirements that provide a foundation for understanding the estate, business and compensation planning techniques discussed in the following chapters.

Under Section 1361(b), certain restrictions are placed on a "small business corporation." These are:

(1)   Restrictions on the number of shareholders. Prior to 1997, an S corporation may have no more than 35 shareholders; however, for taxable years beginning after December 31, 1996, this number is increased to 75;

(2)   An S corporation must be owned by individuals who are not nonresident aliens, except that an estate and certain types of trusts may own stock;

(3)   An S corporation must be a domestic corporation;

(4)   An S corporation may have only one class of stock.

Certain types of corporations are not eligible to be classified as small business corporations. Prior to 1997, an S corporation shareholder may not be a member of an "affiliated group."[11] Under the Small Business Job

Protection Act of 1996, for tax years beginning after December 31, 1996, an S corporation may own 80% or more of the stock of a C corporation and may own a qualified subchapter S subsidiary. A qualified subchapter S subsidiary is defined as a domestic corporation that is not an ineligible corporation pursuant to Code section 1361(b)(2) if:

(i) 100% of the stock of such corporation is held by the S corporation, and

(ii) the S corporation elects to treat such corporation as a qualified subchapter S subsidiary.[12]

The Small Business Job Protection Act of 1996 also expanded eligible shareholders of S corporation stock to include qualified plans and certain charitable organizations. Effective for tax years beginning after December 31, 1997, Code section 1361(c)(7) provides:

(7) CERTAIN EXEMPT ORGANIZATIONS PERMITTED AS SHAREHOLDERS. — for purposes of subsection (b)(1)(B), an organization which is —

(A) described in section 401(a) or 501(c)(3), and

(B) exempt from taxation under section 501(a)

may be a shareholder in an S corporation.

The purpose of this provision is to ensure that the stepped-up basis in S corporation stock acquired from a decedent is reduced by the extent to which the stock value is attributable to items consisting of income in respect of a decedent. The provision puts S corporation shareholders on par with partners under a comparable basis rule for partnerships.

Special Rules

The Code provides certain "special rules" for purposes of applying the requirements of a "small business corporation."[13] For purposes of counting shareholders within the number of shareholder limitation, a husband and wife (and their estates) are treated as one shareholder.[14] If a spouse dies, the surviving spouse and the decedent's estate are still counted as one shareholder. With regard to the requirement that an S corporation may have only one class of stock, "differences in voting rights" among the shares of common stock *are* permitted.[15] Thus, one owner of an S corporation may have voting common stock and another shareholder may have nonvoting common stock within the one class of stock rule. In certain cases, as discussed in Chapter 5, gifts of nonvoting stock from father to son, for example, may offer estate and business planning advantages that present the opportunity to shift value within a family business without a loss of control by the senior generation.

One Class of Stock Requirement

A C corporation may have both common and preferred stock issued to its shareholders. In general, preferred stock shareholders have superior rights to that of the common stock shareholders with respect to the payment of dividends by the corporation, or a higher priority as to the receipt of proceeds in the event of a liquidation. Differences in voting rights may also exist between classes of common and preferred stock, or between different classes of common stock or preferred stock. In contrast, an S corporation may only have one class of stock, although differences in voting rights may exist so that shares of S corporation stock may be voting or nonvoting. The original rationale supporting the one class of stock requirement for S corporations was to ensure that the flow through system of taxation for S corporations could be administered on a straight-forward basis. In other words, the absence of a corporate tax bracket and the direct taxation of shareholders was thought to require a uniform method of ownership in order to permit a simple and fair administration of the tax system contemplated by the S corporation form.

The regulations to Code section 1361 describe the principles that control the determination of whether an S corporation has a single class of stock.[16] The requirement that an S corporation may have only one class of stock is satisfied if all of the outstanding shares of stock of the corporation confer identical rights to distribution and liquidation proceeds to the shareholders. An S corporation may not issue any instrument or obligation, or enter into any arrangement, that would have the effect of creating a second class of stock. In order to determine whether identical rights to distribution and liquidation proceeds are provided to the shareholders, reference may be made to the governing provisions of the corporate charter, the articles of incorporation and bylaws, binding agreements of the corporation or its shareholders, and applicable state law. In addition, even if the governing provisions of such corporate documents provide for identical rights to distributions, any actual, constructive, or deemed distributions that differ in timing or amount will be treated for tax purposes according to the facts and circumstances involved. In this regard, leases, employment agreements, or loan agreements, are not considered to be governing provisions of the corporation for purposes of determining whether rights to distributions from an S corporation are identical.[17]

The regulations to Section 1361 specify several key areas of shareholder rights that either conform to or violate the one class of stock requirement. The following is a brief review of particular rights that S corporation shareholders may have under the regulations.

Voting Rights. In addition to permitting voting stock and nonvoting stock, the regulations allow differences in voting rights for certain specified purposes. For example, a class of stock may vote only on particular issues, such as the right to elect members of the corporation's board of directors.

Redemption Agreements. Shareholders may enter into agreements to redeem or purchase stock in the event of death, divorce, disability, or termination of employment without violating the single class of stock requirement, provided that such an agreement:

(1)   does not have a principal purpose to circumvent the one class of stock requirement; and

(2)   does not establish a purchase price that, at the time the agreement is entered into, significantly deviates from the fair value of the stock.

The application of these standards to the design and operation of buy-sell agreements for S corporation shareholders is discussed in Chapter 5.

Deferred Compensation Plans. In addition to delineating permitted differences between shareholders as to rights with respect to stock ownership, certain plans of deferred compensation may, or may not, be regarded as constituting outstanding stock under the terms of the regulations. Under the regulations, an instrument, obligation or arrangement will not constitute outstanding stock for purposes of deferred compensation plans if it:

(1) does not convey the right to vote;

(2) is an unfunded and unsecured promise to future payment;

(3) is issued to an employee or to an independent contractor for the performance of services to the corporation; and

(4) is issued pursuant to a plan with respect to which the employee or independent contractor is not currently taxed on the income.[18]

This portion of the final regulations is discussed in Chapter 7.

Sections 1361(c)(2) and (d) furnish detailed definitions of those trusts that are permitted to own S corporation stock. These rules are covered in Chapter 6, which discusses estate planning considerations for S corporation shareholders.

Election

A corporation becomes an S corporation when its shareholders elect S status under the requirements of Code section 1362. As with most other elections under the federal tax law, those who benefit from the election must also accept the burden of various requirements and limitations.

In order for the S corporation election to be valid, all of the shareholders (on the day of the election) must consent to it.[19] Barring the acquisition of shares by an ineligible shareholder, the election continues whether the original shareholders continue to consent to it, and whether subsequent shareholders consent to it. The election to become an S corporation may be made at any time during the taxable year, but it will not be effective until the succeeding taxable year unless it is made on or before the 15th day of the third month of the current taxable year. Thus, an S corporation that will use the calendar year as its taxable year must complete its election by March 15 in order for it to apply in the current year.

The shareholders of an S corporation may revoke the election, provided that those owning more than one-half of the shares on the day on which the revocation is made consent to it.[20] Both voting shares and nonvoting shares are counted for this purpose.

Inadvertent Terminations

The requirements necessary for initial and continuing qualification for the S corporation election may be violated through an innocent act on the part of a shareholder. Section 1362(f) provides the following measure of relief:

(f) INADVERTENT INVALID ELECTIONS OR TERMINA-TIONS. — If —

(1) an election under subsection (a) by any corporation —

(A) was not effective for the taxable year for which made (determined without regard to subsection (b)(2)) by reason of a failure to meet the requirements of section 1361(b) or to obtain shareholder consents, or

(B) was terminated under paragraph (2) or (3) of subsection (d),

(2) the Secretary determines that the circumstances resulting in such ineffectiveness or termination were inadvertent,

(3) no later than a reasonable period of time after discovery of the circumstances resulting in such ineffectiveness or termination, steps were taken —

(A) so that the corporation is a small business corporation, or

(B) to acquire the required shareholder consents, and

(4) the corporation, and each person who was a shareholder in the corporation at any time during the period specified pursuant to this subsection, agrees to make such adjustments (consistent with the treatment of the corporation as an S corporation) as may be required by the Secretary with respect to such period,

then, notwithstanding the circumstances resulting in such ineffectiveness or termination, such corporation shall be treated as an S corporation during the period specified by the Secretary.

In practice, the Service has varied in its willingness to grant relief to S corporation shareholders who have invoked the inadvertent termination provision in ruling requests.[21]

In the event that an S corporation election is terminated under Section 1361(d), the corporation generally may not make another S election until the fifth taxable year which begins after the first taxable year for which the termination is effective.[22]

Calendar Year/Business Purpose Requirement

Most S corporations are established on a calendar year basis. Section 1378 provides that the taxable year of an S corporation shall be a "permitted year," which is a year ending on December 31 or any other accounting period for which the corporation establishes a business purpose to the satisfaction of the IRS.[23] Any deferral of income to shareholders will not be treated as a business purpose.

A full discussion of the "business purpose" requirement is beyond the scope of this chapter. However, the IRS has provided guidance in this area through the publication of Revenue Procedure 87-32.[24] That procedure sets forth two mechanical tests and a "facts and circumstances" test, which permits the IRS to exercise its discretion in determining whether a business purpose is established. The three tests described in Revenue Procedure 87-32 are:

1. The "natural business year/25% test," in which a corporation may use a non-calendar fiscal year if 25% or more of gross receipts are recognized in the last two months of the period, and that requirement has been met for three consecutive 12-month periods.

2. The "ownership tax year test," in which a non-calendar fiscal year is permitted if shareholders holding more than one half of issued and outstanding shares of stock have, or are currently changing to, the same tax year.

3. The "facts and circumstances test," in which the IRS may permit the use of a non-calendar fiscal year, but a clear business purpose must be established and it can be expected that the Service will be vigilant in its scrutiny of possible deferral or distortion of income.

In addition Revenue Ruling 87-57[25] illustrates several examples of the "business purpose" test and Notice 88-10[26] provides guidance for the election of taxable years by S corporations, partnerships and personal service corporations.

In general, the filing of the S corporation election by a corporation that had not previously adopted a specific taxable year will result in calendar year reporting, unless a particular fiscal year is requested and the corporation can satisfy the applicable requirements.

The standards indicated in Revenue Procedure 87-32 have been modified by the Service in administrative action taken in recent years. The modification pertains to the standards used to determine whether the IRS will grant an extension of time to make a fiscal year election when the election's due date is fixed by regulation or other published guidance. The election to use a tax year other than a required tax year qualifies for an automatic 12-month extension.[27]

Accounting Methods

Under Code section 448, significant limitations on the election of the cash method of accounting are in effect for certain types of C corporations. An S corporation generally is not subject to the same rules (unless it is classified as a "tax shelter" as defined under Code section 461(i)(3)).

In addition to the cash receipts and disbursements method, an S corporation may also use:

1. the accrual method;

2. the installment method; or

3. any method that clearly reflects income.[28]

THE "FLOW THROUGH" CONCEPT

The S corporation tax rules are built around the general principle that the shareholder, rather than the S corporation, is taxed on the income of the business, after deductions are taken into account. In many ways, the rules governing income and deductions for S corporations are the same as those governing C corporations. However, because an S corporation is not a separate entity, a series of rules have been developed in the Code with respect to the taxation of an S corporation's shareholders. An S corporation is often described as being a conduit or a "flow through" entity for income tax purposes. Although the corporation is not a separate entity for income tax purposes, the tax consequences that the shareholders ultimately experience begin at the corporation's level. In other words, income and deductions, or gains and losses, are determined at the entity level before being allocated to the shareholders. The income, deductions, etc. of the corporation are either passed through to the shareholders directly, or are passed through to the shareholders, but subject to further qualification at the shareholder level. The Code distinguishes between *separately* and *nonseparately* computed items of income, loss, deduction or credit.

Specifically, Section 1366(a)(1) states that the shareholders must take into account a pro rata share of the corporation's "(A) items of income (including tax-exempt income), loss, deduction, or credit, the separate treatment of which could affect the liability for tax of any shareholder, and (B) nonseparately computed income or loss."

In typical fashion, the Code backs into a definition of "nonseparately computed income or loss." Section 1366(a)(2) defines *nonseparately* computed income or loss as gross income minus deductions allowed to the corporation, determined by excluding all *separately* computed items.

In general, a separately computed item is taken into account by itself because it can affect the tax treatment of an individual shareholder. Examples of separately computed items include capital gains and losses, charitable contributions, tax-exempt interest, and investment interest expenses. The S corporation reports separately stated items to each shareholder, who then takes the item into account on his or her income tax return.

EXAMPLE. George and Herman are each 50% shareholders of an S corporation. The corporation borrows money to finance the purchase of an investment asset and incurs $12,000 of investment interest expense. An allocation of $6,000 of investment interest expense is made to each shareholder. That expense will be fully or partially deductible, or nondeductible, in the current year, depending upon whether each shareholder has investment income against which it may be offset, under the rules contained in Section 163(d) limiting the deductibility of investment interest expense.

In effect, nonseparately computed income or loss represents a "basket" approach to determining the amount of income or loss realized by the corporation that is allocable to each shareholder. All items that do not require separate allocation are lumped together, so that deductions are offset against income in order to determine a net income or loss figure. A detailed list of examples of separately stated items is contained in IRS Publication 589, "Tax Information on S Corporations."

Unless an election is made to terminate the S corporation's taxable year,[29] Section 1377(a)(1) indicates that items of taxable income or loss etc., are computed on a "per share, per day" basis. All of the tax items are allocated to each shareholder on a pro rata basis according to the number of shares owned by the shareholder compared to the shares outstanding on each day of the taxable year.

EXAMPLE. An S corporation earns $300,000 of net income in its taxable year (which is the calendar year). From January 1 until June 30, Elise is the corporation's sole shareholder. On July 1, Schaefer and Shelby each acquire a 25% interest in the corporation. The allocation of income to the three shareholders would be as follows:

SHAREHOLDER	OWNERSHIP	DAYS IN PERIOD	PRO RATA SHARE
Elise	100%	181/365	49.6%
Elise	50%	184/365	25.2%
Schaefer	25%	184/365	12.6%
Shelby	25%	184/365	12.6%
Total Percentage			100%

Character of Income

Code section 1366(b) indicates that the character of any item included in a shareholder's pro rata share is determined as if the shareholder had realized the item directly from its source or incurred it in the same manner as the corporation. Generally, this means that the character of income, that is, whether it is taxable or tax exempt, is determined at the corporate level, and that character is also passed through to the shareholder.

EXAMPLE. An S corporation owns a $600,000 insurance policy on the life of a 50% shareholder. If the insured shareholder dies, the corporation receives $600,000 of life insurance proceeds, which are tax exempt under Code section 101(a). The tax exempt income is passed through to the shareholders according to the "per share, per day rule."

OBSERVATION. The determination of the character of the income is made according to how it is incurred at the corporate level. The "character rule" is consistent with the "flow through" principle, which generally applies to S corporation shareholders. However, further transactions may alter the tax treatment to a shareholder. For instance, life insurance proceeds are tax exempt to the shareholder because the nontaxable character of the proceeds is passed through to the shareholder. A subsequent disposition of the proceeds, such as payment of compensation to an employee, or a capital investment by the corporation, or a redemption of stock from a shareholder's estate, will produce tax consequences consistent with the additional event.

BASIS

A shareholder's basis in S corporation stock is initially determined in the same manner as for the owner of a C corporation. Basis consists of property transferred to the corporation in exchange for the S stock, or, if stock is purchased from another person, basis is equal to the price paid for the stock. However, tracking basis over a period of time for the owner of an S corporation is considerably more complicated than for the owner of a C corporation. In a sense, tracking basis is the price paid by a shareholder for the benefit of avoiding a corporate tax. The basis of the S corporation shareholder is subject to constant adjustment according to the financial experience of the corporation.

Code section 1367 sets forth the general rules for basis adjustments. A shareholder's basis is *increased* by both separately computed and nonseparately computed items of income. In addition, basis is increased by the excess of depletion deductions over the basis of property subject to depletion. *Furthermore, basis is increased whether income is taxable or tax-exempt.* Thus, for example, life insurance proceeds payable to an S corporation increase a shareholder's basis in stock (according to the amount of income allocated to the shareholder under the per share, per day rule).

In general, a shareholder's basis is *decreased* by the total of the following items determined with respect to the shareholder:[30]

1. Distributions by the corporation which were not includable in the shareholder's income;

2. Separately computed items of loss and deduction;

3. Any nonseparately computed loss;

4. Any expense of the corporation not deductible in computing its taxable income and not properly chargeable to capital account; and

5. The amount of the shareholder's deduction for depletion for any oil and gas property held by the S corporation to the extent such deduction does not exceed the proportionate share of the adjusted basis of such property allocated to such shareholder under Section 613A(c)(11)(B).

A shareholder's basis in stock cannot be reduced below zero, that is, it cannot be a negative number. If a shareholder's basis in S stock is reduced to zero, further reductions in basis (because of items specified in Section 1367(a)(2)(B)-(E) (separately and nonseparately computed loss items, nondeductible expenses, etc.)) are applied to reduce the shareholder's basis in any indebtedness of the corporation to the shareholder. However, just as for the shareholder's basis in stock, the shareholder's basis in debt also cannot be reduced below zero.[31] Following a reduction in the shareholder's basis in debt, any net increases in basis are applied to restore the shareholder's basis in debt before it may be used to increase the shareholder's basis in stock.[32]

The basis rules generally reflect a pattern that a shareholder's basis is increased as income is received by the corporation and basis is decreased as expenses or losses are incurred, or with respect to basis in stock, as nontaxable distributions are made to the shareholder. To step back from the detail of the basis rules for a broader view, the underlying concept is that the S corporation shareholder's basis is constantly expanding and contracting in reaction to the corporation's financial flow. Increases in basis are a reflection of events that make stock in the corporation more valuable as income is received, and decreases in basis reflect loss of value as expenses or distributions are paid.

EXAMPLES: MR. MONEY AND MR. WORK

Many of the rules governing S corporation taxation may seem artificial and hard to understand when viewed in isolation. Perhaps a series of examples is the best way to illustrate the operation of the fundamental rules governing the income and expenses of the S corporation and the effect on its shareholders. The purpose of the following examples is to provide a working understanding to those who are interested in being involved in the estate, business and benefit planning of S corporation owners without getting lost in the minutiae of the tax rules that regulate the financial comings and goings of S corporations and their owners.

Formation

Mr. Money and Mr. Work decide to set up an S corporation for a new business venture. Mr. Money contributes $80,000 to the corporation and receives 80 shares of stock; Mr. Work contributes $20,000 and receives 20 shares of stock. Mr. Money and Mr. Work will both be employed by the S corporation. However, Mr. Work, true to form, will spend far more time in providing services to the corporation than will Mr. Money, who has provided most of the capital to the business.

S Corporation Income

Assume that the corporation earns $100,000 in the first year of its existence and that it has no expenses. The taxable income of the S corporation will pass through to Mr. Money and Mr. Work in proportion to their stock ownership. Therefore, as the owner of 80% of the stock, Mr.

Money will have $80,000 of taxable income. Mr. Work, as the owner of 20% of the stock, will have $20,000 of taxable income.

It is important to realize that Mr. Money and Mr. Work will be taxed on these amounts *whether or not the income is distributed to them*! For the moment, however, we will assume that all income of the corporation to which they are entitled as shareholders is distributed to them.

Salaries

Suppose that Mr. Money and Mr. Work decide to draw salaries from the corporation for their services. Mr. Money, the controlling stockholder, decides that his salary should be $20,000. However, in recognition of Mr. Work's contributions, he allows Mr. Work to have a salary of $30,000.

The $50,000 of salary expense is deductible to the S corporation under Code section 162 just as it would be if the business were a C corporation. After deducting $50,000 of salary expense from the S corporation's gross income of $100,000, the taxable income of the corporation is $50,000. *As shareholders*, Mr. Money and Mr. Work are charged with $40,000 and $10,000 of income, respectively, in proportion to their stock ownership.

At the end of the year, each has the following income from the corporation:

Mr. Money

Salary	$20,000
Shareholder Income	40,000
Total Income	$60,000

Mr. Work

Salary	$30,000
Shareholder Income	10,000
Total Income	$40,000

The salaries paid to Mr. Work and Mr. Money represent amounts received by them *as employees* for services rendered to the S corporation. Compensation paid to employees, whether in the form of salary or bonus, is deductible to the S corporation provided that it is reasonable, that is, it is an ordinary and necessary business expense under Section 162. However, to the extent that the S corporation realizes taxable income after deducting compensation and other items, it is taxed to the shareholders in proportion to their stock ownership, rather than at the entity level.

OBSERVATION. A shareholder employed by an S corporation generally receives both salary and dividends from the business. A couple of thoughts to keep in mind regarding the allocation of salary and dividends:

1.   Dividends are generally avoided by the shareholder of a closely held corporation because income taxation occurs at both the corporate and shareholder levels. Typically, a shareholder-employee of a C corporation will receive a bonus within the limits of "reasonable compensation" under Section 162, if possible, rather than allow a dividend to be paid to him or her. Dividends paid by an S corporation are simply another form of income to a shareholder-employee, taxed only at the individual level. If the S corporation is owned by a sole shareholder, the choice between a bonus or the receipt of a dividend does not usually make much difference in regard to income tax consequences.

2.   When two or more shareholders own stock in an S corporation, the payment of a bonus for services rendered to a shareholder-employee necessarily reduces the dividends available for distribution to *all* shareholders. Maintaining a consistent policy regarding the allocation of salary, bonus and dividend payments to shareholder-employees can become a critical issue, especially in multi-shareholder situations or in cases involving shareholders having different levels of participation in the business as employees.

The issue of whether compensation is reasonable, and therefore, deductible, is, generally, not as critical for an S corporation as it is for a C corporation when payments are made to a shareholder employee. However, characterization of payments as shareholder distributions or compensation may make a great deal of difference in life insurance planning. These differences are explored in greater depth in later chapters. For the moment, let's return to the tax treatment received by Mr. Work and Mr. Money in dealing with their S corporation.

Basis

A shareholder's basis in S corporation stock is constantly affected by the income received and expenses incurred by the corporation. Specifically, basis is *increased* as income is received and *decreased* as expenses are paid. A crucial fact of life in S corporation compensation planning is that the shareholder is taxed on income earned by the corporation, *whether or not the income is received by the shareholder*. This apparently harsh rule of taxation without receipt is balanced by the rule governing calculation of the shareholder's basis. Specifically, income that is received by the S corporation and taxed to its shareholders, but not distributed to them, will proportionately increase the basis of each shareholder's stock. If the income remains in the corporation, the shareholder's basis is higher than if it is distributed to him or her.

Let's return to Mr. Money and Mr. Work in order to illustrate this point. The basis of the two shareholders is calculated as follows:

1. Initial contribution of cash in exchange for stock

	Mr. Money	**Mr. Work**
Contribution	$80,000	$20,000
Basis	$80,000	$20,000

2. Increase basis by S corporation income of $100,000

	Mr. Money	**Mr. Work**
Basis	$ 80,000	$20,000
Plus Income	$ 80,000	$20,000
Basis	$160,000	$40,000

3. Decrease by expenses (salaries) of the S corporation of $50,000

	Mr. Money	**Mr. Work**
Basis	$160,000	$40,000
Less Expenses	$ 40,000	$10,000
Basis	$120,000	$30,000

If the corporation did not distribute its $50,000 of net income ($100,000 income minus $50,000 expenses) to the shareholders, the basis of each shareholder would remain at the level shown. Nonetheless, the shareholders would be taxed on the corporation's net income even though they did not receive the money as a distribution. However, if the $50,000 were distributed to the shareholders, the basis of each shareholder would be decreased proportionately, as shown below.

4. Decrease by $50,000 distribution

	Mr. Money	**Mr. Work**
Basis	$120,000	$30,000
Distribution	$ 40,000	$10,000
Basis	$ 80,000	$20,000

As a result, as far as basis is concerned, Mr. Money and Mr. Work are back to where they started! It is worth mentioning that both the compensation paid to them *as employees* and the distributions made to them *as shareholders* result in a lower basis to Mr. Money and Mr. Work. Thus, each shareholder's basis has returned to its starting point whether the corporation compensated them as employees or paid distributions to them as shareholders. Either form of payment by the corporation reduces basis proportionately to the shareholders.

However, from the standpoint of how money is *received* by a shareholder-employee (i.e., as compensation to an employee or a distribution to a shareholder), different considerations apply. Distributions made to S corporation shareholders are necessarily in direct proportion to the respective amounts of stock owned by each shareholder (see next section of this chapter in regard to S corporation distributions). Salaries and other forms of compensation are paid by the S corporation to an employee (who may also be a shareholder) for services rendered without regard to stock ownership.

If an S corporation pays out all of its income in a particular year in the form of compensation and distributions, the basis of each shareholder returns to the same amount as it had been at the start of the year. Compensation payments will naturally vary according to services performed, but distributions must necessarily be paid in direct proportion to stock ownership. If a greater amount of the corporation's net income is paid as a bonus, that much less is available for a dividend distribution to the owners.

For example, suppose that the remaining $50,000 of the corporation's income had been paid as a bonus to Mr. Work, rather than in the form of shareholder distributions to him and Mr. Money. Each owner's basis would still be reduced to the same amount, but the total compensation to each would be:

5. Pay $50,000 bonus to Mr. Work

	Mr. Money	Mr. Work
Salary	$20,000	$30,000
Bonus	$ 0	$50,000
Distribution	$ 0	$ 0

If Mr. Money were not so magnanimous, and the remaining $50,000 were distributed to the shareholders, the allocation of salary and dividends would be as follows:

6. Distribute $50,000 to Shareholders

	Mr. Money	Mr. Work
Salary	$20,000	$30,000
Distribution	$40,000	$10,000
Total Income	$60,000	$40,000

Effective for decedents dying after August 20, 1996, the Small Business Job Protection Act of 1996 added the following special rule pertaining to basis adjustments for inherited S corporation stock. Code section 1367(b)(4)(A) and (B) provides:

(4) ADJUSTMENTS IN CASE OF INHERITED STOCK. —

(A) IN GENERAL. — If any person acquires stock in an S corporation by reason of the death of a decedent or by bequest, devise, or inheritance, section 691 shall be applied with respect to any item of income of the S corporation in the same manner as if the decedent had held directly his pro rata share of such item.

(B) ADJUSTMENTS TO BASIS. — The basis determined under section 1014 of any stock in an S corporation shall be reduced by the portion of the value of the stock which is attributable to items constituting income in respect of the decedent.

DISTRIBUTIONS

The tax treatment resulting from a distribution by an S corporation to a shareholder varies according to whether or not the corporation has earnings and profits (E&P).

S Corporations Having No Earnings and Profits

The rule governing the taxation of a distribution by an S corporation having no E&P is straightforward and simple. Code section 1368(b) indicates that, in such a case, a distribution:

(1)   reduces adjusted basis, and

(2)   to the extent that the distribution exceeds adjusted basis, the excess is taxed as gain from the sale or exchange of property.

How is the determination made as to whether an S corporation has E&P? Earnings and profits is a function of the experience of a C corporation. A newly-formed business that elects to be an S corporation does not have any concern with regard to E&P (assuming that the S election was made after 1982).

Income earned by an S corporation increases the basis of its shareholders. If a shareholder is taxed upon income that is *not* distributed to him, his basis remains increased, thereby permitting a subsequent distribution of such income to be nontaxable. On the other hand, income that is distributed to a shareholder in the same year in which it is earned causes a corresponding decrease in the shareholder's basis in the same taxable year.

Thus, a shareholder receiving a distribution from a corporation having no E&P simply reduces basis, and, if basis is exhausted, treats the remaining portion of the distribution as capital gain.

S Corporations Having Earnings and Profits

An S corporation having E&P falls into one of three categories:

(1)   operation as an S or C corporation prior to 1983;

(2)   operation as a C corporation after 1982 and prior to S corporation election; or

(3)   acquisition of another corporation having earnings or profits.

In the vast majority of situations, an S corporation with E&P has carried over the earnings and profits from its existence as a C corporation. A distribution by an S corporation having E&P must necessarily take into account such earnings and profits before the usual rule governing S corporation distributions can apply. Otherwise, the mere conversion of a C corporation to an S corporation would permit the S corporation owner to have an unfair tax advantage in comparison to the result that would have occurred if C corporation status had been maintained.

Simply put, if a distribution to a C corporation shareholder would have been a dividend before the S election, it will remain a dividend after the S election is in effect. In fact, the rules applicable to the taxation of a shareholder who receives a distribution by an S corporation with E&P are identical to those governing a distribution by a C corporation to a shareholder. In defining the general rule for taxation of S corporation distributions, Code section 1368(a) refers to Code section 301(c), which establishes a system ordering the tax treatment of C corporation distributions, as follows:

(1)   to the extent of earnings and profits, a dividend includable in the gross income of the shareholder;

(2)   a reduction in the shareholder's adjusted basis; and

(3)   in excess of adjusted basis, gain from the sale or exchange of property.

As a matter of convenience, tax planning practitioners loosely refer to distributions made to a (C corporation) shareholder on account of stock ownership as "dividends." That characterization is correct, as far as it goes. Dividends are a direct product of earnings and profits that are available for distribution. However, a distribution may exceed the E&P of a corporation. Distributions that exceed E&P amount to a distribution of property from the original or ongoing contribution of capital to the shareholder, that is, from basis, and, if sizable enough, from the appreciated value of such contributed property, that is, gain in value of the corporation.

The Small Business Job Protection Act of 1996 adopted a rule pertaining to an S corporation's accumulated earnings and profits, effective for tax years beginning after December 31, 1996. The following House Committee Report describes the effect of the provision:

Elimination of Certain Earnings and Profits. The provision provides that if a corporation is an S corporation for its first taxable year beginning after December 31, 1996, the accumulated earnings and profits of the corporation as of the beginning of that year is reduced by the accumulated earnings and profits (if any) accumulated in any taxable year beginning before January 1, 1983, for which the corporation was an electing small business corporation under subchapter S. Thus, such a corporation's accumulated earnings and profits are solely attributable to taxable years for which an S election was not in effect. This rule is generally consistent with the change adopted in 1982 limiting the S shareholder's taxable income attributable to S corporation earnings to his or her share of the taxable income of the S corporation.

The intent of the provision is to eliminate unnecessarily complicated corporate record keeping.

The Accumulated Adjustments Account

Life becomes more complicated when an S corporation with E&P defers a distribution of income until a year subsequent to the taxable year in which it is recognized to the shareholders. If a corporation has E&P, and its shareholder is taxed on income which is not distributed, that income is accounted for by the maintenance of an accumulated adjustments account

(AAA). AAA is equal to an S corporation's income that is taxed to its shareholders for all S corporation years minus the amount of income that has been distributed to its shareholders. AAA is tracked primarily to avoid taxing a shareholder twice on the same income.

Section 1368(e)(1) defines AAA as being an S corporation account which is adjusted in a manner similar to basis under Section 1367, with certain exceptions. Unlike basis, no AAA adjustments are made for tax exempt income. In addition, adjustments may be made without regard to the "not below zero" rule limiting basis reductions for a shareholder's indebtedness, and adjustments cannot be made for federal taxes attributable to taxable years when the corporation was a C corporation.

AAA was devised as part of the Revision Act of 1982. To a great extent, it serves the same function that was provided by the previously taxed income (PTI) concept of pre-Revision Act law. A review of the differences between the PTI concept that pertained under former law and AAA that applies to the operation of S corporations after 1982 is beyond the scope of our purpose in this chapter. However, one difference that deserves mention is that, unlike PTI, AAA is *transferable* to another shareholder. In other words, if shares are sold or otherwise transferred by an S corporation owner to another shareholder, the new shareholder assumes ownership of the AAA that was allocated to the shares of the former shareholder. The shareholder who assumes the AAA allocated to the newly-acquired shares also receives the corresponding right to have a tax-free distribution of income that AAA allows.

AAA is maintained for S corporations with E&P in order to keep track of income which has been taxed to shareholders, but not distributed to them. For an S corporation *without* E&P, there is no need to maintain AAA. In that case, if income is earned by the corporation and taxed to its shareholders, but not distributed to them, basis remains increased until a distribution is made in a subsequent year. The need to maintain AAA is triggered by the presence of E&P in the S corporation. When distributions are made by an S corporation that has E&P and AAA, Code section 1368 imposes an overlay of rules upon the general principle of "basis first, then gain" that is the foundation for distributions by *any* S corporation.

Specifically, Section 1368(c) establishes a system designed to prevent double taxation of a shareholder while also requiring a distribution of E&P to be taxed as a dividend in the same manner as if it were made from a C corporation. In tracking distributions made by an S corporation with E&P and AAA, the following rules of traffic direct the taxation of such distributions:

(1)   A distribution reduces AAA according to the "basis first, then gain" rule;

(2)   Any distribution in excess of AAA is treated as a dividend to the extent that it does not exceed the accumulated E&P of the corporation;

(3)   Any adjusted basis remaining after the reduction attributable to (1) is further reduced; and

(4)   After basis has been reduced to zero, the remaining distribution is treated as gain from the sale or exchange of property.

EXAMPLE. Daniel is the sole owner of a corporation which had $100,000 of accumulated earnings and profits at the time an S election was made in 1987. In 1990, Daniel was charged with $50,000 of taxable income earned by the corporation, but not distributed to him. As a result, the $50,000 became assigned to AAA. Prior to a $350,000 distribution to him in 1991, he had an adjusted basis of $200,000 in his S corporation stock. The 1991 distribution to Daniel is taxed in the following manner:

$350,000 DISTRIBUTION	CHARACTER	BASIS (AFTER DISTRIBUTION)
1. First $50,000	Tax free; Eliminates AAA; reduces basis	$150,000
2. Next $100,000	Dividend	$150,000
3. Next $150,000	Tax free; Reduces basis	0
4. Final $50,000	Capital gain	0

The structure of the rules governing distributions dictates that AAA is reduced first because the shareholder has already been taxed on the AAA amount. However, Section 1368(e)(3) permits an S corporation to elect to have E&P taxed prior to any reduction of AAA. It should be noted that the election is described as being available to the S corporation "...with the consent of all of its affected shareholders." An "affected shareholder" means any shareholder to whom a distribution is made by the S corporation during the taxable year.[33] Generally, S corporation shareholders will not elect to receive taxable dividends rather than tax-free distributions from AAA.

S corporations that have PTI carried over from pre-1983 years, as well as post-1982 AAA, and accumulated E&P have to consider PTI within the ordering of distributions described above. In those cases, *cash* distributions in excess of AAA are considered to be from PTI; after PTI is exhausted, further distributions are considered to come from accumulated E&P.

If an S corporation incurs losses, it is possible that AAA could become a *negative* balance. Unlike basis, which cannot be reduced below zero, AAA may reach a negative level as continuing adjustments attributable to losses and deductions reduce it below zero. If that happens, the negative AAA must be restored to a positive figure before tax-free distributions can be made.

The Small Business Job Protection Act of 1996 modifies certain rules pertaining to AAA and distributions. Specifically, with respect to any distribution made during the taxable year, the adjusted basis of stock is to be determined with regard to basis increases specified in Code section 367(a)(1), which includes items of S corporation income, etc. Basis adjustments for distributions are taken into account prior to applying the loss limitation for the year. Consequently, distributions reduce adjusted basis for determining the allowable loss for a year, but the loss for a year does not reduce the adjusted basis for purposes of determining the tax status of distributions made during that year.

In addition, in determining the amount of AAA for purposes of determining how distributions are taxed to a shareholder of an S corporation with accumulated E&P, net negative adjustments (i.e., the excess of losses and deductions over income) for that taxable year are disregarded.

The operation of these provisions is illustrated by the following examples contained in the House Committee Report to Section 1309 of the Small Business Job Protection Act of 1996:

EXAMPLE 1. X is the sole shareholder of corporation A, a calendar year S corporation with no accumulated earnings and profits. X's adjusted basis in the stock of A on January 1, 1998, is $1,000 and X holds no debt of A. During 1998, A makes a distribution to X of $600, recognizes a capital gain of $200 and sustains an operating loss of $900. Under the bill, X's adjusted basis in the A stock is increased to $1,200 ($1,000 plus $200 capital gain recognized) pursuant to section 1368(d) to determine the effect of the distribution. X's adjusted basis is then reduced by the amount of the distribution to $600 ($1,200 less $600) to determine the application of the loss limitation of section 1366(d)(1). X is allowed to take into account $600 of A's operating loss, which reduces X's adjusted basis to zero. The remaining $300 loss is carried forward pursuant to section 1366(d)(2).

EXAMPLE 2. The facts are the same as in Example 1, except that on January 1, 1998, A has accumulated earnings and profits of $500 and an accumulated adjustments account of $200. Under the bill, because there is a net negative adjustment for the year, no adjustment is made to the accumulated adjustments account before determining the effect of the distribution under section 1368(c).

As to A, $200 of the $600 distribution is a distribution of A's accumulated adjustments account, reducing the accumulated adjustments account to zero. The remaining $400 of the distribution is a distribution of accumulated earnings and profits ("E&P") and reduces A's E&P to $100. A's accumulated adjustments account is then increased by $200 to reflect the recognized capital gain and reduced by $900 to reflect the operating loss, leaving a negative balance in the accumulated adjustments account on January 1, 1999, of $700 (zero plus $200 less $900).

As to X, $200 of the distribution is applied against X's adjusted basis of $1,200 ($1,000 plus $200 capital gain recognized), reducing X's adjusted basis to $1,000. The remaining $400 of the distribution is taxable as a dividend and does not reduce X's adjusted basis. Because X's adjusted basis is $1,000, the loss limitation does not apply to X, who may deduct the entire $900 operating loss. Accordingly, X's adjusted basis on January 1, 1999, is $100 ($1,000 plus $200 less $200 less $900).

These provisions put the treatment of distributions by S corporations during loss years on par with the applicable rules for partnership taxation. As a result, because the adjustment for distributions is made before adjustments to basis, in a loss year, S corporation shareholders have a broadened opportunity for tax-free treatment of a distribution.

AAA and Stock Redemptions

If an S corporation redeems stock in a manner that qualifies as an exchange under Code sections 302 or 303, AAA is also adjusted when the stock is redeemed. Specifically, a portion of AAA is reduced in the same proportion as the amount of stock that is redeemed.[34]

EXAMPLE. Yolanda and Zeke own 60 shares and 40 shares, respectively, of an S corporation that has $200,000 of AAA. Following Zeke's death, the corporation completely redeems the stock held by his estate in a manner that qualifies as an exchange under Section 302. The ratio of the number of shares redeemed in comparison to the number of shares owned by both shareholders is 40% (Zeke's 40 shares ÷ 100 shares). Correspondingly, AAA is reduced by 40% of $200,000, or $80,000. After the redemption, Yolanda owns all 60 shares outstanding and her shares have $120,000 of AAA attributed to them.

S CORPORATIONS AND LLCS

Recently another business form which provides for flow through taxation, the limited liability company or LLC, has received much attention. Nearly all states have passed legislation recognizing this type of business entity. Like an S corporation, an LLC offers its owners the flow through taxation of a partnership while at the same time providing the corporate characteristic of limited liability.

An LLC does not have partners or shareholders, but rather those owning an interest in the LLC are termed "members." All of the members of the LLC may have a say in the management of the business in a manner similar to the partners in a partnership. On the other hand, the LLC may be structured so that the day-to-day management activities are handled by a few managers. These managers may also be members and thus are referred to as member-managers. However, for the most part there is no requirement that a manager be a member of the LLC.

Before looking further at the characteristics of the LLC, it should be noted that since the LLC is a relatively new type of business form, some issues surrounding its use may not yet be firmly settled.

Creating the Business Entity

As mentioned earlier in this chapter, an S corporation must file an election to be granted S corporation status. There is no similar requirement for an LLC. However, because an operating agreement must be drawn up for an LLC, the process of creating this type of business entity may take more time than the process of creating an S corporation.

After the LLC is established, the chances of losing the flow through taxation of a partnership are less than the chances of, even inadvertently, terminating the S corporation election. On the other hand, if the owners or members of the entity want to terminate the flow through taxation, it is fairly easy for an S corporation to do so by violating the eligibility rules. It is not as simple for an LLC to be restructured so that it is taxed as a corporation.

Number and Type of Owners

Under Code section 1361, S corporations are limited to a certain number of shareholders. Prior to 1997 this number was 35. For taxable years beginning after December 31, 1996, the maximum number of shareholders for an S corporation is 75. In contrast, LLCs are not limited as to the number of persons or entities that may own an LLC interest. Generally, an LLC must have at least two members[35] while an S corporation may have only a single shareholder.

Furthermore, an S corporation may not have certain persons and entities as shareholders. Only individual United States residents, estates, and certain types of trusts can hold shares in an S corporation without triggering a termination of the S corporation election. For taxable years beginning after 1997, an S corporation may have tax-exempt organizations as described in Code sections 401(a) and 501(c)(3) as shareholders.[36] An LLC may be owned by all these individuals and entities plus nonresident aliens, partnerships, and corporations.

Prior to 1997, an S corporation was prohibited from being a member of an affiliated group.[37] Thus, an S corporation could not own 80% or more of the stock in a subsidiary. For taxable years beginning after 1996, an S corporation can own more than 80% of the stock in a C corporation. Also, an S corporation may own a qualified subchapter S subsidiary.[38] An LLC can own a subsidiary.

One Class of Stock Requirement

An S corporation may have only a single class of stock while an LLC is not saddled with a similar restriction. Thus, an S corporation's stock must confer identical rights to distributions and liquidation proceeds.[39] An LLC may have numerous classes of membership interests. Thus, an LLC may issue ownership interests with different dividend or liquidation rights.[40]

Also, LLCs can make special allocations under Code section 704(b). Thus, an LLC may allocate items of gain, loss, and deduction in any manner it wishes as long as the method of allocation has "substantial economic effect." If an S corporation permitted such allocations, it would find itself in violation of the one class of stock rule. Instead, taxable income or loss of an S corporation must flow through to the shareholders in proportion to the ownership of the S corporation stock.[41]

Income Taxation

Depending upon how it is structured, an LLC can be taxed either as a corporation or as a partnership. For the most part, the partnership classification is more desirable since the flow through nature of the partnership eliminates the double taxation common to the corporate form.

Whether an LLC is taxed as a partnership or as a corporation is a function of four critical business entity attributes. These are: (1) continuity of life; (2) free transferability; (3) centralized management; and (4) limited liability. An entity which possesses either three or four of these attributes is classified and taxed as a corporation. On the other hand, an entity which possesses only one or two of these characteristics is classified and taxed as a partnership. In 1995, the Internal Revenue Service indicated that a safe harbor may soon be available under which the entity could simply choose the manner of its taxation.[42]

One other taxation difference between S corporations and LLCs involves basis. Under Code section 1367, S corporation shareholders cannot include any part of the S corporation's liabilities as part of their basis in their S corporation shares. Thus, debt obtained by an S corporation does not have any effect upon the shareholders' basis in their shares. Generally, this is not true for members of LLCs where debt is usually includable in a member's basis in his interest in the LLC.[43]

FOOTNOTE REFERENCES

1. P.L. 85-866, Technical Amendments Act of 1958, Sec. 64, (1958).
2. P.L. 97-354, Subchapter S Revision Act of 1982, (1982).
3. P.L. 99-514, Tax Reform Act of 1986 (TRA '86), (1986).
4. *General Explanation of the Tax Reform Act of 1986*, pp. 7-11.
5. Another factor that tended to promote the election of S corporation status was the repeal of the "General Utilities" doctrine, which meant that taxation can occur at both the corporate and the shareholder level in the event of the liquidation of a C corporation, rather than tax at one level for an S corporation (except for the built-in gains tax under Section 1374). In addition, tax law commentators have also pointed to the following factors as disfavoring operation as a C corporation, and therefore, indirectly favoring S status: the enactment of the alternative minimum tax on C corporations; the limited availability of the cash method of accounting for C corporations; and the repeal of the long-term capital gains deduction. At the same time, the built-in gains tax, restrictions on the ability of S corporations to elect fiscal years and passive loss limitations applicable to a shareholder who does not "materially participate" in the operation of the business have presented an obstacle to a possible S corporation election.
6. P.L. 100-203, Revenue Act of 1987, Sec. 10224(a), (1987).
7. P.L. 101-508, Omnibus Budget Reconciliation Act of 1990, Sec. 11101(a), (1990).
8. Assumes that the $50,000 paid to Big Kath in Year 2 is a deductible bonus, not a nondeductible dividend to the corporation
9. See Section 1363(a), which provides:
    SEC. 1363. EFFECT OF ELECTION ON CORPORATION.
    (a) GENERAL RULE. — Except as otherwise provided in this subchapter, an S corporation shall not be subject to the taxes imposed by this chapter.
    Also, see Section 1363(b).
10. Section 1371(a)(1) states that, "Except as otherwise provided in this title, and except to the extent inconsistent with this subchapter, subchapter C shall apply to an S corporation and its shareholders."
11. For tax years beginning prior to 1997, Section 1361(b)(2)(A) specifies that a member of an affiliated group (determined under Section 1504 without regard to the exceptions contained in subsection (b) thereof) is an "ineligible corporation." Section 1361(b)(2) also specifically itemizes other ineligible corporations.
12. IRC Sec. 1361(b)(3)(B).
13. IRC Sec. 1361(c).
14. IRC Sec. 1361(c)(1).
15. IRC Sec. 1361(c)(4).
16. Reg. §1.1361-1(l).
17. Reg. §1.1361-1(l)(2).

18. Reg. §1.1261(b)(4).
19. IRC Sec. 1362(a)(2).
20. IRC Sec. 1362(d)(1)(B).
21. See Letter Rulings 9001050, 8807037, 8812018, 8812045, 8621013 and 8620027 for examples of situations in which the Service granted relief from inadvertent terminations. But compare Letter Rulings 9115026 and 8832055 in which the Service was less sympathetic. These rulings currently have little relevance since they were issued prior to the enactment of the Small Business Job Protection Act of 1996, which eased some of the prior restrictions on inadvertent terminations. The amendments made in the Small Business Job Protection Act of 1996 to Code section 1362(f) are to be effective with respect to elections for taxable years beginning after December 31, 1982. See Code section 1362(c) reproduced in Appendix A.
22. IRC Sec. 1362(g).
23. IRC Sec. 1378(b).
24. Rev. Proc. 87-32, 1987-2 CB 396.
25. Rev. Rul. 87-57, 1987-2 CB 117.
26. Notice 88-10, 1988-1 CB 478.
27. Rev. Proc. 92-85, 1992-2 CB 69, modifying Rev. Proc. 87-32, 1982-2 CB 396, and modified by Rev. Proc. 93-28, 1993-2 CB 344, and Rev. Proc. 95-1, 1995-1 CB 313.
28. Reg. §1.446-1(c).
29. IRC Sec. 1377(a)(2). Also, see the discussion contained in Chapter 6 in regard to utilizing the election to terminate the taxable year of the S corporation in conjunction with planning the redemption of stock from the shareholder's estate.
30. IRC Sec. 1367(a)(2)(A)-(E).
31. IRC Sec. 1367(b)(2)(A).
32. IRC Sec. 1367(b)(2)(B).
33. IRC Sec. 1368(e)(3)(B).
34. IRC Sec. 1368(e)(1)(B).
35. Rev. Proc. 95-10, 1995-1 CB 501.
36. IRC Sec. 1361(c).
37. IRC Sec. 1361(c)(2)(A).
38. IRC Sec. 1361(b).
39. Reg. §1.1361-1(l)(1).
40. See IRC Sec. 1361(b)(1)(D).
41. See IRC Sec. 1366(a).
42. See Notice 95-14, 1995-1 CB 297.
43. See IRC Sec. 752.

Chapter 2

BONUS PLANS

S corporation owners have all the same *needs* for life insurance protection that C corporation owners have. Specifically, income replacement, estate liquidity, buy-sell funding and key employee indemnification needs are among the primary areas for which life insurance provides a uniquely appropriate solution. While the S corporation shareholder's needs are apt to be no different than if a C corporation were involved, the tax rules governing S corporations demand, in some instances, that a different approach may be needed to achieve the same result as for a C corporation.

Throughout the discussion in this chapter, any reference to a "shareholder" assumes that the shareholder is a full-time employee of the S corporation (or, if the context requires, a C corporation). For the most part, the owners of closely held businesses that have elected S corporation status are actively employed in the operation of the business. Of course, an S corporation may have one or more owners who are passive investors. They may be otherwise employed, or, may be donees or beneficiaries of S corporation stock as a result of income tax planning or estate planning activities of family members. Throughout other chapters of the book, certain topics are naturally focused on corporate expenses or issues pertaining to stock ownership that are likely to be of concern to "pure shareholders," that is, those who are only owners and not employees of S corporations. However, in this chapter, the focus is on the more frequent case in which an S corporation shareholder is a full-time employee.

Life insurance planning techniques featuring corporate owned insurance, split dollar plans and ownership by an irrevocable trust are extensively described in later chapters of this book. For the moment, we will focus on the ins and outs of the "bonus plan," that is, an arrangement in which compensation paid by the corporation to an employee for services rendered is the source of premiums for a personally owned life insurance policy.

"BONUS PLANS"

A bonus plan may also be called a "Section 162 plan," a "whole dollar plan," a "Section 162 bonus plan," or some other descriptive label. In any event, a life insurance premium is furnished by the payment of tax deductible compensation by the corporate employer. The compensation may be a true bonus, that is, the payment of an additional amount because of an employee's performance; or, it may involve earmarking a portion of current compensation as dedicated to the payment of a life insurance premium. For S corporations, a bonus plan is a highly attractive method of paying for life insurance protection, not because any particular tax leverage is possible, but because of its simplicity and versatility. In short, it's an easy concept to communicate. The virtue of simplicity should not be underestimated. While making a concept easy to understand does not necessarily mean that it is easy to sell, it is also true that when the sale has been derived from the prospect's *need* for coverage, an easily explained idea is better than a complex approach that strains the attention span and enthusiasm of the prospect.

The simplicity of the bonus plan approach is apt to be appreciated by the closely held business owner who has had to jump through the hoops and over the hurdles of tax qualified benefit planning arrangements. Qualified pension and profit sharing plans offer an ongoing example of legislative and regulatory tinkering with the tax law. The rules disallowing favorable tax treatment for certain benefits provided to two-percent shareholders restrict benefit planning possibilities for S corporation owners, or, at least, make such planning more complicated and expensive than if a C corporation were involved.[1] Against this backdrop, the life underwriter who promotes the bonus plan concept should emphasize its ease of installation, ownership and administration.

Bonus plans do not have nondiscrimination rules as to eligibility, coverage or vesting. A bonus plan may provide benefits exclusively for highly compensated employees and for any amount of coverage (subject to limitations on reasonable compensation, as discussed below). Of course, the reason that bonus plans are not restricted is that they do not offer any particular tax benefit, that is, no need for legislative or regulatory qualification exists (other than to stay within the bounds of reasonable compensation).

BONUS PLANS FOR S OR C CORPORATIONS

In the case of a closely held C corporation, amounts paid as compensation for life insurance premiums offer tax leverage to the corporation (and therefore, to its insured shareholder) to the extent that the corporate tax bracket is higher than the marginal individual tax bracket. For example, assume that a corporation has a combined federal and state income tax bracket of 40%. At the same time, suppose that an insured shareholder is in the 30% tax bracket. From the corporation's standpoint, $10,000 of compensation paid for life insurance premiums would have an after-tax cost of $6,000. The insured would have an after-tax benefit of $7,000 ($10,000 minus the $3,000 tax cost incurred in a 30% tax bracket). The $1,000 spread between the $6,000 after-tax cost to the corporation and the $7,000 after-tax benefit to the insured constitutes the tax "leverage." To the extent that the insured is both shareholder *and* employee, he realizes the leverage enjoyed by the corporation because of his stock ownership.

Other than for a larger corporation that has a relatively high corporate tax bracket (perhaps made even higher by state or local income taxes) the concept of tax leverage based on a differential between corporate and individual rates no longer has much application, especially since individual tax rates have risen during the past several years. The original driving force behind widespread S elections was the thought that *all* income taxation would be incurred at historically low individual tax rates. However, many corporations have elected S status in situations for which the difference between corporate and individual rates might be insignificant. In many situations involving highly compensated shareholder-employees, the individual tax rate may have risen during the past several years to exceed the highest corporate tax rate otherwise applicable if a C corporation were in place. Nonetheless, despite the presence of certain technical rules, which are discussed in Chapter 1, S corporation elections have remained popular because no thought need be given to a corporate tax bracket.

The simplicity of the bonus plan approach dictates that the great number of insurance sales on the lives of S corporation shareholder-employees will simply be paid as another form of employee compensation. In determining how to meet the premium expense of a personally owned policy, the key point is that amounts paid as deductible compensation can offset corporate income that would otherwise cause the entity to be taxed in the case of a C corporation, or the shareholders to be taxed in the case of an S corporation. If an S corporation is involved, the prospect of a bonus plan does not involve a comparison of tax brackets. Instead, it may represent a choice between a payment to an employee as a shareholder, or, if the insured is a sole shareholder-employee, a choice between income paid as compensation or as a corporate distribution.

BONUS PLAN APPLICATIONS

The insured S corporation shareholder may purchase a life insurance policy to satisfy any of the funding needs discussed above: estate liquidity, income replacement, etc. In addition, other planning situations may result in the bonus plan approach being utilized. A few examples of these include:

A Cross Purchase Plan

In this case, the bonus is paid to each shareholder who is the owner and beneficiary of a policy on the life of another shareholder of the S corporation. Whether a cross purchase plan is appropriate in a given case is examined more thoroughly in Chapter 5, which discusses business continuation planning for S corporation shareholders. In any event, the bonus is paid to the owner of the policy as compensation and is deducted by the S corporation, thereby reducing the taxable income otherwise charged to the shareholders.

A One-Way Buyout

The sole shareholder of an S corporation may agree to sell his stock to a key employee in the event of death. The corporation can pay a bonus to the key employee that will be sufficient to meet the expense of the premiums on a life insurance policy insuring the shareholder. The payment of the bonus will naturally reduce the corporate income otherwise available for distribution to the shareholder. However, the insurance funding provides a guarantee to the owner that the value of the business will be converted to cash for the benefit of his family in the event of his death.

A Group Term Replacement Plan

During the past several years, the Section 79 nondiscrimination rules governing group term life insurance plans have provided an impetus for employers to establish alternative plans that can be designed to favor highly compensated employees. Typically, group term life insurance in excess of $50,000 of coverage is replaced by permanent protection under a bonus plan, or possibly, a split dollar plan. The same motivation for replacing group term life applies to the S corporation marketplace, with the added incentive that shareholders owning more than a two percent interest are precluded from being treated as employees for purposes of Code section 79, in any event.[2] Because of the latter rule, S corporations have probably not utilized group term plans to the same extent as C corporations. However, it may be advisable for S corporations to confine participation in group term plans to nonshareholder-employees, and to pay a bonus to provide life insurance for shareholders on a wholly selective basis, that is, without any restriction as to type or amount of coverage.

Individually Owned Policies for Retirement Funding

During the past several years increasingly onerous restrictions on qualified pension and profit sharing plans have motivated some businesses to either terminate or limit the funding of qualified plans. Many S corporation owner-employees have considered various forms of accumulating for retirement other than through a qualified plan. Furthermore, while traditional nonqualified deferred compensation plans may have a role in the benefit planning of certain S corporations (see Chapter 7), many S corporation shareholders are reluctant to establish these types of plans because of concerns about maintaining direct personal control over retirement funds. Apart from a lack of tax savings appeal, other factors also make it likely that corporate sponsored nonqualified deferred compensation plans will have limited application in the S corporation marketplace.

Thus, even if an S corporation sponsors, say, a Section 401(k) plan in which a shareholder-employee participates, the shareholder who is concerned about accumulating for retirement is likely to turn to other methods of funding. Personal investments in stocks, bonds, and for many individuals, mutual funds, have become increasingly attractive. The life insurance industry has targeted the appeal of personal choice and investment flexibility by promoting variable life insurance policies to business owners and other individuals.

A shareholder-employee can purchase a personally owned life insurance policy that will accumulate a substantial cash value by age 65, or other applicable retirement age. The policy may be a universal-variable life policy sold for its contribution flexibility and accumulation. Alternatively, it may simply be a fixed premium policy that has a relatively expensive premium that, in turn, generates substantial cash value and dividends. These policies are generally structured to avoid being classified as modified endowment contracts (MECs), given the expectation that withdrawals or partial surrenders of cash value will be made tax-free (until basis is recovered) following the insured's retirement. An S corporation may furnish the premiums to fund these policies through a bonus plan established on an entirely selective basis for the benefit of both shareholders and key employees.

FOOTNOTE REFERENCES

1.   IRC Sec. 1372.
2.   IRC Sec. 1372. See discussion in Chapter 7.

Chapter 3

CORPORATE OWNED LIFE INSURANCE

The owner of a closely held corporation, whether S or C, typically pays all types of business expenses from the corporation. The business may provide funding for a wide range of benefits, including life and disability insurance. An insurance policy on the life of a shareholder-employee may be personally owned and funded by compensation paid to the insured, as in the case of a bonus plan, discussed in Chapter 2. Such a policy may be owned by the insured or may be assigned to a trust for estate planning purposes. Or, a policy could be subject to a split dollar agreement (see Chapter 4 for a full discussion), which is really a hybrid arrangement between personally owned and corporate owned life insurance. This chapter covers the various aspects of life insurance policies owned by and payable to S corporations. Since corporate owned policies and personally owned policies exist at opposite ends of the spectrum, both the purposes and tax planning implications of corporate owned policies dictate a separate treatment of the subject.

INSURANCE NEEDS OF S AND C CORPORATIONS

S corporations purchase insurance on the lives of shareholders and key employees for many of the same reasons as C corporations. A short list of needs would include key employee indemnification, loan liquidation and credit line maintenance, stock redemptions under Section 302 pursuant to a buy-sell agreement with a shareholder and partial stock redemptions for the payment of estate taxes and other costs under Section 303. Providing informal funding for various types of nonqualified deferred compensation arrangements is less likely to occur in the S corporation marketplace than in the C corporation context, for reasons discussed in Chapter 7.

Other than nonqualified plans, S corporations need death benefit protection on the life of a shareholder or key employee for the usual range of needs that apply to any closely held C corporation.

Many S corporations are owned by one, two, or a few shareholders and do not have great management depth. Consequently, the death of an owner or a key employee may profoundly affect the course of a business, and even its viability as an entity. In many closely held businesses, one individual's relationship with customers, suppliers, staff and lenders may be critical to the financial health of the operation. The infusion of capital derived from a corporate owned insurance policy may support a business that would otherwise collapse from financial strain.

In addition, corporate owned insurance for S corporations offers certain advantages not available for C corporations. These will be covered both in this chapter and in Chapter 5, which deals with business continuation planning. Additionally, certain drawbacks of the C corporation marketplace, such as the corporate alternative minimum tax, are not a factor for S corporations.

NONDEDUCTIBILITY OF PREMIUM PAYMENTS

Both S corporations and C corporations are subject to the limitation contained in Section 264(a)(1), which provides:

(a)   GENERAL RULE.— No deduction shall be allowed for —

(1) Premiums paid on any life insurance policy covering the life of any officer or employee, or of any person financially interested in any trade or business carried on by the taxpayer, when the taxpayer is directly or indirectly a beneficiary under such policy.

An income tax deduction for the payment of premiums on a corporate owned policy is not permitted because of the fact that the proceeds are received income tax free by the corporation. The purpose of the rule, similar to the restriction on deductibility of expenses incurred to produce tax exempt income,[1] is to prevent the ownership of a business owned insurance policy from yielding a double tax benefit, both for premiums and proceeds.

Premiums for an insurance policy owned by and payable to an S corporation are usually paid from the income taxable to a shareholder. At times, it is said that premiums on a policy owned by an S corporation cause income to be taxable to a shareholder. This statement is not technically correct and may leave the impression that the payment of premiums somehow *creates* taxable income. In fact, premiums paid by an S corporation as the owner and beneficiary of a policy on the life of a shareholder or employee are paid *from* income taxable to the shareholders. The income is taxable to the shareholders whether it is distributed to them directly or expended for a nondeductible expense, such as a premium for a corporate owned life insurance policy. A premium paid for a corporate owned policy does not reduce the income of the business that is ultimately taxable to the shareholders, as would an ordinary and necessary business expense deductible under Section 162.

EXAMPLE. Jonathan owns 75% and Kay owns 25% of the outstanding stock of an S corporation, which purchases a $1,000,000 insurance policy on Jonathan's life. Before its payment of the premium, the corporation has the following income and expenses:

S Corporation:

Income $1,000,000
Expenses .... $ 900,000
Net Income .... $ 100,000

Shareholders	Ownership	Income
Jonathan	75%	$75,000
Kay	25%	$25,000

If the corporation pays a $24,000 premium for the policy, Jonathan and Kay must still report $75,000 and $25,000, respectively, of the $100,000 of income taxed to them as shareholders. Of that $100,000, $24,000 is sent to the insurance company and $76,000 remains available for distribution. The $24,000 premium is charged to, and the $76,000 remains available to, Jonathan and Kay, in proportion to their stock ownership. If the $76,000 is distributed, Jonathan will receive $57,000 and Kay will receive $19,000, although they will be taxed on $75,000 and $25,000, respectively.

Since the S corporation is not a taxable entity, its taxable income, and nondeductible expenses paid from taxable income, flow through to the shareholders. The premium expense is charged pro rata to the shareholders in accord with their stock ownership. Naturally, a shareholder who owns more of the stock will absorb a correspondingly greater portion of the cost of the coverage. Or, it may happen that the corporate owned coverage will benefit one shareholder more than another. In any case, the shareholders may adjust compensation or take other steps to produce an equitable allocation of income between or among them. In the case of an S corporation owned by a sole shareholder, the nondeductible premium paid for corporate owned insurance is equivalent to an "after-tax" dollar paid for a personally owned policy. In both cases, the premium is paid from income taxable to the shareholder, whether taxable as a distribution or received as compensation for services rendered.

EFFECT OF PREMIUMS ON BASIS

In Chapter 1, it was noted that a shareholder's basis in stock is *increased* by the income earned by an S corporation and *decreased* by its expenses. Basis is increased whether the income is taxable or tax exempt.[2] Conversely, basis is decreased by expenses, whether they are deductible or nondeductible to the S corporation. The payment of a premium for a corporate owned life insurance policy is a nondeductible expense.[3] Therefore, it should follow that the premium expense for a corporate owned policy directly reduces the basis of the shareholders in S corporation stock. The reduction in basis clearly applies to the payment of a premium for a corporate owned term insurance policy. And, the reduction in basis directly reflects the stock ownership of the shareholders, in the same manner that the premium expense is charged to the shareholders in direct proportion to their stock ownership.

EXAMPLE. Hondo is the sole shareholder of an S corporation. The corporation obtains $1 million of term insurance on Hondo's life in order to satisfy the credit line requirements of Bilgewater Bank. The summary in Figure 3.01 is based upon the term insurance premiums projected for Hondo over the next 25 years.

Obviously, the reduction in basis in each succeeding year directly reflects the escalating cost of term insurance during the period. At some point, it may be more economical for the corporation to purchase a permanent policy[4] on Hondo's life. The determination of whether term or permanent insurance is appropriate for Hondo's coverage should be made according to the same standards that govern any term vs. permanent comparison. The usual factors apply, such as the insured's age, the purpose of the coverage, the projected duration of the insurance need, the policy owner's ability to pay premiums, etc. However, in certain cases, the

Figure 3.01

Male, age 40
Preferred, non-smoker
$1,000,000 death benefit
S Corporation is owner and beneficiary

Insured is 100 percent owner of S Corporation

TERM INSURANCE

Year	Annual Premium	Annual Basis Reduction
1	1,350	1,350
5	2,120	2,120
10	3,680	3,680
15	5,670	5,670
20	9,190	9,190
25	15,200	15,200
Total at Age 65	148,280	148,280

effect that each type of corporate owned insurance will have on an S corporation shareholder's basis may also have to be taken into account.

PERMANENT INSURANCE AND BASIS

If an S corporation is the owner and beneficiary of a permanent life insurance policy on the life of a shareholder or key employee, the premium is a nondeductible expense. However, unlike the situation with term insurance, the premium expense does not necessarily reduce the basis of the shareholders by the full amount of the premium. As a matter of accounting practice, the cash value increase in each year may partially or fully offset the premium paid, and correspondingly offset the basis reduction attributable to the expense. The actual accounting practice followed may matter because the Code does not provide a clear answer to the basis reduction question. By patching together an analysis of applicable Code sections, tax law principles and accounting methods, it is the author's opinion that a conclusion to the problem can be reached. However, this is one of those areas where there is room for differences of opinion and different practices based upon both accounting methods and interpretations of the tax law.

An example showing the premiums and cash values of a life insurance policy offers a reference point for a discussion of the basis reduction issue. Figure 3.02 indicates the actual premiums and cash values of a policy provided by a major life insurance company for a hypothetical insured.

Figure 3.02

Facts

Insured: Male, age 40
Preferred, non-smoker rates
$1,000,000 initial death benefit
Vanishing premium plan
S corporation is owner and beneficiary
Insured is 100 percent owner of S corporation

Annual

Year	Premium	Cash Value Increase	Basis Reduction*
1	$16,570	$ 540	$16,030
2	$16,570	$ 9,158	$ 7,412
3	$16,570	$15,931	$ 639
4	$16,570	$17,912	$ 0
5	$16,570	$19,583	$ 0
6	$16,570	$21,383	$ 0
7	$16,570	$23,130	$ 0
8	$16,570	$25,029	$ 0
9	$ 8,277	$18,083	$ 0

Cumulative

Premiums	Cash Value	Basis Reduction*
$140,837	$150,750	$24,081

*Basis Reduction is equal to "Net Insurance Expense"
(Annual Premium - Annual Cash Value Increase).

The numbers shown in Figure 3.02 represent the premium expenses and cash value growth for a policy that is designed to produce a rich cash value accumulation. The policy was selected in order to provide a contrast to the basis reduction for a term insurance policy illustrated in Figure 3.01. In Figure 3.01, term insurance premiums are paid by the S corporation over a 25 year period, causing a substantial reduction in the shareholder's basis. Figure 3.02 assumes that a "vanishing premium" arrangement will be in place. The total premium outlay in this case is nearly the same over the nine year period as over the 25 year period in Figure 3.01, but the basis reduction is significantly less in Figure 3.02. And, of course, if the policy performs as projected, no further premiums will be required and both the cash value and the death benefit will remain substantial in later years and upon the death of the insured.

Figure 3.02 does not present the entire picture for determining the shareholder's basis for a whole life policy owned by an S corporation. The effect of policy dividends on basis has been intentionally omitted, for the moment, in order to isolate the analysis of the alternative methods of dealing with premiums and cash values in regard to basis reduction. The effect of policy dividends will be covered later in this chapter. As is, Figure 3.02 may offer a fair representation of the reduction in basis that a *nonparticipating* policy might yield. Before considering the fit of policy dividends in the basis reduction puzzle, we will first examine the extent to which cash value may offset premiums within the framework of the tax law and accounting practices.

The basis reduction indicated in Figure 3.02 is not the only approach that can be followed. In order to support the numbers shown in the basis reduction column, some background discussion is necessary. Code section 1367(a)(2) states that the basis of a shareholder's stock in an S corporation is decreased by the sum of the following items pertinent to this discussion:

(A)   distributions not includable in the shareholder's income (generally items that are a tax free recovery of basis);

(B)   separately computed items of loss and deduction;

(C)   nonseparately computed loss; and

(D)   *"any expense of the corporation not deductible in computing its taxable income and not properly chargeable to capital account..."*

Subsection (D) is quoted with emphasis because it offers the most direct reference available in the Code for determining the answer to the basis reduction question for permanent life insurance policies owned by S corporations. In analyzing the language of subsection (D), let's first consider its application to the basis reduction resulting from corporate owned term insurance. Section 264 dictates that the payment of a life insurance premium for a corporate owned policy is a nondeductible expense. A term insurance premium for a corporate owned policy fits the category of an expense "...not deductible in computing...taxable income..." A premium for a corporate owned permanent insurance policy is also nondeductible, but only a portion of the premium is "...not properly chargeable to capital account."

The annual cash value increase that results from the payment of a permanent insurance premium *is* "properly chargeable to capital account." In this context, "capital account" should be interpreted to apply within the meaning of "capitalized" as opposed to "expensed." In general, one year is the dividing line for the accounting test of whether an expenditure will be consumed or used in that period, or should be capitalized because it provides an asset having value beyond the current year. Unless otherwise restricted, the cash value of a corporate owned permanent policy is carried as an asset of either an S or a C corporation. In the context of determining a reduction in basis resulting from the payment of a premium for a policy owned by an S corporation, "capital account" refers to the cash value of the policy, which is an asset that has a value beyond the insurance coverage provided in the current year.

For purposes of tracking basis, the annual premium paid by an S corporation for a corporate owned policy may be divided into two parts: that portion of the premium equal to the annual increase in cash value and the remainder of the premium. If the cash value increase is equal to the amount "properly chargeable to capital account," the remainder of the premium constitutes the amount by which basis should be reduced. The remainder of the premium is referred to in this chapter as the "net insurance expense," although that is merely a convenient term for purposes of tracking basis and its meaning should be confined to its context in this chapter. Thus, without regard to policy dividends for participating policies, the basis reduction resulting from the premium payment by an S corporation for a corporate owned policy should be limited to the amount of the annual premium minus the annual cash value increase in each year.[5]

This method of calculating basis reduction has the virtue of having Code language to support it. However, it also has the shortcoming of being unresponsive to the prospect of a basis *increase* in later policy years when the cash value increase exceeds the premium.

BASIS, CASH VALUE AND THE TAX LAW

Figure 3.02 indicates that the cash value increase in year 4 is $17,912. The cash value increase exceeds the annual premium of $16,570 by $1,342. In other words, the basis reduction in year four should be a negative $1,342. In mathematical terms, a negative of a negative figure should be a positive figure. (Put in linear terms, the "negative" of a negative figure is simply a change in direction that yields either a lower negative figure or a positive figure.) However, a positive figure in this context means an increase in basis. Section 1367(a)(1) provides for *increases* in a shareholder's basis. Section 1367(a)(2) provides for *decreases* in a shareholder's basis. By offsetting the annual cash value increase against the annual premium, the amount of basis reduction ("net insurance expense") can be determined. If the cash value increase *exceeds* the premium, a negative basis reduction should not produce an *increase* in basis under Section 1367(a)(2). The interpretation of that Code provision seems particularly strained if it is read to authorize a basis *increase* while expressly describing items that permit a basis *decrease*.

However, adhering to a strict interpretation of statutory language leads to a result that falls short, in terms of symmetry and fairness. As the summary indicates, in year four and later years, the cash value increase exceeds the premium. If basis is reduced to zero, but not increased by the "excess" cash value increase (that amount in excess of the premium), it becomes lost in the process. (It is possible that the "lost basis" will be accounted for after the death of the insured when proceeds are received, as discussed below in this chapter.) If the "reduce to zero" theory of tracking basis is disregarded and $33,993 of "excess" cash value is permitted to *increase* basis in Figure 3.02, the net effect over the nine year period would be to *increase* basis by $9,912, rather than to *decrease* basis by $24,081.

Figure 3.02 assumes that a vanishing premium arrangement will be followed. The objective of such a plan is to limit the period during which premiums must be paid by the policy owner "out of pocket," until premiums are paid by dividends and partial surrenders of cash value in later years. Suppose, instead, that premiums will be paid for 25 years. Clearly, if the "excess" cash value were taken into account throughout the period, the insured shareholder's basis at the end of the period would be increased considerably.

An ideal solution to the problem of how to treat the "excess" cash value would satisfy both the letter of the tax law and provide an equitable method of avoiding the "lost basis" problem. As stated above, permitting "excess" cash value to *increase* basis seems to be a fair means of tracking basis as premiums are paid by the S corporation during the insured's lifetime. Extracting support for that position from the language of the Code (or other tax law authority such as regulations, rulings, etc.), however, is a difficult proposition. In the author's opinion, the question of whether the "excess" cash value may be permitted to increase basis narrows down to the following analysis. Section 1367(a)(2)(D) appears to permit annual cash value increases to offset annual premiums in determining basis reduction because cash value increases are "properly chargeable to capital account." Alternatively, the entire increase in annual cash value, that is, "excess" cash value as well as the cash value increase equal to the annual premium, could restore basis if it constitutes income within the meaning of Section 1367(a)(1), which provides for increases in a shareholder's basis.

Section 1367(a)(1) permits a shareholder's basis to be increased by items of income described in Section 1366(a)(1)(A). Such items of income include both taxable income and tax exempt income.

An item of taxable income is both *realized* by the taxpayer and *recognized* as taxable. For example, suppose that an individual purchases shares of publicly traded stock for $10,000 and sells the shares a few years later for $15,000. During the period of stock ownership, the shares appreciated in value. The increase in value is unrealized appreciation until the shares are sold. The sale of the shares is a taxable event, that is, the sale determines the point at which income is *realized* to the investor. As a "taxable event," actual taxation will follow — income will be *recognized* as taxable — unless recognition does not occur because a specific exclusion applies. (Or recognition may occur, but be offset by a deduction such as the long term capital gains deduction applicable under former law. Under current law, capital gain in the example above is fully recognized, but the rate of federal income taxation on the gain may not exceed 28%.)

The sale of shares in the example above produces income in the form of taxable gain that is both realized and recognized to the investor. On the other hand, the investor might have purchased a municipal bond. Income received by the investor from the bond is realized but not recognized to the taxpayer because it is excluded from taxation under Code section 103. In addition, the principal value of the bond will fluctuate inversely with the direction of interest rates following the time of its purchase. Thus, if interest rates drop substantially over time, the principal value of the bond should correspondingly increase. However, just as in the case of the shares of stock, the increase in value is *unrealized* appreciation until the bond is sold. Upon the sale of the bond, capital gain attributable to the increase in principal value is both realized and recognized for income tax purposes.

Life insurance policies traditionally have been accorded various forms of special treatment under the income tax law. For example, death proceeds of a policy are excluded from federal income taxation under Section 101(a)(1). Death proceeds received by an S corporation from a policy owned on the life of a shareholder-employee, for example, are excluded from income taxation under Section 101(a)(1). The proceeds are *realized* as income, but not *recognized* because of the Section 101(a)(1) exclusion. Apart from death proceeds, life insurance policies are also protected from income taxation during the insured's lifetime, as well. Any amount received under a life insurance policy, including a dividend, surrender or withdrawal of cash is included in the policy owner's gross income "...only to the extent it exceeds the investment in the contract."[6] During the past several years, that protection from income taxation has become more qualified, and limited, in certain cases, as Congress has responded to the proliferation of a more diversified range of life insurance policies.[7] Among other developments, more investment oriented insurance products have been introduced to the marketplace as major changes have occurred within various segments of the financial services industry.[8] However, the additional conditions that have been imposed during the insured's lifetime upon the income tax treatment of life insurance policies have not altered one fundamental fact. Under current federal income tax law, cash value increases are neither recognized, nor realized, as income, while the cash value remains within a policy that satisfies the definition of life insurance under Section 7702.

That protection provided under the income tax law to the growth in cash value, or "inside buildup," is unquestionably a matter of legislative grace. If Congress were so inclined, the inside buildup within the policy could become not only realized, but recognized to the policy owner, by a stroke of the pen. Nonetheless, under the current tax law, the inside buildup is exempt from income taxation. (And, as a practical matter, the inside buildup is likely to remain tax exempt, given the social policy reasons for the exemption, as well as the political forces that would resist the "stroke of the pen.") In the author's view, cash value increases constitute a form of unrealized appreciation, or growth in principal value that does not qualify as "income" within the meaning of Code section 1366(a)(1). Thus, cash value increases that are allowed to remain within a life insurance policy should not be treated as income and allowed to increase the basis of the shareholders under Section 1367(a)(1).

On the other hand, amounts received by the S corporation as a policy owner that are either recognized as taxable income under a particular Code provision, or realized, but not recognized can be classified as income under Section 1366(a)(1). For example, if an S corporation incurs taxable income because it surrenders a permanent life insurance policy and receives cash value in excess of its basis in the policy, the gain resulting from the surrender is clearly within the category of "income" under Section 1366(a)(1). Similarly, a withdrawal of cash value from a universal life policy in excess of basis in the policy is also treated as income both realized and recognized for income tax purposes.

Conversely, a partial surrender or withdrawal from a policy in which the cash value received is less than the basis of the policy reduces the policy owner's basis in the policy, but does not ordinarily produce taxable income to the policy owner, unless the amount received exceeds the policy owner's basis or unless one of the exceptions to the general rule of "basis first, then income" applies.[9]

If cash value surrendered or withdrawn from a policy produces income that is realized and recognized, that is a function of the S corporation's *basis in the policy*. Taxable income that is incurred by the corporation as the result of a policy surrender or withdrawal increases the basis of the shareholder *in the stock*. Surrenders or withdrawals received from a policy that do not result in income realized or recognized do not increase a shareholder's basis because they are not "income" for purposes of Sections 1366(a)(1) and 1367(a)(1).

The net result of not permitting "excess" cash value increases within a policy, nor withdrawals or surrenders not constituting taxable income, to be treated as income under Section 1366(a)(1) is the following:

1. Cash value increases left within the policy may offset premium expense to limit basis reduction under 1367(a)(2)(D), but "excess" cash value is not accounted for until the death of the insured, (or possibly, during the insured's lifetime if a surrender or withdrawal happens to produce taxable income); and

2. A surrender or withdrawal of cash value from a policy that constitutes taxable income to the S corporation can increase basis under Section 1367(a)(1) because it is income under Section 1366(a)(1). Nonetheless, whether a surrender or withdrawal produces taxable income to the corporation is determined according to the *aggregate* amounts paid into and surrendered or withdrawn from a policy. In contrast, because cash value accumulation *within* the policy is treated as asset growth on an annual basis (and is offset against the premium on an annual basis for purposes of determining basis reduction), the "excess" cash value may or may not be taken into account upon a surrender or withdrawal of the policy.

The apparent inequity resulting from the "lost basis" that occurs when the "excess" cash value is not taken into account during the insured's lifetime is a product of Code sections and tax law principles that simply do not square evenly in all situations. To the extent that there is room for adjustments to basis to be made according to a judgment based upon accounting practice, "excess" cash value may simply be treated as "income" by the S corporation's CPA. However, in the author's opinion, while that interpretation may achieve rough justice, it is not supported by the terms of the tax law.

POLICY DIVIDENDS

The owner of a participating whole life policy can expect to receive policy dividends over a period of years, as premiums are paid. Dividends represent a return of premium to the policy owner, based upon the insurance company's experience, with the actual cost of the insurance developed as a function of interest, mortality and expenses of the company's policies in the aggregate. Dividends from a whole life policy, roughly speaking, are somewhat like dividends from an individual stock, or a mutual fund; they constitute the current yield, or income, of the policy. Cash value can be characterized as principal; dividends provide a form of return, or income, from the policy.

To the extent that policy dividends are actually or constructively received by the S corporation as discussed below, they should increase the S corporation shareholder's basis in the stock. For purposes of Section 1366(a)(1), dividends may be characterized as income, and therefore, can increase the shareholder's basis under Section 1367(a)(1). From the standpoint of the S corporation's income tax treatment with respect *to the policy*, dividends are received tax free to the extent that they do not exceed the policy owner's basis *in the policy*; cumulative dividends in excess of basis are taxable income.[10] If taxable, dividends represent income that is both realized and recognized to the policy owner. If not taxable, dividends are treated as a return of investment to the policy owner under Section 72.

However, for purposes of being classified as income under Sections 1366(a)(1) and 1367(a)(1) dividends represent amounts received by the S corporation that should be permitted to restore stock basis otherwise reduced by the payment of premiums. Cash value accumulation represents the growth of an asset, that is, an amount "chargeable to capital account" under Section 1367(a)(2)(D). For purposes of tracking basis, the growth in cash value remaining within the S corporation offsets premium expense, subject to the "reduce to zero" limitation discussed in the preceding section of this chapter. On the other hand, policy dividends are paid directly to the S corporation as a form of return on premiums, or income to the S corporation, realized by the corporation outside of the policy (e.g., when received in cash), without regard to whether or not dividends are recognized as taxable income under Section 72. In the author's opinion, dividends should be treated as realized income, and, therefore, income under Section 1366(a)(1) and an increase in stock basis under Section 1367(a)(1).

The summary in Figure 3.03 illustrates the interplay of premiums, cash value and dividends for a participating whole life policy.

Figure 3.03

Facts

Insured: Male, age 45
Preferred, non-smoker rates
$1,000,000 death benefit
S corporation is owner and beneficiary
Insured is 100 percent owner of S corporation
Dividends are paid in cash to S corporation

ANNUAL

Policy Year	Premium	-	Cash Value Increase	=	Basis Decrease(-)	+	Dividends (Increase Basis)	Net Basis Decrease(-)/ Increase(+)
1	$16,920	-	$ 0	=	- $16,920	+	$ 0	- $16,920
2	$16,920	-	$ 1,000	=	- $15,920	+	$ 352	- $15,568
3	$16,920	-	$14,000	=	- $ 2,920	+	$ 822	- $ 2,098
4	$16,920	-	$15,000	=	- $ 1,920	+	$ 1,271	- $ 649
5	$16,920	-	$16,000	=	- $ 920	+	$ 2,178	$ 1,258
6	$16,920	-	$16,000	=	- $ 920	+	$ 3,348	$ 2,428
7	$16,920	-	$16,000	=	- $ 920	+	$ 4,552	$ 3,632
8	$16,920	-	$17,000	=	$ 0	+	$ 5,632	$ 5,632
9	$16,920	-	$18,000	=	$ 0	+	$ 6,719	$ 6,719
10	$16,920	-	$17,000	=	$ 0	+	$ 7,797	$ 7,797
11	$16,920	-	$19,000	=	$ 0	+	$ 8,953	$ 8,953
12	$16,920	-	$18,000	=	$ 0	+	$10,287	$10,287
13	$16,920	-	$19,000	=	$ 0	+	$11,643	$11,643
14	$16,920	-	$20,000	=	$ 0	+	$12,882	$12,882
15	$16,920	-	$20,000	=	$ 0	+	$13,804	$13,804
16	$16,920	-	$21,000	=	$ 0	+	$14,560	$14,560
17	$16,920	-	$20,000	=	$ 0	+	$15,210	$15,210
18	$16,920	-	$22,000	=	$ 0	+	$15,844	$15,844
19	$16,920	-	$21,000	=	$ 0	+	$16,444	$16,444
20	$16,920	-	$22,000	=	$ 0	+	$17,056	$17,056

CUMULATIVE: 20 YEARS

Premiums	Cash Value Increase	Dividends	Net Increase In Basis
$338,400	$332,000	$169,354	$128,914

As Figure 3.03 indicates, in year eight, dividends create a net increase in basis that overcomes the decrease in basis that the "net insurance expense" (premium - cash value) would otherwise yield. The net basis increase or decrease represents the sum of the net insurance expense (which, in any year, is either a negative figure that decreases basis, or zero) and dividends (which are income that increases basis).

Policy dividends, of course, may be applied by the policy owner to any (one or more) of several purposes. Typically, a dividend election by the policy owner may direct dividends:

1.   To be paid in cash;

2.   To accumulate at interest;

3.   To reduce the premium;

4.   To purchase paid-up additional insurance; or

5.   To purchase term insurance.

In addition, these elections can be combined. For example, in the later years of a vanishing premium arrangement, dividends may be applied to reduce the premium, and the amount of dividend in excess of the premium may be applied to purchase paid-up additional insurance.

Dividend Election

The reference in the following paragraphs to dividends as constituting "income" paid to the S corporation is made with respect to income for purposes of Section 1366(a)(1), and increases in stock basis of the shareholders under Section 1367(a)(1), not in regard to whether dividends constitute taxable income to the corporation as a policy owner under Section 72.

Paid in Cash

In Figure 3.03, the S corporation elected to receive dividends in cash. As income paid to the S corporation, dividends increase basis.

Accumulate at Interest

Dividends left with the insurer to accumulate at interest are income that increases stock basis and the interest earnings therefrom also constitute income of the corporation that increases the basis of the shareholder.

Reduce the Premium

If dividends are applied to reduce the premium, the same treatment as a cash election should result. The election to reduce is equivalent to a cash election in which the dividend is constructively received and automatically deposited into the policy for the policy owner's convenience. Thus, the dividend is income that increases basis, but is applied to cover the cost of premium (and the full amount of the premium is taken into account otherwise for purposes of determining the "net insurance expense" discussed in the preceding section of this chapter).

Purchase Paid-Up Additional Insurance

Dividends that are applied to purchase paid-up additions are income that is constructively received by, and available to, the S corporation policy owner, and therefore, increases basis. However, the election to purchase paid-up additions means that dividends are invested in the policy to purchase insurance coverage in addition to that provided by the payment of the required premium for the original face amount. The effect on basis resulting from the purchase of paid-up additions mirrors the "net insurance expense" system that applies to the payment of the required premium. The application of the dividend to purchase the paid-up addition generates cash value within the addition. That cash value offsets the premium cost of the paid-up addition and the difference is the net insurance expense, which again, in each year, will decrease basis or could be zero, but should not be a positive figure. However, the cash value resulting from the purchase of a paid-up addition is combined into the overall cash value in a typical insurance illustration. And, in determining the net insurance expense for purposes of tracking basis, the aggregate cash value increase resulting in each year from both the base coverage and the paid-up additions should be subtracted from the sum of the premium for the base coverage plus the dividend applied to purchase paid-up additions.

Purchase Term Insurance

The dividend increases basis because it is constructively received as income to the policy owner. Applying it to purchase term insurance creates "net insurance expense" and causes a direct reduction of the shareholder's stock basis.

TAX LAW AND ACCOUNTING PRACTICE

Given that the tax law is less than crystal clear on the issue of basis reduction for permanent insurance policies owned by S corporations, and also considering the inequity presented by the "reduce to zero" limitation, how should basis be accounted for? The following methods are most likely to be followed in practice:

1. *Reduce basis by the full premium.* This method would be favored by tax law practitioners who cannot find a clear answer to the problem in the Code. The cash value baby gets tossed out with the premium bath water with no room for further interpretation.

2. *Reduce basis by the "net insurance expense."* The annual premium is reduced by the annual cash value increase, but only "to zero," with no *increase* in basis allowed in years when the cash value increase exceeds the premium. This approach seems justified by the language of Section 1367(a)(2)(D) ("...expense of the corporation not deductible...and not properly chargeable to capital account..."). However, as shown in Figure 3.03, a net increase in basis may result in certain years when policy dividends are treated as income to the corporate policy owner for purposes of Sections 1366(a)(1) and 1367(a)(1).

3. *Reduce basis by the "net insurance expense" and permit an* **increase** *in basis when cash value increase exceeds the premium.* This approach is most beneficial to the S corporation shareholders in that it avoids the "lost basis" dilemma that the "reduce to zero" method cannot accommodate. It tempers a literal reading of Code language with an effort to reach a common sense result as a matter of accounting practice. However, common sense notwithstanding, permit-

ting an increase in basis because of the cash value increase is difficult to justify under Section 1367. An increase should not be allowed by the provisions governing a decrease in basis; the cash value growth should not be shoe horned into the definition of "income" that permits an increase in basis.

As discussed later in this chapter, the basis that is "lost" may actually be deferred, rather than lost, if the S corporation owns the policy until the death of the insured (and the same shareholders continue to own the corporation).

THE IMPORTANCE OF BASIS

The S corporation shareholder's basis in stock is significant in two situations: (1) a corporate distribution and (2) a sale by the shareholder of the S corporation stock. In both cases, basis serves to shield the shareholder from incurring taxable income.

Distributions

Chapter 1 describes the system of taxation that applies to corporate distributions under Section 1368. As a general rule, a larger basis permits a greater distribution to be made to a shareholder. In that regard, income that is taxed to the shareholders but not distributed allows basis to remain at an increased level, thus permitting subsequent distributions to be made on a tax free basis. Having a greater basis to absorb tax free distributions is obviously an advantage to S corporation shareholders if it is anticipated that major distributions will be made in the future.

Any number of situations can be imagined in which it might be useful for a shareholder to receive a tax free distribution from the corporation (including, from the life underwriter's perspective, a distribution to fund a premium for a personally owned policy or split dollar plan, as well as a corporate owned policy). As the summaries contained in this chapter illustrate, a corporate owned whole life policy will permit the insured shareholder to maintain a higher basis in subsequent policy years at older ages, rather than the term insurance alternative which bleeds basis as mortality costs cause premiums to rise exponentially at older ages.

Maintaining a higher basis in anticipation of corporate distributions is a more significant issue for S corporation owners than for C corporation owners. However, the role of basis in the event that stock will be sold is an important aspect of planning for the owners of both S and C corporations.

Sale of Stock

Many closely held business owners, whether S or C corporation stock is involved, expect to "die with their boots on." Or, at least, they may expect to hold their stock until death, whether or not they remain employed or active in the management of the business. This outlook is particularly apt to be expressed if a succeeding generation will be in place to inherit the stock or if the owner has an entrepreneurial obsession with building the business or has a highly pronounced work ethic. However, in many situations, an S corporation owner may have an expectation that stock will be sold during the owner's lifetime. The following example offers a classic case in which planning for a lifetime sale may occur.

EXAMPLE. Lenny and George are the owners of Icemice, a rodent extermination company subject to an S corporation election. George is a scientist and a typical "inside" employee, devoted to perfection of the mousetrap. However, having found that mere invention did not cause the world to beat a path to his door, he formed an association with Lenny, a "marketing genius." Lenny has developed a customer base, but George fears that the company is vulnerable to "high tech" developments and a fickle attitude on the part of the buyers of their product. Without Lenny, George would "cash out" and retire. For his part, Lenny will admit that he needs a supporting organization in order to sell mousetraps, and expects that the product might become obsolete if George could not maintain technological competitiveness.

Both Lenny and George are interested in maintaining the level of their stock basis in the event that the other owner dies or becomes disabled. A higher basis reduces the amount of taxable gain that the remaining shareholder would have to report for income tax purposes in the event of a sale of the S corporation stock. In addition, the sale of the stock may be triggered by a forced retirement or a period of unemployment until a new business opportunity is developed. In other words, the sale of stock may not constitute the windfall that some closely held business owners envision. Instead, it may provide a sum of money or a stream of income that will be utilized as a source of financial support. In such a case, the credo "it's not what you earn, it's what you keep" will directly apply. A higher stock basis will "sweeten the deal" by nearly 40%. (Receiving $1.00 rather than $.72 after applying a 28% capital gains rate offers almost 40% more return in relation to each dollar of *profit* (not overall investment), based on: $1.00 - $.28 = $.72; $.28 ÷ $.72 = 38.9%.

BASIS AND THE INSURANCE SALE

To summarize, the payment of a premium for a life insurance policy owned by an S corporation reduces its shareholder's basis; the reduction in basis is significantly less over a period of years for a whole life policy rather than a term policy; and an S corporation shareholder would prefer to have a higher basis, rather than a lower basis, in the S shares because of the prospect of corporate distributions or sales of stock. How are these conclusions relevant to the life underwriter from the standpoint of insurance planning for the S corporation owner? Where do these thoughts fit in the planning process?

First of all, the *need* for corporate owned life insurance must be established independently of the basis reduction issue. Before addressing the question of which type of policy is most appropriate, the purpose of the coverage must be established: key employee indemnification, stock redemption funding, etc. After the function of the coverage is clear, the duration of the need should be considered. In that process, situations at either extreme — clearly short term or clearly long term — will readily dictate the appropriate form of insurance. The decision to select the "right" policy becomes more difficult if one of the following situations is involved:

1. The need for insurance is a period of "intermediate" range, say, five to ten years, without a clear indication of whether the need will continue at the end of the period;

2. An initial need is clear for a limited period (e.g., indemnification to cover a corporate credit line) and may be followed by a succeeding need that is not currently established, but probable (stock redemption funding); or

3.   The duration of the need is clearly long term, but cash flow is a problem *and* the corporation's access to the policy's cash value is a plus.

Obviously, these situations are only examples. Other circumstances may apply or variations of those described above may come into play. The advantages of a lesser basis reduction offered by a whole life policy will carry the day in those cases when "everything else is equal." In other words, if the need for coverage is on the cusp between term and permanent, keeping basis at a higher level may dictate the selection of whole life coverage.

SALES POINT. Blending a complex concept into the conversation with a prospect (or an adviser) requires great communication skill on the part of the life underwriter. The topic of basis reduction for a corporate owned policy certainly does not fall in the category of a "door opener." The agent must build a foundation upon which the basis reduction issue can rest. However, without getting lost in technical deep grass, it is worth pointing out that the basis question can provide a segue to a discussion of buy-sell planning.

The S corporation may only need term insurance, but the discussion of basis may trigger a broader examination of business continuation planning and funding. That discussion may come full circle if the unique advantage of S corporation funding for a stock redemption is considered. (See Chapter 5.)

DEATH PROCEEDS

If an S corporation owns a policy on the life of a shareholder, the insurance proceeds paid upon the shareholder's death are tax free to the corporation under Code section 101. (Assuming, of course, that no exception applies to create income taxation, such as a violation of the transfer for value rule.) Proceeds paid to a C corporation would also be tax exempt under Section 101. However, in the case of a C corporation, insurance proceeds may be subject to taxation because of the application of the corporate alternative minimum tax (AMT). A discussion of that tax is beyond the scope of our purpose in this chapter, but it can be said that the application of the tax to the C corporation may be triggered by the receipt of the insurance proceeds, or may be generated by independent items of income and deduction that cause the tax to apply. In any event, the possible application of the corporate AMT is not a factor for S corporations. No need for a parallel system of corporate taxation exists because the S corporation is generally not a taxable entity under the regular system of corporate taxation. The absence of the corporate AMT as a factor in the S corporation marketplace can be contrasted to the world of C corporations, even if it only falls into the "small favors" category.

DEATH PROCEEDS AND BASIS

As previously stated, under Section 1367(a)(1)(A), a shareholder's basis in S corporation stock is increased by, among other things, items of income described in Section 1366(a)(1). Again, those items of income include tax-exempt income, such as life insurance proceeds. Thus, if an insured shareholder of an S corporation dies, the proceeds paid to the corporation are not taxable and increase the basis of the surviving shareholders in the corporation's stock. However, a question arises as to the extent by which the proceeds increase the basis of the surviving shareholders. The answer to the question necessarily draws us back into the thick of the basis reduction issue.

Before proceeding with that analysis, it should be noted that the stock basis of an insured shareholder will be stepped up to its fair market value at death under Code section 1014(a)(1). The "step up" rule provided under that Code section overrules the effect on basis that would otherwise occur because of the corporation's receipt of death proceeds. Thus, if the insured is the sole shareholder of an S corporation, the extent to which death proceeds are considered income in the calculation of basis becomes a moot point. On the other hand, if more than one shareholder is involved, the proceeds paid to the S corporation are taken into account, pro rata, according to stock ownership. In that case, the significance of the extent to which proceeds increase basis will be directly related to the respective stock ownership of the surviving shareholders. (Nevertheless, as a practical matter, the focus of life insurance planning in regard to the effect on stock basis may be more centered on premiums than proceeds simply because the payment of premiums is more immediate and the receipt of proceeds is more remote to the shareholders.)

An S corporation may also purchase insurance on the life of a key employee who is not a shareholder. For ease of explanation, it is assumed in the following summaries that the insured is a key employee, but not a shareholder, of the S corporation. Therefore, the receipt of proceeds by the corporation will directly affect the stock basis of the shareholders according to one of the methods described in the following discussion.

The term "tax-exempt income" contained in Section 1366(a)(1) is not qualified or further defined. On its face, it suggests that stock basis is increased by the amount of the entire insurance proceeds paid to the S corporation upon the insured's death. A full increase in stock basis would be a symmetrical tax result if basis had been decreased by the full amount of the premium paid in each year during the insured's lifetime. Once again, if an S corporation owns a term insurance policy, a reduction in basis by the amount of the entire premium seems warranted. Conversely, basis should be increased, or restored, by the full amount of the death proceeds of term insurance received by the corporation.

If the S corporation owns a permanent insurance policy, the treatment of premiums and proceeds in regard to the basis question should have the same symmetry as for term insurance. The three methods described above of reducing basis because of premium payments by the S corporation necessarily produce three methods of increasing basis when proceeds are received by the corporation at the insured's death, if consistency in tracking basis is to be maintained. These three methods are discussed below under the headings of: (1) Increase Basis by Full Amount of Death Proceeds; (2) Increase Basis by Book Income Plus "Lost Basis"; and (3) Increase Basis by Death Proceeds Minus Cash Value.

Increase Basis by Full Amount of Death Proceeds

To begin with the easy case, if cash value increases are disregarded and basis is reduced by the entire amount of the premium during the insured's lifetime, basis should be correspondingly increased by the full amount of the proceeds upon the insured's death. This approach disregards the "not properly chargeable to capital account" Code language that supports a lesser basis reduction in regard to the payment of the premium. However, a full increase offers the virtue of simplicity: death proceeds are considered to be income without any need for qualification because of the treatment accorded premiums during the insured's lifetime. Figure 3.04 illustrates the effect on the shareholder's basis when death proceeds are paid to the S corporation upon the insured employee's death. The summary is based upon the same policy used in Figure 3.03, but assumes that the shareholder's basis was fully reduced by the amount of each premium payment (no offset for cash value). Following the insured's death, basis is increased by the entire amount of proceeds paid to the corporation. The direct reduction in basis caused by premium payments and corresponding basis increase attributable to proceeds operates in the same manner as if a term insurance policy were involved, (except for the reference in the following example to policy dividends).

Figure 3.04

Facts

Insured: Male, age 45
Preferred, non-smoker rates
$1,000,000 death benefit
S corporation is owner and beneficiary
Insured is key employee of S corporation

Initial basis = $500,000
Dividends are paid in cash to S corporation
Premiums fully reduce basis in each year
Death occurs after end of year 19

Years	Total Premiums	Total Dividends
19	$321,480	$152,298

Calculation: Basis Before Death

Initial Basis	—	Total Premiums (Decreased)	+	Total Dividends (Increase)	=	Basis Before Death
$500,000	—	$321,480	+	$152,298	=	$330,818

Calculation: Basis After Death

Basis Before Death	+	Death Proceeds (Full Amount)	=	Basis After Death
$330,818	+	$1,000,000	=	$1,330,818

Increase Basis by Book Income Plus "Lost Basis"

As suggested above, as premiums are paid during the insured's lifetime, reducing basis by only the "net insurance expense" with a "reduce to zero" limitation seems to be the best method available to comply with the terms of the applicable tax law. Following the insured's death, the basis of the surviving shareholders should be increased by the portion of the policy proceeds deemed to be income under Sections 1366(a)(1) and 1367(a)(1). The full amount of the proceeds are tax exempt income to the S corporation under the general rule of Section 101(a)(1). However, the entire proceeds should not be treated as income for purposes of Section 1367(a)(1), for the sake of consistency. If basis is increased by the full amount of the proceeds, the shareholders are effectively able to use cash value increases to create a lesser basis reduction when premiums are paid and to count a portion of the cash value again to increase their basis following the insured's death. One method of curbing an unwarranted increase in basis would be to offset cash value against proceeds received at death. This approach is similar to the "book income" concept formerly used by the corporate alternative minimum tax.[11] In addition, it has the appeal of seeming to be the real measure of *income* to the S corporation in the year of the insured's death. On the day before the insured's death, the corporation carries the cash value of the policy on its balance sheet as a corporate asset. On the day after the insured's death, the corporation's wealth is increased by the difference between the proceeds received and the cash value. (The "income" is limited because the cash value has already been taken into account as an offset to basis reduction during the insured shareholder's lifetime.)

However, if the "reduce to zero" limitation applies to the tracking of basis as premiums are paid, basis may be "lost" at the insured's death unless the corporation's measurement of "income" is appropriately adjusted. While the notion of "book income" as the measurement may offer a certain appeal, it overlooks a portion of basis that should be accounted for at death. The "lost basis" problem may be solved by an adjustment to the "income" received by the S corporation in the year of the insured's death.

As shown in Figure 3.05, the potential for "lost basis" begins in policy year eight when the cash value increase initially exceeds the premium. At that point, the "reduce to zero" limitation is in full swing: the "net insurance expense" is actually a negative number (and therefore, could potentially *increase* basis), but for purposes of determining a basis reduction, it is deemed to be zero. In policy years eight through 19, the annual cash value increase exceeds the annual premium, with the "lost" basis totaling $28,960.

Figure 3.05

Facts
Insured: Male, age 45 Preferred, non-smoker rates $1,000,000 death benefit S corporation is owner and beneficiary Insured is key employee of S corporation

Initial basis = $500,000
Dividends are paid in cash to S corporation
Premiums reduce basis by "net insurance expense"
Death occurs after end of year 19

Year	Cash Value Increase	— Premium	= "Lost" Basis
8	$17,000	$16,920	$ 80
9	$18,000	$16,920	$1,080
10	$17,000	$16,920	$ 80
11	$19,000	$16,920	$2,080
12	$18,000	$16,920	$1,080
13	$19,000	$16,920	$2,080
14	$20,000	$16,920	$3,080
15	$20,000	$16,920	$3,080
16	$21,000	$16,920	$4,080
17	$20,000	$16,920	$3,080
18	$22,000	$16,920	$5,080
19	$21,000	$16,920	$4,080

Cumulative "Lost" Basis = $28,960

At the end of year 19, the cash value of the policy is $310,000. If the insured dies at that time, the S corporation will receive $1,000,000 of death proceeds. The book income of the corporation generated by the payment of the death benefit is $1,000,000 - $310,000 or $690,000. However, the "income" for purposes of Section 1367(a)(1), of the corporation in the year of death should be $718,960, consisting both of book income ($690,000) plus the cumulative amount of basis that had not been accounted for during the insured's lifetime ($28,960). This method of calculating the S corporation's income takes into account the excess cash value increase that was not permitted to reduce basis in each year that premiums were paid. It is based on establishing symmetry and reflects the system for determining reduction in basis as premiums were paid.

Increase Basis by Death Proceeds Minus Cash Value

If the cash value accumulation of the policy is somehow characterized as income for purposes of tracking basis as premiums are paid, the annual cash value increase is permitted not only to offset the annual premium, but to *increase* basis when it exceeds the premium. As discussed above, the terms of Section 1367(a)(2)(D) (dealing with a basis reduction) and the difficulty of characterizing "excess" cash value as income, make it difficult to justify an increase in basis because the cash value increase exceeds the premium. However, if the *entire* cash value is allowed to restore basis as premiums are paid, the measurement of "income" when death proceeds are received should take that into account. In order to avoid a windfall to the shareholder that would result if basis is increased twice, the measurement of the corporation's income from the proceeds should be limited to book income, as illustrated in Figure 3.06.

In this case, the total cash value may be used to offset the proceeds received at death in order to calculate the increase in basis to the shareholders. This adjustment can be contrasted to the method followed in Figure 3.05, in which the "excess" cash value not permitted to reduce basis during the insured's lifetime is added back to determine the basis increase to the shareholders following the insured's death.

Figure 3.06

Facts

Insured: Male, age 45
Preferred, non-smoker rates
$1,000,000 death benefit
S corporation is owner and beneficiary
Insured is key employee of S corporation

Initial basis = $500,000
Dividends are paid in cash to S corporation
Premiums reduce and cash values increase basis in each year
Death occurs after end of year 19

Calculation: Basis Before Death

Initial Basis	Total Premium — (Decrease)	+	Cash Value (Increase)	+	Total Dividends (Increase)	=	Basis Before Death
$500,000 —	$321,480	+	$310,000	+	$152,298	=	$640,818

Calculation: Basis After Death

Basis Before Death +	Book Income*	=	Basis After Death
$640,818	+ $690,000	=	$1,330,818

*Book Income means Death Proceeds minus Cash Value.

FOOTNOTE REFERENCES

1. IRC Sec. 265.
2. Code section 1367(a)(1)(A) refers to Code section 1366(a)(1)(A), which provides that items of income include tax-exempt income.
3. IRC Sec. 264.
4. The term "permanent policy" or "permanent insurance" is used to refer to any form of policy having a cash value, whether it is a traditional participating whole life policy, a nonparticipating universal life policy or a variation of either type of policy.

5. "Each year" in this context means the taxable year of the S corporation, that is, in most cases the calendar year. In determining the amount of basis reduction, assuming that premiums are paid annually, the premium paid at the beginning of a new *policy* year would be offset by the cash value increase that accrues at the end of the immediately preceding policy year. For example, assume that a $10,000 annual premium is paid on June 1 for a corporate owned policy that is in force for five years on that date. The payment of the $10,000 premium that is due at the beginning of the sixth policy year (a nondeductible expense) should be offset by the accrual of the cash value increase (chargeable to capital account) that occurs on the last day of the fifth policy year. The net difference between the premium paid and the growth in cash value should be the amount of basis reduction applicable under the terms of Section 1367 (a)(2)(D). (In the same manner, a policy dividend that is actually or constructively received by the S corporation during the calendar year constitutes (nontaxable or taxable) income that increases basis, as discussed below.)

6. IRC Sec. 72(e)(5)(A).

7. See Code section 7702(f)(7), which provides that if a cash distribution is made from a policy resulting in a reduction in benefits during the first 15 years that it is in force, the distribution is taxed according to a "gain first, then basis" rule rather than the "basis first" rule generally applicable under Section 72(e)(5)(A). Also, see Code section 7702A, which describes the conditions under which a policy may be deemed to be a "modified endowment contract"(MEC).

8. In 1982, TEFRA introduced the first statutory definition of life insurance into the Internal Revenue Code under Section 101(f), which set forth rules governing flexible premium life insurance policies. Section 7702, enacted in 1984 as part of the Deficit Reduction Act, provides a detailed definition of how much cash value accumulation can be permitted within a contract that qualifies as a life insurance policy. The MEC rules contained in IRC Section 7702A were enacted generally in response to the promotion of single premium life insurance policies as quasi-investment products.

9. Code section 72(e)(5)(A) states the general rule, but see footnote 7 in regard to exceptions.

10. IRC Sec. 72(e)(5)(A).

11. IRC Sec. 56(f) prior to repeal by Section 11801(a)(3) of P.L. 101-508, The Omnibus Budget Reconciliation Act of 1990.

Chapter 4

SPLIT DOLLAR PLANS

INTRODUCTION

A split dollar plan involves an arrangement between two parties in which rights and responsibilities are divided with respect to the premiums, cash value and death benefit of a life insurance policy. The textbook cliche regarding a split dollar plan is that it is a *method* of purchasing life insurance, not a reason for buying a policy. In addition, it is a form of life insurance plan which may be funded by any type of whole life policy: traditional whole life, universal, variable, interest sensitive whole life, participating, non-participating, etc.

Typically, a split dollar plan is entered into by an employer and an employee as a form of fringe benefit or compensation planning technique. Usually, split dollar plans are established by corporations, rather than partnerships or sole proprietorships. Within the corporate marketplace, a split dollar plan may be established by virtually any type of corporation from the smallest closely held corporations, including professional corporations, to large publicly held companies. Apart from a business setting, two individuals may enter into a "private" or "family" split dollar agreement in order to split the costs and benefits of life insurance coverage. The focus in this chapter will be on the split dollar plan for the closely held corporation. The advantages and disadvantages of split dollar in the S corporation setting will be compared and contrasted to the fundamental aspects and varieties of split dollar plans for C corporations.

Most frequently, a split dollar plan is set up as either a collateral assignment or an endorsement plan. In the collateral assignment plan, the insured employee is the applicant and owner of the policy and assigns to the corporate employer the right to receive the premiums it has paid, or the cash value (or the greater or lesser of the two) in the event of the employee's death, or termination of the plan during the employee's lifetime. An endorsement plan features the employer as the applicant and owner of the policy. The employer *endorses* to the employee the right to name the beneficiary of that portion of the death benefit in excess of the employer's interest. Again, the employer's interest is generally its premiums paid or the policy's cash value.

Another form of plan is a "true split," in which each party applies for and owns separate portions of the policy without any endorsement or collateral assignment. Regardless of the means by which each plan is established, the end result usually involves the employer having rights in the policy's cash value and the net death benefit (face amount minus cash value) made payable to the employee's beneficiary.

Insurance Needs

A split dollar plan may be established in response to one or more needs for life insurance coverage such as family income continuation, estate planning, business continuation, corporate fringe benefit planning, etc. Interest in a split dollar plan may be generated both by the financial resources of each party, as well as their respective needs for insurance. The agent selling the coverage may actively promote a split dollar plan when it seems appropriate, such as with a particular alignment of corporate and individual income tax brackets, or the parties may "back into" split dollar because neither a personally owned policy nor a corporate owned policy is suitable to both of them.

Once the need for coverage is clearly established, the corporate employer may entertain the suggestion that a split dollar plan be initiated for the following reasons:

1. Cost Recovery: The employer has the ability to recover its premium payments during the insured's lifetime, or upon death. Essentially, the employer gives up the use of its funds that are expended for premium payments. Once again, the employer may be entitled to the cash value, its premiums (or an alternative measure, such as premiums plus interest at a specified rate.)

2. Discrimination Permitted: Unlike many other benefit plans, a split dollar plan may discriminate in regard to eligibility, type and amount of coverage provided. The plan may cover

only the most highly paid employees, or shareholder-employees, or, for that matter, a shareholder who is not employed by the sponsoring corporation. (A split dollar plan is a "welfare benefit plan" for purposes of the Employee Retirement Income Security Act of 1974 (ERISA), but most plans need be concerned only with the provisions covering fiduciary responsibility and administration and enforcement of the plan.[1])

3.   Simplicity: A split dollar plan is not difficult to establish and administer. Typically, the employer executes a corporate resolution and enters into a split dollar agreement with the insured which defines the respective rights and obligations of the parties with regard to the split of premiums, cash values and death proceeds. In addition, the agreement should include provisions that are designed to comply with the provisions of ERISA that require designation of a fiduciary, specification of a funding policy and description of a claims procedure.[2]

4.   Flexibility in Plan Design: Freedom from nondiscrimination requirements, as well as the nature of a divisible premium, means that the employer may choose to pay the entire cost of the plan (frequently the case for a shareholder-employee) or may require a contribution by the insured (more typical for a key employee). Split dollar permits significant flexibility in plan design and enables the employer to coordinate its features with other benefits furnished to its employees. In addition, upon the employee's retirement, the plan may be terminated and the policy may be "rolled out" of the plan, that is, transferred to the exclusive ownership of the employee.

5.   Funding Corporate Obligations: The corporation's interest in the policy can fulfill its need for indemnification in the event of the death of the insured shareholder or key employee. While its share of the proceeds will not be significant in the first several years that the plan is in effect, the cash value can appreciate substantially over a longer period. While the rollout of the policy is more commonly directed to exclusive ownership of the policy by the insured, it is also possible that

the rollout may be to the corporation. At that point, the policy may be used to provide informal funding in order to support the corporation's obligation under a nonqualified deferred compensation plan to pay retirement income to the employee or a death benefit to the employee's family.

6.   Corporate Access to Cash Value: If the split dollar agreement permits the corporation to maintain control of the policy's cash value, the corporation's bank, CPA, or others requiring disclosure of its financial status may appreciate the fact that the corporation carries the cash value as an asset. Depending upon the terms of the split dollar agreement, the corporation can have the ability to borrow, surrender, or withdraw cash value during the insured employee's lifetime, as well as receive its portion of the proceeds upon the insured's death.

Before discussing the advantages of a split dollar plan to the insured employee, as well as its role in S corporation life insurance planning, a brief review of the income tax aspects of split dollar is in order.

INCOME TAXATION OF SPLIT DOLLAR PLANS

To the Corporation (or Shareholders)

Under Section 264, the corporation's premium payment is nondeductible because it is a beneficiary of the policy. The premium is nondeductible regardless of whether it is paid by a C corporation or an S corporation. Conversely, upon the death of the insured, the C or S corporation's receipt of its share of the policy's death benefit is income tax free under Code section 101.

If a C corporation is involved, the nondeductible premium payment is made from the corporation's taxable income (or possibly from other sources if it has no taxable income because it incurs a net operating loss). Once again, because an S corporation is not a taxable entity, nondeductible premium payments are paid from corporate income that is taxable to the shareholders. In effect, the premium is paid as a corporate "dividend" taxable to the shareholders which is sent to the insurance company, rather than distributed to the shareholders.

To the Insured

The income taxation of the insured employee who receives insurance protection under a split dollar plan is well defined in the tax law. The IRS originally viewed a split dollar plan as an interest-free loan for income tax purposes.[3] Specifically, the payment of a premium by the employer for a particular type of split dollar plan was originally described by the Service, as "...such arrangement is regarded, for Federal income tax purposes, as though an interest-free loan is actually made by the employer to the employee in amounts equal to the annual increases in the cash surrender value of such policies. The mere making available of money does not result in realized income to the payee or a deduction to the payer."[4]

Several years later, the Service reconsidered its position and decided that the employer's premium payment conferred a currently taxable economic benefit upon the insured employee. In Revenue Ruling 64-328,[5] the IRS stated its position in regard to the income taxation of the insured employee:

> In the typical "split dollar" arrangement, then, the purpose is, and the effect is, to provide an economic benefit to the employee represented by the amount of the annual premium cost that he should bear and of which he is relieved. It is well settled that the providing of life insurance results in an economic benefit to the insured...An employee who receives an economic benefit under an arrangement with his employer generally must include in his gross income the value of the benefit received...In a situation such as this, in which the economic benefit to the employee is a continuing annual benefit so long as the "split dollar" arrangement is kept in force, the amount to be included annually is the annual value of the benefit received by the employee under the arrangement, which is held to be an amount equal to the 1-year term cost of the declining life insurance protection to which the employee is entitled from year to year, less the portion, if any, provided by the employee. The cost of life insurance protection per $1,000, as shown in the table contained in Revenue Ruling 55-747, *supra*, may be used to compute the 1-year term cost.[6] (Citations omitted.)

In Revenue Ruling 66-110,[7] the Service refined the measurement of the economic benefit received by the insured, and specified that:

In any case where the current published premium rates per $1,000 of insurance protection charged by an insurer for individual 1-year term life insurance available to all standard risks are lower than those set forth in Revenue Ruling 55-747, such published rates may be used in place of the rates set forth in that Revenue Ruling for determining the cost of insurance in connection with individual policies issued by the same insurer and used for "split dollar" arrangements or held by trusts qualified under section 401(a) of the Code.[8]

Since the publication of Revenue Rulings 64-328 and 66-110, the income taxation to the insured employee resulting from the coverage received under a split dollar plan provided by a corporate employer has been clearly defined. As the insurance industry has evolved, the "insurer's rates" used to measure the term insurance value of the economic benefit have been substantially reduced in recent years. For example, the term insurance rates used by many insurers are only about 20% to 25% of the "PS 58" rates published in Revenue Ruling 55-747.[9] Coupled with the drop in individual tax rates that have been in place after the enactment of the Tax Reform Act of 1986, the cost of coverage is only 12% to 20% of its level during the late 1970s.[10] As a result, split dollar plans are significantly more attractive from the insured's viewpoint today than ever before, provided that they make sense in the particular planning circumstances involved.

With regard to the income taxation of the insured employee, it is immaterial whether the insurance protection is furnished by a C or an S corporation. The economic benefit, that is, the term insurance value of the coverage, is measured in exactly the same manner. Whether or not the insured is a shareholder, if the split dollar benefit is furnished to the insured for services rendered as an employee, the same income tax treatment results without regard to whether the plan is sponsored by a C corporation or an S corporation. If the benefit is provided for a shareholder who is not an employee of the corporation, its measurement remains the same, although it is treated as a dividend, rather than as compensation.[11] Strictly in regard to the taxation of the economic benefit to the shareholder, whether a C or an S corporation sponsors the plan has no bearing on the income tax result.

A split dollar plan may be structured as an "employer-pay-all" plan in which the corporation furnishes the entire premium with no contribution by the employee. (In fact, the employer may also reimburse the employee for the income tax cost created by the plan through the payment of a bonus, and may even pay an additional bonus to cover both the income tax liability generated by the bonus, as well as by the economic benefit.) Alternatively, the employee could be required to contribute to the cost of the plan. Usually, the contribution will be equal to the term insurance cost of the death benefit payable to the beneficiary named by the employee. In other words, the contribution is equal to the income that the employee would otherwise report, thereby negating the income tax liability that would result under an "employer-pay-all" plan.

Comparison of Income Tax Brackets (C Corporation)

Unless other factors dictate how premiums will be paid in a particular situation, a comparison of income tax brackets may favor the use of a split dollar plan. Traditionally, the comparison has been made between the corporate income tax bracket of a C corporation and the personal income tax bracket of the insured. In its simplest form, the tax bracket comparison can be made for an insured employee who is also the sole shareholder of a C corporation when the choice is between a split dollar plan and a bonus plan. The decision to choose either type of plan in these circumstances is easily supported if the tax brackets offer a clear contrast.

BONUS PLAN
$10,000 ANNUAL PREMIUM

Insured Employee

Compensation Before Tax	Personal Bracket	Tax	Compensation After Tax
$14,285	30%*	$4,285	$10,000

Corporation

Compensation	Corporate Tax Bracket	Tax	After Tax Cost
$14,285	45%*	$6,428	$7,857

* Combined federal and state income tax rate.

As shown above, the insured employee in a 30% income tax bracket would need $14,285 of compensation in order to wind up with $10,000 of net income available for the payment of a premium. On the other side of the ledger, if the corporation is in a 45% income tax bracket and pays $14,285 of compensation to the employee, its after tax cost for the payment is $7,857. When the insured employee is also the sole shareholder of the corporation, the bonus plan approach provides tax leverage to the corporation because its deduction exceeds the tax cost of the compensation to the employee. To the extent that the corporation's tax bracket exceeds the insured employee's tax bracket, the "bonus plan" approach will be attractive. (See Chapter 2 for a full explanation of bonus plans.)

On the other hand, if the corporation is in a lower income tax bracket than the insured, a split dollar plan will have greater appeal than a bonus plan. Suppose, for example, that the corporation is in a 15% bracket as shown in below.

Corporation

Compensation	Corporate Tax Bracket	Tax	After Tax Cost
$14,285	15%	$2,143	$12,142

In this case, the value of the corporate tax deduction is significantly diminished. If a split dollar plan is installed, the premium will be nondeductible to the corporation. However, in a lower corporate tax bracket, the corporate deduction has less value. As a result, the nondeductibility of the premium is more acceptable than if the corporation were in a higher tax bracket.

From the insured employee's standpoint, the income tax cost of a split dollar plan is considerably less than for a bonus plan. The income subject to taxation is only the term insurance cost, rather than the full premium. For example, if the premium is $10,000, the term insurance cost, depending upon the insured's age, might be only $1,000. In a 30% tax bracket, the tax cost to the insured employee would be $300 if the employer paid the entire premium.

Thus, when comparing corporate and individual tax brackets, the rule of thumb for selecting a bonus plan or a split dollar plan as the preferred method is summarized below.

Corporate Tax Bracket	Personal Tax Bracket	Preferred Plan
Higher	Lower	Bonus Plan
Lower	Higher	Split Dollar

If the difference between the tax brackets is negligible or other factors override a particular alignment of tax brackets, then either type of plan may be acceptable, depending upon the objectives of the corporation and the insured employee.

Income Tax Aspects of Split Dollar in S Corporations

A comparison of income tax brackets is fine when a C corporation is involved. How should the comparison be made when the owner of an S corporation evaluates a choice of insurance plans to provide personal coverage? Does split dollar make sense as a method of purchasing insurance in the S corporation marketplace?

The owner of an S corporation may favor a split dollar plan for many of the same reasons discussed above that influence the owner of a C corporation (cost recovery, no nondiscrimination rules, etc.). Apart from its income tax status, an S corporation is an entity with financial needs and purposes that are separate from its owners and employees. However, when income tax factors are taken into account, the evaluation of a split dollar plan for an S corporation introduces a number of variables that do not apply if the owners of a C corporation are considering a split dollar plan.

The feasibility of split dollar in an S corporation will depend upon whether the insured employee is a sole shareholder, a majority or minority shareholder, or simply a key employee who owns no stock in the corporation. In addition, the insured may be a shareholder who is not employed by the corporation. The income tax planning efforts of those various ownership and employment categories are summarized in the following pages.

Sole shareholder-employee. If the S corporation pays the entire premium, it is a nondeductible expense that is paid from income taxable to the insured shareholder. In addition, as an employee, the insured receives an economic benefit that is measured according to the term insurance cost of the coverage. The insured suffers a certain amount of double taxation because he is both a shareholder and an employee. The numbers might look like this:

S Corporation Income Taxable to Shareholder $100,000
    Premium ....$ 10,000
    Economic Benefit (Term Cost) ....$ 1,000

Income Taxable to Shareholder - Employee:
    As Shareholder ....$ 10,000
    As Employee ....$ 1,000
    Total Income ....$ 11,000

The "double charge" for the term insurance cost seems inequitable, but to the author's knowledge no relief is available from the Code, the income tax regulations, IRS rulings or court cases. The nondeductible expense of the premium paid by the corporation passes through to the shareholder and is separate from the current benefit of the coverage provided to the employee for services rendered. While there is no question that the insured employee enjoys an ongoing benefit from the protection that is provided, the absorption of the taxable income to the shareholder occurs because the corporation is not a taxable entity. If the insured is a nonowner employee of an S corporation or if the corporation is a C corporation, the cost of the entire premium and the economic benefit are allocated to two different parties. While S corporation status certainly has its advantages, an "employer-pay-all" split dollar plan brings out its dark side.

Nonetheless, the "double tax" result can be avoided if the premium contribution by each party is properly arranged. Specifically, the insured should pay the term cost of the policy and the corporation should pay the balance of the premium. This type of arrangement, sometimes called a "PS 58 offset plan" or simply a contributory plan, is designed to eliminate reportable income to the insured. If the employer pays the entire premium, the insured must report the term cost of the coverage as income under Revenue Rulings 64-328 and 66-110. Both rulings also indicate that any premium contributions by the insured employee will offset the amount of income otherwise reportable. If the insured sole shareholder-employee in our example contributes the $1,000 term cost "out-of-pocket," the tax treatment lines up as follows:

Premium Allocation for Contributory Plan
Premium .... $ 10,000
Shareholder Pays Term Cost .... $ 1,000
Corporation Pays Balance of Premium .... $ 9,000

Income Taxable to Shareholder - Employee
As Shareholder .... $ 9,000
As Employee .... $ 0
Total Income .... $ 9,000

By contributing the term cost otherwise taxable to him as an employee, the insured eliminates $1,000 of income (although he must earn enough income to cover the term cost). At the same time, the S corporation is required to pay only $9,000 from its taxable income and that portion of the cost to the insured as a shareholder is correspondingly reduced.

The true cost to the S corporation shareholder-employee of the contributory arrangement can be illustrated by comparing it to a split dollar plan established by a C corporation. Suppose that a C corporation and its shareholder-employee enter into an "employer-pay-all" split dollar plan in which the employer will also pay a "double bonus" to cover the employee's income tax cost. The employer will pay the entire premium plus a bonus sufficient to reimburse the employee's income tax cost attributable to both the economic benefit from the plan and the bonus itself. Using the same figures illustrated above, the employee's income tax treatment is as follows:

Premium Paid by Corporation .... $ 10,000
Bonus Paid by Corporation .... $ 429

Employee's Income:
Economic Benefit (Term Cost) .... $ 1,000
Bonus .... $ 429

Total Income .... $ 1,429
Income Tax @ 30% Rate .... $ 429

(When a 50% tax rate was in effect, the term "double bonus" was appropriate because a $2 bonus was necessary to provide the employee with $1 after paying $1 of income tax. However, since individual tax rates have been reduced, it might be more appropriate to refer to an "extra bonus.") The $429 bonus covers the $300 of income tax generated by the $1,000 of economic benefit plus $129 of tax resulting from the bonus itself.

A contributory split dollar plan for an insured who is the sole shareholder-employee of an S corporation may also be compared to an employer-pay-all plan for a C corporation *without* the "extra bonus." Rather than follow the extra bonus approach to make the employee whole after the tax, suppose that the employee will bear the $300 tax resulting from the $1000 of income charged to him when the C corporation pays the premium. In the same manner, when the employee contributes the term cost for the S corporation plan, the employer is presumably the source of funds for the contribution. The employee derives his $1,000 contribution from other compensation paid by the employer (which may or may not be earmarked as a bonus) and absorbs the $300 income tax liability.

To this point, the discussion has dealt only with the insured's income tax consequences as an employee, rather than as a shareholder. On the other side of the equation, the corporate cost of the premium is borne by the C corporation or by the sole shareholder of the S corporation. If the cost in both cases is not identical, it is at least consistent with the general pattern of taxation that each type of entity creates; the nondeductible cost is borne by the corporation at its tax rate or by the shareholder at his personal tax rate.

When the income tax costs on both the shareholder and the employee sides of the ledger are combined for an S corporation split dollar plan, the total is the same as for a personally owned policy under a bonus plan. As discussed above, the insured's contribution to the premium as an employee presumably stems from a compensation payment ("bonus") that may or may not be sufficient to cover his income tax liability. The balance of the premium payment is paid from income that is taxable to the S corporation shareholder. If the premium were paid under a bonus plan, the entire amount would be taxable to the employee as compensation. At the same time, the payment would be deductible to the corporation and would reduce its income, thereby reducing the shareholder's income. However, since the shareholder and the employee are the same individual, either form of plan results in income taxed at the same rate to the same person, albeit classified differently (with a possible difference in the shareholder's basis, as discussed below). In such a case, if a bonus plan would be just as effective as a split dollar plan from the standpoint of income tax planning, then other factors, such as the corporation's need to control the cash value, should apply to justify the use of a split dollar plan. If other factors supporting the use of a split dollar plan do not apply, then a personally owned policy paid under a bonus plan may be more suitable.

More Than One Shareholder. If an S corporation is owned by more than one shareholder, the allocation of cost is a bit more complicated than in the sole shareholder situation. The term cost remains taxable to the insured shareholder-employee unless the insured avoids taxation by contributing to the cost of the plan. The balance of the premium, however, is allocated to the shareholders in direct proportion to their ownership of stock.

EXAMPLE. Wally owns 60% and Eddie owns 40% of C & H Enterprises. They decide to have the corporation sponsor a split dollar plan for Eddie to which he will contribute the term insurance cost of the coverage. The premium would be allocated to Wally and Eddie as follows:

Premium	$10,000
Eddie's Contribution (Term Cost)	$ 1,000
Balance of Premium	$ 9,000

Allocation of Balance from Shareholder's Income:

Wally: 60% ë $9,000	$ 5,400
Eddie: 40% ë $9,000	$ 3,600

Upon disclosure of the allocation of costs, Wally decides that he would also like to be covered by an identical policy. The costs would continue to be allocated according to the same percentages shown above, except, of course, Wally would contribute his own term insurance cost.

In effect, Wally pays a greater portion of the balance of the premium than Eddie does because he owns more shares and the taxable income that is the source of the premium is allocated according to stock ownership. Certainly, in regard to Eddie's policy, he might feel that he is personally subsidizing a benefit for Eddie. As in the case of any other fringe benefit, if one owner believes that the other owner receives a disproportionate benefit, other adjustments to compensation can be made if the business is profitable enough and the owners can comfortably negotiate with each other. For instance, if only Eddie were covered by the plan, and each of the shareholders otherwise received a bonus, Wally's bonus might be increased to rectify any perceived imbalance in compensation caused by Eddie's coverage. (However, given that the imbalance is a product of *shareholder* income, any attempt to redress the difference should be independently justifiable as a matter of compensation paid to an employee for services rendered. A purported compensation payment that is determined by the IRS to be a dividend may run afoul of the rules defining the one class of stock requirement and lead to termination of S corporation status.)

Nonowner Key Employee. Suppose that C & H Enterprises offers split dollar coverage to Theodore, a key employee. Although Theodore might be required to contribute the term cost of his coverage, Wally and Eddie are bearing the brunt of the cost from income that is taxable to them as shareholders. Are Wally and Eddie crazy? What dark secrets must Theodore know about the shareholders to persuade them to include him in the plan?

Far from being crazy, Wally and Eddie may actually be shrewd employers. As discussed in Chapter 7, it may be preferable to pay greater cash and benefits to a valued key employee than to transfer stock of an S corporation to him. Any subsequent transfer by Theodore to an ineligible shareholder may jeopardize S corporation status. Such a transfer could be prevented or rendered inoperative by a restrictive provision in the shareholders' buy-sell agreement. Even so, the perils of minority ownership that apply to both S and C corporations may steer the shareholders away from sharing equity with a key employee.

There are a few reasons why Wally and Eddie may consider split dollar protection for Theodore. Before doing so, however, assuming that they agree that providing life insurance coverage for Theodore is an appropriate form of fringe benefit, they may first entertain the bonus plan format discussed in Chapter 2. While the premium would be deductible to C & H Enterprises, other factors may outweigh that advantage. Wally and Eddie may not be confident that Theodore will be sufficiently "handcuffed" to the corporation because of the coverage. If Theodore were to leave the company, he could take the policy with him. On the other hand, if C & H Enterprises owns the cash value of a policy held under a split dollar plan, Theodore could be obligated to purchase the corporation's interest in the policy under the terms of a split dollar agreement. If, instead, Theodore stays with the company over the long term, the policy could be rolled out of the plan to Theodore upon retirement (or sooner) subject to terms that would fairly reward his service over the period.

The terms of the split dollar agreement enable the corporation to protect its investment in the policy and limit Theodore's access to the cash value. The investment feature is secondary to the role of the policy as an employee benefit. The purpose of the plan is to provide a death benefit to a key employee, but if circumstances change, the corporation can recover its premium outlay plus interest if the employee purchases the policy for its cash value upon termination of the plan. By following this approach, Wally and Eddie are more likely to be willing to subsidize the overall cost of the coverage as shareholders because they can recoup their investment if Theodore leaves sooner than they had expected.

Shareholder Only (Not an Employee). An S or a C corporation may enter into a split dollar agreement with a shareholder who is not employed by the corporation. The premium is paid as a nondeductible expense of the corporation. Revenue Ruling 79-50[12] describes the income tax consequences that flow from a split dollar arrangement established for the benefit of the shareholder of "a corporation" (presumably a C corporation). The ruling states that the economic benefit provided to a shareholder because of the corporation's payment for the term insurance cost constitutes a distribution by the corporation to the shareholder with respect to his or her stock under Section 301(c). The distribution is a dividend to the extent of the earnings and profits of the corporation.

If an S corporation provides life insurance coverage under a split dollar plan for a nonemployee shareholder, the same pattern of income taxation specified in Revenue Ruling 79-50 should apply, within the framework of the S corporation rules. The premium paid by the S corporation is also a nondeductible expense, effectively paid from income taxable to the shareholders. If the corporation is owned by a sole shareholder, he absorbs the cost of the premium out of income taxable to him or her as a shareholder. (Thus, the cost is apt to be the same as for a personally owned policy under a bonus plan. Given an equal cost for either type of plan, a clear need for the S corporation to have access to cash value or to receive a death benefit would have to be established to justify a split dollar plan.) On the other hand, if the S corporation is owned by more than one shareholder, the taxable income from which the premium is paid would be prorated among the shareholders according to stock ownership.

Just as in Revenue Ruling 79-50, the term insurance portion of a premium paid by an S corporation for split dollar coverage provided to a shareholder is also a distribution to the shareholder with respect to his or her stock. However, the tax consequences of the distribution to the S corporation shareholder are governed by Section 1368 (rather than Section 301(c) for the C corporation shareholder). Apparently, it is possible that a sole shareholder of an S corporation having earnings and profits (E&P) could incur double taxation on the term insurance cost in a manner analogous to a sole shareholder-employee covered by an employer-pay-all split dollar plan. The premium is paid from corporate income taxable to the shareholder and the term insurance cost is a distribution, apart from the premium payment. If the S corporation has E&P, the term insurance cost is taxable to the shareholder as a dividend (unless the distribution is treated as made from the accumulated adjustments account (AAA)). Nonetheless, for S corporations having no E&P, the distribution deemed to occur because of the term insurance cost simply reduces the shareholder's basis. Since the premium payment by the C corporation is paid from income taxable to the shareholder in any event, the distribution issue can be avoided if the shareholder directly pays the term insurance cost "out of pocket" and the S corporation pays the balance of the premium. Just as with an S corporation shareholder-employee, the contributory approach cuts off the potential for double taxation or, at least, eliminates the possibility of a deemed distribution to the insured shareholder, whether taxable, or nontaxable as a reduction in basis.

One Class of Stock Requirement. In Letter Ruling 9318007, Revenue Ruling 79-50 was cited by the Service in the context of whether a split dollar plan provided for the benefit of an S corporation shareholder would create more than one class of stock. The facts of the ruling involved the establishment of a split dollar plan for an S corporation for the benefit of one of its shareholders (who was also the president and chief executive officer of the corporation). The plan was contributory. The shareholder's irrevocable trust would pay for the economic benefit, or term insurance value, of the coverage and the corporation would pay for the balance of the premium.

In its ruling request, the corporation asked the Service to address the issue of whether the proposed split dollar life insurance plan would create more than one class of stock within the meaning of Code section 1361(b)(1)(D). The Service pointed to pertinent provisions of Regulation Section 1.1361-1(b) regarding the one class of stock requirement. These regulations are concerned with whether all outstanding shares of stock confer identical rights with respect to distribution and liquidation proceeds. Regulation Section 1.1361-1(l)(i) states that a commercial contractual agreement, such as a lease, employment agreement, or loan agreement, is not a binding agreement relating to distribution and liquidation proceeds (and thus is not a "governing provision" for such purpose) unless a principal purpose of the agreement is to circumvent the one class of stock requirement under Section 1361(b)(1)(D). The Service cited Revenue Ruling 79-50 with respect to the question of whether the payment of a split dollar benefit by the corporation for a shareholder was a corporate distribution.

In Letter Ruling 9318007, the IRS concluded that the corporation's proposed split dollar agreement would not create more than one class of stock. The contributory nature of the plan seemed to be a significant factor in the Service's holding, as indicated by the following statement:

> Because the arrangement provides that, at the time X pays the premiums, A, or the irrevocable trust established by A, must reimburse X to the extent the payment confers an economic benefit to that shareholder, X's split dollar arrangement does not alter rights to distribution and liquidation proceeds.

It is worth noting that, while the ruling describes the insured as both a shareholder and president/chief executive officer, it ignores the possibility that the premium payment by the corporation (if the plan were employer-pay-all rather than contributory) would be treated as employee compensation. Perhaps other facts not described in the ruling would cause the economic benefit of the coverage to be characterized as a shareholder distribution rather than compensation. However, unless a shareholder-employee has otherwise reached the threshold of exhausting the limits of reasonable compensation, it is more likely that the economic benefit should be classified as employee compensation, rather than as a shareholder distribution. Treating the economic benefit as compensation, rather than as a dividend, should foreclose any possible concern with regard to the one class of stock rule.

It is likely that the taxpayer in Letter Ruling 9318007 had specific reasons to believe that the split dollar plan would be viewed as a benefit provided to a shareholder rather than to an employee. That classification, in turn, apparently led to the application of Revenue Ruling 79-50, which was clearly directed to the tax treatment accorded a shareholder covered under a split dollar plan. In any event, it is better to have a split dollar benefit provided to an S corporation shareholder-employee on a contributory basis, rather than employer-pay-all, to avoid both double taxation on the term insurance benefit, as well as the possibility that shareholder distributions could raise the one class of stock issue.

Shareholder's Basis in Split Dollar Plans. The premium payment by an S corporation for a policy held under a split dollar plan has an effect on a shareholder's basis in his stock that is similar to the effect on basis for a corporate owned policy. Suppose that a split dollar plan is adopted by an S corporation for its sole shareholder-employee and that the corporation will pay the entire premium. As discussed in Chapter 3, the shareholder's basis in the S corporation stock should be decreased by the "net insurance expense," that is, the difference between the premium and the annual increase in cash value in each year. If the cash value increase exceeds the premium, no reduction in basis occurs, but, in the author's opinion, no *increase* in basis may occur because of the excess amount.[13] If dividends received under a participating policy are paid to the S corporation, the shareholder's basis in stock is increased correspondingly. For example, dividends received by the S corporation in cash should be classified as tax-exempt income (unless the corporation's basis in the *policy* is exceeded, in which case policy dividends are taxable), and the shareholder's basis in stock should be increased accordingly. Further variations that are equally relevant to corporate owned policies or those held under a split dollar plan are discussed in Chapter 3.

If the insured contributes to the cost of the split dollar plan, basis is calculated a bit differently than it is with a corporate owned policy. As discussed above, it is preferable for the sole shareholder-employee of an S corporation to contribute the term cost of the policy in order to avoid being taxed "twice" on the economic benefit of the coverage. In such a case, the starting point for determining the "net insurance expense" of the corporation is the balance of the premium paid by the S corporation, rather than the entire premium. Furthermore, if dividends are paid to the insured, rather than to the corporation, the shareholder's basis in S corporation stock will not be increased.[14]

It is also worth mentioning that the calculation of the "net insurance expense" will be affected by the corporation's interest in the cash value under the terms of the split dollar plan. If an S corporation owns a life insurance policy, it owns the entire cash value of the policy. It is more likely that the S corporation's cash value ownership in a policy held under a split dollar plan will be limited to the extent of its premium payments, rather than the full cash value, if the insured is a shareholder-employee of the corporation. In calculating the amount of the "net insurance expense" for purposes of determining the effect of the S corporation's premium payment, only that portion of the annual cash value increase to which the corporation is entitled should offset its premium payment for purposes of computing the extent to which the "net insurance expense" may reduce the basis of the shareholder in the S corporation stock. If the S corporation shares are held by more than one shareholder, the effect on basis will be correspondingly prorated according to stock ownership.

Split Dollar "Rollouts"

In recent years, many split dollar plans have been established in contemplation of a future transfer or "rollout" of the policy to the exclusive ownership of the insured. Prior to the restrictions on the deductibility of interest that were imposed by the Tax Reform Act of 1986 (TRA '86), split dollar plans were often designed to have the corporation pay four of the first seven annual premiums. In the beginning of the eighth policy year, the policy would be "rolled out" of the split dollar plan and transferred to the insured employee. At that time, the insured would borrow an amount from the cash value that would be sufficient to repay the corporation for its premium payments. Thereafter, the insured would continue to borrow from the policy's cash value in order to pay premiums and the tax leverage obtained from deducting interest at a 50% personal tax rate would permit the insured to maintain the policy in force without having to pay premiums "out of pocket." Another factor favoring the rollout technique was the motivation to avoid the increasingly expensive term insurance costs that are imposed at older ages if the insured remains within the split dollar plan.

Since the introduction of TRA '86, financed insurance has joined multiple write off limited partnerships in tax shelter heaven. Split dollar rollouts are still being illustrated, but they are now more typically designed to operate within a "vanishing premium" arrangement. Rising term insurance costs at older ages continue to favor the use of a rollout, although the year of rollout may be extended because of the widespread use of lower illustrative term insurance rates by many insurers[15] and lower income tax brackets. While lower term rates and tax rates provide some relief, at older ages it generally becomes advantageous to terminate the split dollar plan. Even if premiums are not paid by the S corporation because a vanishing premium arrangement is utilized, the insured would still be taxed on the economic benefit of receiving the insurance protection within the split dollar plan as long as it remains in effect.

Many split dollar plans that are set up for the benefit of shareholder-employees or key employees are structured as "equity plans." Under an equity plan, the corporation typically has a secured interest in the cash value to the extent of its premium payments, rather than ownership of the full cash value. To the extent that the total cash value exceeds the corporation's premium payments, the "excess" cash value ("equity") accrues to the benefit of the insured. In the event that the split dollar plan is terminated and the policy is rolled out to the insured, the cash value of the policy is transferred to the insured. The prospect that the insured employee of a C corporation will incur a substantial income tax liability upon the transfer of cash value in the year of rollout has been a concern to tax planning practitioners. In two private letter rulings,[16] the IRS has indicated that an insured employee must report income in the year of rollout equal to the cash value of the transferred policy offset by any amount contributed by the employee toward the purchase of the policy (apparently including his or her term insurance contributions, as well). The position of the IRS is that the transfer of the cash value constitutes a transfer of property by an employer to an employee that is subject to Code section 83.

Some commentators have argued that Section 83 should not apply to a rollout if the plan is established on a collateral assignment basis. The argument is based upon the premise that the employee is the initial owner of the policy and the release of a collateral assignment to the corporation should not be classified as a transfer of cash value for purposes of Section 83. The proponents of the view that a rollout is not a taxable event also find solace in the fact that neither of the private letter rulings issued by the IRS dealt with a collateral assignment plan. In the author's opinion, that argument overlooks the economics of a rollout, regardless of whether the plan is established as a collateral assignment, an endorsement, or other-

wise. In analyzing the tax treatment of a rollout from a collateral assignment plan, the Service could reissue its catchall statement from Revenue
Ruling 64-328 (addressed to taxation of the split dollar plan's economic
benefit, but equally applicable in the context of a rollout):

> The same income tax results obtain if the transaction is cast in
> some other form resulting in a similar benefit to the employee.

If the rollout of the policy from a split dollar plan is to the insured
employee (or shareholder-employee) of an S corporation, the income tax
consequences to the insured should be the same as if a C corporation were
involved. However, with an S corporation, the income tax consequences
to the shareholders should also be taken into account. The private letter
rulings regarding rollouts indicate that the employer is entitled to a
deduction under Code section 162 equal to the amount included in the
insured's income. In other words, if a rollout creates income for the
insured, it permits a corresponding income tax deduction to the corporation. If a split dollar plan is sponsored by an S corporation for the benefit
of its sole shareholder-employee, the transaction amounts to a wash. The
insured is charged with income as an *employee*. On the other side of the
equation, the deduction taken by the S corporation will reduce its income,
and therefore, the taxable income of the insured as a *shareholder*.

Whatever conclusion may be reached regarding the issue of income
taxation to the insured upon a rollout, the potential for taxation has to be
recognized. The "wash" result that occurs if a sole shareholder-employee
of an S corporation is the insured neutralizes the threat of future taxation.
The deduction that benefits the S corporation, and therefore, the shareholder, offsets the income to the insured as employee. However, as with
other aspects of split dollar generally, the tax consequences of rollouts
play out differently depending upon whether an S corporation is owned by
one shareholder or more than one shareholder, and whether the insured
employee is a shareholder or a nonowner key employee. If more than one
shareholder is involved, the value of the deduction is directly proportional
to the percentage of stock owned by the insured. And, if the insured is not
a shareholder, the prospect of charging the insured with income upon a
rollout is directly opposed to the shareholders' benefit from a corporate
deduction.

UPDATE ON EQUITY SPLIT DOLLAR PLANS

For many years, tax planning practitioners have been concerned that the rollout of a policy to the sole ownership of the insured covered under an equity split dollar plan might result in income taxation of the insured under Code section 83. As mentioned in the last section of this chapter, opinion has been divided between those who believe that Section 83 might apply and those who maintain that a rollout should not be viewed as a taxable event, at least in the case of a collateral assignment split dollar plan. The defense to the prospect of taxation advanced by those in the latter camp has been based upon the argument that Section 72, rather than Section 83, should control the income tax treatment of the insured. The proponents of the Section 72 viewpoint contend that, under a collateral assignment plan, the insured owns the policy from the time of issue and simply continues that ownership after the rollout. Thus, the argument goes, a rollout is not a taxable event because the insured's ownership is unbroken from the inception of the policy to its aftermath following a rollout. According to that view, Section 72 governs whether, how and when an insured is taxed with respect to ownership of a life insurance policy. Under the Section 72 theory, the termination of an equity split dollar plan, in which the corporation receives only its premiums and the insured owns cash values generated as a result of payments by the corporation, should not cause the insured to be taxed. Apart from that, if the insured surrenders the policy and realizes gain in doing so, Section 72 should control income tax consequences to the insured.

Those who believe that Section 83 should apply to a rollout have also been concerned that the insured under an equity split dollar arrangement could be taxed well in advance of a rollout. In general, Section 83 addresses the taxation of an employee who receives property in return for services. "Property," in this context, might mean stock or other intangible rights, tangible goods, or other items of a non-cash nature that might be transferred by an employer to an employee. Regulation Section 1.83-3(e) specifically provides that property includes a beneficial interest in assets (including money) that are transferred or set aside from the claims of the creditors of the corporation, such as in a trust or escrow account. In the case of transfer of a life insurance policy, the term property includes only the cash surrender value of the policy. The transfer of all, or a portion of, the cash value of an insurance policy by an employer to an employee is clearly subject to the application of Section 83. For example, if an S (or a C) corporation owned an insurance policy on the life of a key employee and transferred it to the employee as a bonus, the employee would be taxed on the cash surrender value of the policy.

Suppose that an employer owns a policy with a cash value of $100,000 on the life of its key employee. If the employer transfers the policy to the employee, the insured employee would be taxed on the $100,000 cash value. If the employee pays $20,000 for the policy, he should be taxed on only $80,000. Or, if the employer borrows $40,000 from the cash value before assigning the policy to the insured, the latter's income would be only $60,000.

In the case of an equity split dollar plan, the proponents of Section 83 assert that the insured should be taxed upon receipt of a vested right to the cash value of a life insurance policy to the extent that the "equity" portion of the cash value in any year exceeds the amount paid by, or taxed to, the insured — even before a rollout. Under that rationale, the insured would be taxed even if a rollout never occurs. Until a recent pronouncement by the IRS, taxation prior to rollout was a theoretical possibility, but not an imminent concern because the Service had previously considered the taxation of the insured under Section 83 only in the context of a rollout.

Technical Advice Memorandum 9604001:
Income Taxation of the Insured Under an Equity Split Dollar Plan

In Technical Advice Memorandum 9604001, the IRS adopted a new position concerning the application of Section 83 to the insured's equity under a split dollar plan. The facts of Technical Advice Memorandum 9604001 indicate that the insured was the chairman, chief executive officer, and 51% shareholder of a corporation that owned 98% of its subsidiary. The insured established an irrevocable trust, which, together with the subsidiary corporation, entered into the following arrangement:

(1)   The trust purchased two $500,000 insurance policies on the executive's life, which were issued to the trust as owner; and

(2)   The trust and the subsidiary entered into split dollar agreements, pursuant to which the trust executed a collateral assignment in favor of the subsidiary to provide collateral for the trust's obligation to repay the subsidiary for the premiums it paid to each insurance company.

The split dollar agreements specified that the trust owned all incidents of ownership in the policies and was the beneficiary of the policy proceeds. In the event of the insured's death, the subsidiary had an unqualified right to receive its premiums paid from the death proceeds of the policy before any amount would be repaid to the trust. The subsidiary would be reimbursed for its premium payments in the event that the policies were surrendered during the insured's lifetime. The split dollar agreements would be terminated in the event of the subsidiary's bankruptcy, the executive's termination of employment, or at the notification to the subsidiary by the trust or the executive, among other reasons.

The split dollar agreements also directed that policy dividends were to be applied to purchase paid-up additional insurance. Furthermore, the trust had the right to borrow, pledge or assign the cash value of the policy, but only to the extent that the cash value exceeded the amount of the premiums paid by the subsidiary.

In the technical advice memorandum, the IRS was presented with the following issues:

(1)   When the subsidiary paid single premiums for the two insurance policies, what amount of income should be included each year in the executive's gross income?

(2)   If the trust was designated as the owner of the insurance policies, did the executive make a gift subject to the gift tax?

In dealing with the first issue, the Service turned to Code section 83, noting that property transferred for services "...is included in the service provider's gross income in the first taxable year in which the rights of the service provider are transferable or are not subject to a substantial risk of forfeiture." Property is "transferred" under Section 83(a) when a person acquires a beneficial interest in the property.

In analyzing the split dollar agreement between the subsidiary and the executive, the Service referred to Revenue Rulings 64-328 and 66-110. It described the particular split dollar plan in Revenue Ruling 64-328 as "...an arrangement that was popular at the time the revenue ruling was published." Revenue Ruling 64-328 had considered both the endorsement system and the collateral assignment system of split dollar plans, and, with respect to the latter, the technical advice memorandum states:

Under the collateral assignment system, the employee in form owns the policy and pays the entire premium thereon. The employer in form made annual loans, without interest (or below the fair rate of interest), to the employee of amounts equal to the yearly increases in the cash surrender value, but not exceeding the annual premiums. The employee then executes an assignment of the policy to the employer as collateral security for the loans. The loans were generally payable at the termination of employment or the death of the employee.

The technical advice memorandum affirmed the conclusion of Revenue Ruling 64-328 that the insured employee is taxable on the annual value of the economic benefit of the split dollar arrangement, that is, the one-year term cost of the life insurance protection. That portion of the Service's analysis covers familiar ground. However, the following statement represents the launching pad for its position that the taxpayer in Technical Advice Memorandum 9604001 will be taxable on the future growth of the policy's cash values in excess of the employer's share:

In amplifying Revenue Ruling 64-328, Revenue Ruling 66-110 concludes that any benefit received from a split dollar arrangement in addition to the current insurance protection discussed in Revenue Ruling 64-328 is also includable in the employee's gross income. According to Revenue Ruling 66-110, that additional benefit may be a policyholder dividend distributed directly to the employee or it may be paid in the form of additional one-year term insurance, or paid-up life insurance for a period of more than one year.

The technical advice memorandum then states that the holdings of Revenue Rulings 64-328 and 66-110 were not affected by the enactment of Section 83. The term insurance value of the protection is taxable to the executive. As to the growth in the cash value, the portion payable to the subsidiary is not taxable to the executive because it remained a general asset of the corporation subject to the claims of its creditors. However, the technical advice memorandum applies Section 83 to the growth of the executive's equity under the policy, that is, the cash value in excess of the employer's share. The technical advice memorandum states:

The cash surrender values in the policies are not taxable to Taxpayer under Section 83 because they remained subject to the claims of Subsidiary's general creditors and to the claims of Subsidiary as a creditor. Thus they were not "property" "transferred" to an employee. The only income therefore reportable by Taxpayer in the years of issue is the value each year of the cost-free life insurance protection under Section 61. Income will be reportable in later years under Section 83 to the extent that the cash surrender values of the policies exceed the premiums paid by Subsidiary because this is the amount that is returnable to Subsidiary.

Presumably, the technical advice memorandum would apply Section 83 so that each year's increase in cash value would be considered a "transfer" of property to the extent that the annual increase is a portion of the excess of aggregate cash value over aggregate premiums paid by the employer that were not previously taxed. The technical advice memorandum does not provide any further description of how future growth in cash values will be taxed. Further, it does not offer any additional rationale as to the operation of Section 83 in taxing the future cash value growth of the policy.

The technical advice memorandum may not be cited as precedent and only applies to the particular taxpayer to whom it directly refers. However, it offers insight into the thinking of the Service on the subject of equity split dollar plans. The significance of the technical advice memorandum is that it addresses the taxation of the cash value increases under Section 83 *prior to a rollout and without regard to whether a rollout will even occur.* For many years equity split dollar plans have been under a cloud of uncertainty as to the application of Section 83 in the event of a rollout. At the same time, many S and C corporations, both large and small, have established equity split dollar plans for their shareholder-employees and executives. In many cases, the concern about possible income tax consequences in the event of a rollout has been deferred for many years until the rollout actually occurs.

In the typical situation, equity for the insured may develop after the policy is in force for five to ten years. Thus, it is necessary for the insured to deal with the prospect of taxation much sooner than if no taxable event occurs until retirement, or another future event that would terminate the split dollar plan. In addition, if the position of the Service in the technical advice memorandum is correct, income tax reporting occurs on an annual basis after an insured employee develops equity in the policy.

Technical Advice Memorandum 9604001 has reverberated across the life insurance industry and has caused a good deal of reaction (and perhaps, overreaction) among practitioners. Unfortunately, its conclusion will tend to chill the establishment of equity split dollar plans. Beyond its limited value as a technical advice memorandum, as opposed to say, a revenue ruling, it does not articulate what constitutes a "transfer" for Section 83 purposes. Further, it does not offer an explanation of how the catchall statement in Revenue Ruling 66-110 regarding the possible taxation of "any benefit," other than current life insurance protection, should be defined.

Additional definition by the Service as to whether, how and when Section 83 applies to the taxation of equity split dollar plans would be very useful in creating a framework for planning. In the meantime, the effect of the apparent shift in the Service's position regarding equity split dollar plans has the same effect upon the insured employee participating in the plan, without regard to whether a C corporation or an S corporation is involved.

REVERSE SPLIT DOLLAR PLANS

In recent years, reverse split dollar plans have gained some degree of attention (and notoriety) as an alternative form of split dollar plan. As the name implies, the roles of the corporation and the employee are reversed. Typically, the insured employee applies for and owns the policy and endorses to the corporation the right to name itself as beneficiary of the amount at risk (the "risk proceeds"), that is, the difference between the total death benefit and the cash value of the policy. The employee continues to own the cash value of the policy.

The premium is usually split between the parties along the same lines as a conventional split dollar plan, but with a reversal of roles regarding payment based on the respective interests of each party to the death benefit and cash value of the policy. The employer pays a portion of the premium equal to the PS 58 cost or term insurance cost of its portion of the death benefit and the employee pays the balance of the premium.

Regardless of whether a C or an S corporation is involved, the insured contributes the balance of the premium. Presumably, the insured's contribution is derived from compensation received as an employee of the corporation. Thus, the payment of the insured's portion of the premium is from "after tax" income and is comparable to a Section 162 bonus plan arrangement. Of course, the "balance of the premium" may vary in amount depending upon whether the corporation pays the full PS 58 rates or the lower one-year published term rates of the insurer in conformity with Revenue Ruling 66-110.

As term insurance costs increase at older ages, the PS 58 or term insurance rates constitute an increasingly greater portion of the premium. In addition, the actual PS 58 rates may be four to five times greater than the insurer's term insurance rates, which means that the corporation will pay a correspondingly higher premium if the PS 58 rates, rather than the insurer's rates, are used to determine its contribution.

The full PS 58 rates are often used to determine the corporation's contribution, as compared to the lower term insurance rates that are utilized for the employee's contribution to conventional split dollar plans. The PS 58 rates far exceed the actual term cost of the coverage. Reverse split dollar plans are often presented as a way to transfer corporate dollars into the cash value of the policy that is owned by the insured. Increasing the corporation's contribution also means that a greater portion of the premium is nondeductible to the corporation. (Again, the remaining portion of the premium presumably is derived from a deductible payment of compensation by the corporation to the employee.)

No court cases, regulations or rulings are available to provide guidance as to the income tax consequences of reverse split dollar plans. Nonetheless, it seems reasonable to infer from Revenue Rulings 64-328 and 66-110 that the *measurement* of the economic benefit of death benefit should be determined in the same manner as for a conventional split dollar plan, even if the parties' interests in the policy are entirely different. Therefore, it seems that either measurement of the economic benefit — PS 58 or term insurance rates — is permissible under the literal terms of the cited revenue rulings. Even so, given that the insurer's term insurance rate would unquestionably be used for regular split dollar plans, the use of the PS 58 rate may be open to question by the IRS if the circumstances otherwise suggest that an insured shareholder-employee is not dealing at arm's length with his corporation.

For our purposes in this chapter, it is not necessary to support or criticize one method or another of determining how much an employer and an employee should contribute to a reverse split dollar plan. If a C corporation is a party to the plan, using either the lower term or higher PS 58 rates may be a function of how corporate and personal tax brackets are aligned, at least in a situation in which the insured employee is also the sole shareholder. The same comparison cited earlier applies.

If the tax brackets of the C corporation and the insured favor a bonus plan approach, then the corporation should contribute only the lower term insurance cost. That payment is nondeductible and the balance of the premium can be paid by the insured from a bonus that is deductible to the corporation. If the insured is a doctor and the owner of a professional corporation, any taxable income of the corporation will be subject to a 34% tax rate,[17] without the benefit of graduated tax rates. If the doctor is in a 28% or 31% individual tax bracket, at least a limited amount of tax leverage is possible.

On the other hand, a larger contribution by the corporation for its share of the death benefit may be in order if the corporation's tax bracket is lower than the insured's tax bracket. If the corporation contributes according to PS 58 rates, it pays a larger portion of the premium. While that payment is nondeductible, it is also not income to the insured. If the insured is in a higher tax bracket, the tax savings to the insured because of the corporation's contribution are greater than the corporation's tax cost for the larger nondeductible payment.

If an S corporation sets up a reverse split dollar plan for the benefit of a shareholder-employee, the following points should be considered:

1. If the insured is the sole shareholder, the entire premium is paid out of the insured's taxable income. The insured bears the cost of the corporation's contribution as a shareholder and pays the remaining portion of the premium from "after-tax" income derived from compensation. In such a case, the cost to the insured is exactly the same, regardless of whether the corporation pays PS 58 rates or the insurer's term rates. Keeping in mind the lack of authority supporting the tax results of reverse split dollar plans, it would be prudent to use the insurer's term rates to reinforce the arm's length character of the arrangement.

It should be recognized that the insured could have complete ownership of the policy at the same tax cost. Therefore, there should be clear and compelling reasons for the insured to split the policy's benefits with the corporation.

2. The "double tax" concern that arises if an S corporation pays the entire premium for the insured under a regular split dollar plan is not a factor for a reverse split dollar plan. Under the reverse arrangement, the corporation pays for its share of the death benefit and no additional economic benefit is chargeable to the insured as an employee because he pays the remainder of the premium.

3. To the extent that there are shareholders involved other than the insured, the corporation's cost is allocated accordingly out of its income taxable to the shareholders. For example, if the insured owns only 20% of the stock, the corporation might choose to pay only the lower term cost and 80% of the remaining term insurance cost would be derived from corporate income taxable to the other shareholders. The insured, of course, would still be responsible for paying the balance of the premium other than the term insurance cost. If that payment is viewed as being derived from compensation received as an employee, the shareholders enjoy the corresponding deduction by the corporation.

4. If a reverse split dollar plan is established for a nonowner key employee, the same dynamics described in the preceding paragraph would apply, except that the insured would bear no portion of the corporation's cost. Once again, it is likely that the corporation would pay only the lower term insurance cost of the plan (rather than PS 58 rates).

5. A reverse split dollar plan is highly specialized and may be appropriate only in a limited number of situations. One scenario that a reverse plan fits is a case in which the corporation needs key employee indemnification for only a limited number of years with a succeeding need for personal coverage. In that case, the corporation pays only term insurance costs during the period when it would receive a death

benefit. At the end of the period, the corporation relinquishes its interest in the policy to the exclusive ownership of the insured. Unlike a conventional split dollar plan, this type of rollout has no income tax implications for the insured. In assuming complete ownership of the policy, the insured assumes the *obligation* to pay the term insurance portion of the premium in order to maintain the total death benefit of the policy. No transfer of cash value or other form of equity is involved upon the termination of the plan.

6.   The corporation's portion of the premium payment directly reduces the basis of the shareholders in the stock of the S corporation. The basis reduction would generally be insignificant unless a very large amount of coverage were purchased for an older insured.

7.   In the event of the insured's death during the period when a reverse split dollar plan is in effect, the proceeds received by the S corporation would directly increase the stock basis of the shareholders. The basis reduction resulting from premium payments during the insured's lifetime is not offset because of cash value increases, nor is an increase in basis allowed because of dividends received. Therefore, the proceeds received by the S corporation upon the death of the insured simply increase basis with respect to the surviving shareholders. In any event, the "step up" rule of Section 1014 increases the basis of the shares held by the deceased shareholder's estate.

ESTATE AND GIFT TAX PLANNING

Chapter 6 deals with estate planning techniques for an S corporation shareholder or key employee. However, a brief discussion of how a split dollar plan may be particularly useful in the estate and gift tax planning of a shareholder-employee belongs in this chapter. In this case, the technique should be contrasted with the result that might occur if premiums for a policy on the life of a shareholder-employee were paid under a Section 162 bonus plan. In other words, the technique about to be discussed is not peculiarly appropriate to S corporation planning; it works just as well if a C corporation is involved. However, it is responsive to the question of why a split dollar plan should be considered for the S corporation shareholder's estate planning.

EXAMPLE: Milo Megabucks is the sole shareholder and the president of Largedeals, Inc., an S corporation. After conferring with his life underwriter, attorney and CPA, he decides to buy a $5,000,000 insurance policy that requires a $100,000 annual premium. Milo will establish an irrevocable trust and the trustee will be the applicant and owner of the policy.

Milo is married and has three children. His attorney is concerned about the gift tax aspects of Milo's contributions to the irrevocable trust. Milo's three children will be *Crummey*[18] beneficiaries in order to permit contributions to the trust to qualify as gifts of a present interest under Section 2503(b). If the transfers of cash to the trust for the premium payments are gifts of a present interest, Milo can give up to $10,000 ($20,000, assuming that his wife joins in the gift) annually to each *Crummey* beneficiary of the trust. However, Milo's attorney is reluctant to add *Crummey* beneficiaries to the trust because he is concerned that the IRS might classify as gifts of a future interest contributions on behalf of beneficiaries who do not have a "substantial and continuing interest" in trust property. The attorney's concern stems from pronouncements of the IRS regarding the conditions that must be satisfied in order for a gift to an irrevocable trust to qualify for the annual exclusion.[19] His attorney adds that he believes the Service is overreaching beyond the standards set in the *Crummey*[20] case and other rulings that it has previously published in regard to the same issue. Nonetheless, he believes that Milo's planning should be safe from possible challenge by the Service and he recommends that only Milo's children should be designated *Crummey* beneficiaries. Thus, Milo faces the problem of having only $60,000 of an annual gift of $100,000 qualify for the annual exclusion, even if Mrs. Megabucks joins in the gift. Naturally, if Milo or his wife dies while premiums are still being paid, the amount qualifying for the annual exclusion is reduced to $30,000.

It is suggested to Milo that he could consume his unified credit during his lifetime by making gifts to the trust beyond the annual exclusion limitation. Milo rejects that suggestion because he wants to preserve the unified credit for estate tax planning purposes — specifically, to fund a credit shelter trust after his death.

A split dollar plan offers an ideal solution in this situation and for other large premium cases with similar facts. Largedeals, Inc. can enter into a split dollar agreement with the trustee of Milo's irrevocable trust. If Largedeals, Inc. were a C corporation, the corporation may pay the entire premium for the policy. In such a case, Milo is subject to income taxation on the term insurance cost of the death benefit payable to the trust and is deemed to make a gift of the same amount to the trust.[21] In order to avoid any question as to whether the term insurance cost qualifies as a present interest gift, the corporation should transfer cash to pay that portion of the premium to the trustee.

However, as explained above in this chapter, it would be better for Milo, as the shareholder-employee of an S corporation, to contribute the term insurance cost "out of pocket." By doing so, he is able to avoid the prospect of double income taxation for the term insurance cost that would otherwise apply under an employer-pay-all plan. The gift tax value of the gifts to the trust should be significantly less than the full premium. The exact measure of the gifts, of course, will depend on Milo's age and the expected duration of the transfers to the trust. Milo should be able to keep the gifts below $30,000 per year, particularly if a vanishing premium arrangement eliminates the need for future contributions to the trust and the policy is rolled out to the trust when the "vanish" stage is reached. The transfers to the trust can be sustained even if Mrs. Megabucks predeceases Milo and he is limited to a $10,000 annual exclusion per *Crummey* beneficiary, rather than the $20,000 amount that is permitted if his wife joins in the gifts.

If the trustee purchases a joint and last survivor policy on the lives of Mr. and Mrs. Megabucks, the value of the gift will be sharply discounted below the term insurance value of a policy on Milo's life alone. For example, if the term insurance value for gift tax purposes is only 20% of the whole life premium for a single life policy, the term insurance value of a joint and last survivor policy might be only 20% of the term insurance value of a single life policy, for gift tax purposes. Thus, a potential gift of $100,000 for the premium for a single life policy may be reduced to $20,000 for the term insurance cost of the gift to the trust under a split dollar arrangement; that gift might be reduced to only $4,000 for a joint and last survivor policy held under a similar plan.

Regardless of whether a single life or joint and last survivor policy is used to facilitate gift tax planning for Milo or a client like him, several other aspects of planning must be coordinated. These include: avoiding estate taxation of the proceeds because of the possible application of the three-year rule under Section 2035; planning to limit the corporation's interest in order to circumvent the controlling stockholder problem that may arise under Regulation Section 20.2042(1)(c)(6) and Revenue Ruling 82-145;[22] coordinating the insured's repayment of the corporation at the time of rollout in regard to both income tax issues and the expectation that a vanishing premium plan will be in place; continuing the payment of the premium and adapting to the increase in gift tax value if one of the insureds covered under a joint and last survivor policy dies prematurely; and ensuring that the policy and the irrevocable trust are integrated within the overall estate plan of one or both insureds.

The position adopted by the IRS in Technical Advice Memorandum 9604001 (discussed above) represents another factor to be taken into account with respect to gift tax planning for split dollar plans. As described above, a split dollar plan can offer considerable leverage in gift tax planning because the value of the gift to an irrevocable trust is only the term insurance value of the coverage. In many instances however, a split dollar arrangement entered into between an irrevocable trust and an S corporation for the benefit of its owner-employee is designed as an "equity" plan. Consequently, to the extent that the increasing cash value in each year creates equity for the irrevocable trust (or other third party owner, such as an adult child), the insured makes an additional gift beyond the annual term insurance value of the policy. Thus, apart from the income tax consequences of the arrangement, the insured must take into account the increased gifts deemed to be made in each year after the "crossover" point is reached. This is when the aggregate cash value of the policy exceeds the aggregate premiums paid by the employer and the irrevocable trust.

From a gift tax planning standpoint, the significance of the increased gift in a particular situation will be a function of its facts. This includes the amount of the premium, the age of the insured, the number of *Crummey* beneficiaries, the projected duration of the split dollar plan, etc. In many instances the increased gift can still be absorbed within the *Crummey* gift (annual exclusion) limits. In the case of a joint and last survivor policy, the increased gift tax value may fall within the annual exclusion limits because the term cost is minimal, at least, while both insureds are alive. This, in turn, means anticipating the increased gift tax value that may result if one insured dies *and* the policy has passed the crossover point.

Many of the same uncertainties that apply to the income tax aspects of equity split dollar plans also pertain to gift tax planning. After all, while income and gift tax results do not necessarily mirror each other generally, Revenue Ruling 78-420 dictates that in the case of split dollar plans involving third party ownership, the measure of a gift for gift tax purposes is necessarily the same as for income tax purposes.[23] Thus, from a gift tax planning vantage point, many of the same considerations must be taken into account for equity split dollar plans as for income tax planning. For example, a forfeiture provision might be employed to defer additional income taxation until a rollout actually occurs. Also, when equity develops, the split dollar plan might be terminated.

However, even though the measurement of the income or the gift attributable to the equity might be the same, the actual effect of the increased gift tax cost could have a very different meaning to the insured than an increased income tax cost. For example, the increased gift attributable to the equity value may be absorbed as a *Crummey* gift within the annual exclusion limitation. Or, even if the equity value causes a portion of the insured's $600,000 exemption equivalent to be utilized, no out-of-pocket expense is incurred, as would occur from an income tax standpoint. By the same token, the income tax cost can be neutralized if the corporation benefits from a corresponding income tax deduction when the insured owner-employee recognizes income because of the growth in equity. Thus, while the corporation may be willing to reimburse an employee for an income tax cost for which the employer receives the benefit of a deduction, an employer may not necessarily cover an employee's cost when gift tax consequences are involved.

All of the additional issues cited can be successfully addressed by planning on the part of the life underwriter and the client's tax attorney. While the planning in such a case can be complicated, it may be far more acceptable than either the gift tax cost of a bonus plan arrangement or the estate depletion that can result from not having coverage in place for estate liquidity purposes.

FOOTNOTE REFERENCES

1. ERISA, Title I, §(3) and generally Parts 4 and 5.
2. ERISA §§ 402, 503.
3. Rev. Rul. 55-713, 1955-2 CB 23.
4. *Id.* at 23.
5. Rev. Rul. 64-328, 1964-2 CB 11.
6. *Id.* at 13.
7. Rev. Rul. 66-110, 1966-1 CB 12.
8. *Id.* at 14.
9. Rev. Rul. 55-747, 1955-2 CB 228.
10. The range of 12% to 20% is the product of multiplying the term costs (20% to 25%) by a factor of 60% to 80%, which is based on the thought that individual income tax rates of 30% or 40% are about 60% to 80% of the former 50% rate.
11. See Rev. Rul. 79-50, 1979-1 CB 138.
12. *Id.*
13. Code section 1367(a)(2)(D) states that an S corporation shareholder's basis in stock is decreased by "any expense of the corporation not deductible in computing its taxable income and not properly chargeable to capital account..." Increases in basis are separately provided for in Section 1367(a)(1).
14. Generally, dividends should be paid to the corporation if it pays the bulk of the premium or the entire premium under a split dollar plan. Policy dividends paid to the insured will create taxable income under Section 72 if they exceed the insured's basis in the *policy.*
15. In addition to actual reductions in term insurance rates during the past several years, many companies offer a term insurance policy that provides a "yardstick" rate for illustrating split dollar policies. Typically, such a policy literally complies with the terms of Revenue Ruling 66-110, but is priced at a minimum level.
16. Let. Ruls. 7916029, 8310027.
17. The first dollar of taxable income is subject to tax at a 34% rate if the corporation is a "qualified personal service corporation" as defined in Code section 448(d)(2). Most professional corporations are considered to be qualified personal service corporations.
18. *Crummey v. Comm.,* 397 F.2d 82 (9th Cir. 1968).
19. See Let. Ruls. 8727003, 9045002. The position adopted by the Service in Letter Ruling 8727003, for example, may have been a product of its facts. Nonetheless, in that ruling, the Service described the need for a *Crummey* beneficiary to have a "sufficient interest" in the trust in order for a transfer by the donor to qualify as a present interest gift. The "sufficient interest" test can be viewed as a gloss upon the *Crummey* withdrawal right, rather than a mere clarification by the Service. In *Estate of Cristofani v. Commissioner,* 97 TC 74 (1991), the Tax Court appears to have erased that gloss and reaffirmed the fundamental point of *Crummey*: the legal right of a beneficiary to make a demand upon the trustee for a withdrawal is determinative of whether the gift qualifies for the annual exclusion. Whether the right is likely to be exercised, actually exercised (or extended by future economic benefits that amount to a "sufficient interest") does not matter.
20. *Crummey v. Comm.,* 397 F.2d 82 (9th Cir. 1968).
21. See Rev. Rul. 78-420, 1978-2 CB 67.
22. Rev. Rul. 82-145, 1982-2 CB 213.
23. Rev. Rul. 78-420, 1978-2 CB 67.

Chapter 5

BUSINESS CONTINUATION PLANNING

The owner of an S corporation has to plan for its continuation or disposition in the event of the owner's death or a lifetime event, such as disability or retirement, that triggers a sale of the corporation. Many of the same issues that apply to the planning of a C corporation shareholder also figure into continuation planning when an S corporation is involved. In addition, the S corporation election creates opportunities and pitfalls that are not pertinent to C corporation planning.

As the title indicates, this chapter focuses on business *continuation* planning. Beyond the fact that continuation may be thwarted with even the best laid plans, not all business owners can necessarily identify a purchaser for their interest. The prospect of a liquidation will also be covered briefly. However, the chief concern of this chapter is business continuation planning in the event of the death of an S corporation shareholder. To that end, the role of life insurance funding and its coordination with the planning of both seller and purchaser will be examined. Planning the disposition of an S corporation owner's stock in the event of death necessarily ties into the shareholder's estate planning concerns. And, of course, planning for the sale or gift of all or a portion of the S stock during the owner's lifetime must also be addressed.

No Succession After Death. It may happen that no one is available to purchase a shareholder's interest in an S corporation. For example, a sole shareholder may not be able to select a key employee, family member or competitor who would be an appropriate candidate to purchase his shares. If the shareholder is a professional who has incorporated his practice as an S corporation, state law will require that the corporation be owned by a professional licensed in the respective field of expertise. In other circumstances, it may simply be that a logical successor cannot be found because of the nature of the business or the outlook of the owner.

Following the owner's death, the S corporation may be sold if it has value as a going concern without the owner's participation. If the S stock is inherited by the owner's spouse and subsequently sold, the spouse will realize income only to the extent that the sale price exceeds the spouse's basis. The basis of the stock will be stepped up to its fair market value on the date of the owner's death (or the alternate valuation date under Section 2032 or 2032A, if applicable).[1]

If a purchaser of the S corporation shares cannot be found, the corporation might be liquidated. The tax rules governing the liquidation of an S corporation differ somewhat from those applicable to the liquidation of a C corporation. Code section 1371 provides:

SEC. 1371. COORDINATION WITH SUBCHAPTER C.

(a) APPLICATION OF SUBCHAPTER C RULES.

(1) IN GENERAL, — Except as otherwise provided in this title, and except to the extent inconsistent with this subchapter, subchapter C shall apply to an S corporation and its shareholders.

Certain Code provisions regarding the liquidation of a C corporation do not apply to an S corporation liquidation. For example, Section 337 provides that a corporation does not recognize gain or loss when it makes a liquidating distribution under Section 332 to an 80% corporate shareholder. A full discussion of the tax aspects of an S corporation liquidation is outside of the scope of this chapter. Nonetheless, the following basic points should be realized.

Code section 336 provides:

SEC. 336. GAIN OR LOSS RECOGNIZED ON PROPERTY DISTRIBUTED IN COMPLETE LIQUIDATION.

(a) GENERAL RULE. — Except as otherwise provided in this section or section 337, gain or loss shall be recognized to a liquidating corporation on the distribution of property in complete liquidation as if such property were sold to the distributee at its fair market value.

Any gain that is recognized under Section 336(a) by an S corporation because of a liquidating distribution of appreciated assets passes through to the shareholders. Following the repeal of the *General Utilities* doctrine by the Tax Reform Act of 1986, the liquidation of a C corporation creates taxation to both the corporation and its shareholders.[2] In the case of an S corporation, gain recognized at the corporate level passes through to the shareholders; the shareholders' stock basis is increased and they are not subject to additional taxation.

If the tax imposed on an S corporation under Section 1374 is applicable because of net recognized built-in gains, an additional tax liability to the shareholders may be created upon liquidation because of such built-in gains. Also, if an S corporation has accumulated E&P and the corporation is liquidated, an effort should be made to distribute E&P as part of the liquidating distributions of the corporation in order to enable the shareholders to be taxed upon their capital gain, rather than dividend income.

Inheritance After Death. If an S corporation is a family owned business, a decedent's shares may be inherited by the shareholder's spouse or children. A direct inheritance of shares could also be a part of a broader business continuation plan in which shares will also be sold to other family members or unrelated parties. A transfer of shares under a will or trust arrangement can also be the concluding event of a larger estate plan that was initiated by lifetime transfers of stock.

The following points should be kept in mind by an S corporation shareholder who contemplates transferring shares at death to a family member:

1. Any shares that will be held in trust should pass to a trust that is an eligible shareholder of S corporation stock. (See Chapter 6 for a full treatment of this point.)

2. The basis of the S corporation stock inherited by a family member is stepped up under Section 1014 to its fair market value for estate tax purposes in the decedent's estate.

3. The beneficiary receiving the shares may be an active or passive shareholder of the S corporation with respect to involvement as an employee. Some thought may be given to creating voting and nonvoting shares during the owner's lifetime that will be transferred to active and inactive shareholders, respectively.

4.   Nonvoting shares have the same rights as voting shares in all respects other than voting. As a result, a shareholder with nonvoting shares has the same right to "dividend" income as a shareholder with voting stock.

Lifetime Gifts of S Corporation Stock. Before considering how both lifetime and post-death *sales* of stock may be arranged under a shareholder's agreement, we will first address the prospect that *gifts* of S corporation stock may be made in the case of a family business. Gifts of stock are likely to be considered when the following factors are present, assuming that all of the stock is held by one or both of the parents of the prospective donees:

•   One or more of the children is currently active in the business and appears to be willing and able to manage the company after the death of the transferor (which we will assume to be the father of the donees).

•   The donor of the stock is willing to make an irrevocable transfer of a portion of his shares.

•   The donor recognizes that income rights accrue to the owner of the shares. A shifting of dividend income to the donees must be acceptable to the donor. If the donor has reservations about losing dividend income, he could receive a greater payment of compensation as an employee that would reduce the income taxable to him as a shareholder. Compensation planning designed to limit shareholders' income should be justifiable within the meaning of "reasonable compensation" under Section 162. In addition, the donees should not necessarily expect to receive substantial amounts of income as a result of the gift. (However, while not the typical case, it is possible that the donor is willing to shift substantial dividend income to the donees in making a transfer of stock.)

•   As is the case when a gift of any type of property is considered, the difference between the donee's income tax basis resulting from a transfer by gift should be compared to the stepped up basis that an inheritance of the shares would permit. (If shares are transferred by gift, the donee carries over the donor's basis in the event of a sale, unless the donor's basis is greater than the fair market value of the shares on the date of the gift, in which case the donee's basis is the fair market value for purposes of determining loss.)[3] In evaluating the merits of a transfer by gift versus bequest, the age and health of the donor and the likelihood of a future sale by the donee should be taken into account. Other fluctuations in basis arising from the current or projected experience of the S corporation should also be taken into account.

- Frequently, but not always, the father will retain lifetime control of the corporation by maintaining 51% of the voting shares. (Or, depending upon state law and the nature of the business, two thirds of the voting shares may be retained.)

- Shares may be transferred to the donor's children either in one fell swoop in order to consume the donor's unified credit (and possibly the unified credit of the spouse, if the spouse joins in the gift) or in a series of smaller gifts designed to stay within the $10,000/$20,000 per donee annual exclusion limitation for gifts of a present interest. Some combination of annual gifts and a greater or lesser utilization of the unified credit may also be used.

A gift of nonvoting stock or a combination of voting and nonvoting stock may offer considerable flexibility to the senior generation owner of an S corporation. Since the enactment of Chapter 14 of the Internal Revenue Code, any gifts of stock by one family member to another may initiate a review of the Chapter 14 provisions by the donor's tax adviser.[4] Chapter 14 is designed to ensure that an accurate valuation can be determined for gift tax purposes when a donor transfers an interest in stock or other property and retains certain rights. However, if the shareholder of an S (or a C) corporation makes a gift of nonvoting stock and retains voting stock, the valuation rules of Chapter 14 do not apply to the gift.[5]

EXAMPLE. Ray owns 100% of the stock of Walbrook Company, an S corporation. A valuation by a qualified appraiser pegs the value of the company at $1,100,000. Ray would like to transfer a portion of his interest in Walbrook to his son, Charlie. Ray intends to transfer $610,100 of stock to Charlie, thereby utilizing both the $10,000 annual gift tax exclusion, the $600,000 exemption equivalent, and an additional $100 to trigger a small gift tax liability. Ray's wife will not join in the gift. The purpose of the additional $100 gift is to require Ray to pay a nominal amount of gift tax and thereby toll the statute of limitations applicable to the gift tax under Code section 2504(c).[6]

The value of the company, the exemption value of the unified credit and Ray's desire to maintain voting control combine to create a dilemma for Ray. If he simply gives $610,100 of stock to Charlie, he will relinquish voting control of the company, which is not acceptable. A lesser gift, such as $500,000 of stock, permits him to maintain voting control, but does not fully consume the unified credit.

Acting on the advice of his attorney, Ray decides to recapitalize his 100 shares of voting stock into a combination of voting and nonvoting shares. Before doing so, he consults with the appraiser who conducted the valuation of the company. Ray's objective is to exchange his voting stock for a larger number of shares of voting stock and a new issue of nonvoting stock. He intends to divide the voting stock into two blocks: a 51% interest and a 49% interest. The appraiser indicates that the value of the minority interest voting stock should be discounted by 25%, and the value of the nonvoting stock should be discounted by 35%, in comparison to the value of the controlling interest voting stock.[7] The discounts allowed are attributable to differences between the shares in regard to control and marketability. The number of shares to be issued in the recapitalization will be determined on the basis that a gift of stock having a total value of $610,100 will consist of 49% of the voting shares and a certain number of nonvoting shares. The number of nonvoting shares will be determined as a residual value after taking into account both the total value of the voting shares and the appraiser's discounts.

When the corporation is recapitalized, the newly issued shares are allocated so that each type will have the following value per share:

Majority interest voting stock	$100
Minority interest voting stock	$ 75
Nonvoting stock	$ 65

Following the recapitalization of the corporation, 11,000 shares are issued to Ray, based upon a $1,100,000 entity value, and a controlling interest value of $100 per share. Ray needs to determine the number of minority interest voting shares and nonvoting shares that he will give to Charlie. In order to do so, it is best to develop algebraic equations to solve for two unknowns: the number of minority interest voting shares and the number of nonvoting shares. It is necessary to solve for one unknown quantity separately, and to use the answer to determine the second unknown.

Total Shares = 11,000

If x = voting shares and y = nonvoting shares,

then y = 11,000 - x

The following equations can be developed:

49x($75) + y($65) = $610,100

.49x($75) + (11,000 - x)($65) = $610,100

$36.75x + $715,000 - $65x = $610,100

$28.25x = $104,900

x = 3,713 voting shares

y = 11,000 - 3,713

y = 7,287 nonvoting shares

3,713 x 0.51 = 1,894 voting shares

3,713 x 0.49 = 1,813 nonvoting shares

If x is the number of voting shares, then the 49% minority interest to be transferred to Charlie consists of 1,813 shares. Therefore, Ray will keep 1,894 voting shares, which constitutes a 51% interest that enables him to retain control of the Walbrook Company. In addition, Ray will transfer 7,287 shares of nonvoting stock to Charlie. The total value of both voting and nonvoting shares given by Ray to Charlie is $609,630, as follows:

1,813 shares x $75 = $135,975

7,287 shares x $65 = $473,655

Total gift = $609,630*

Thus, when the recapitalization and gift of both types of stock have been completed, the ownership of the Walbrook Company will be:

Shareholder	Common Stock
Ray	1,888 voting shares
Charlie	1,819* voting shares 7,287 nonvoting shares

* To accommodate the $470 of value lost in rounding numbers, Ray could give six more voting shares to Charlie (1,819 shares), which would leave him with voting control, but enable the total gift to be $610,080.

Following the gift, Ray will be entitled to receive 17.2%, and Charlie will be entitled to receive 82.8% of the taxable income of the Walbrook Company.

It is important for a prospective donor of S corporation stock such as Ray to be aware of the potential revocation of the S election. Section 1362 (d)(1)(A) and (B) provides:

(d) TERMINATION. —

(1) BY REVOCATION.

(A) IN GENERAL. — An election under subsection (a) may be terminated by revocation.

(B) MORE THAN ONE-HALF OF SHARES MUST CONSENT TO REVOCATION. — An election may be revoked only if shareholders holding more than one half of the shares of stock of the corporation on the day on which the revocation is made consent to the revocation.

No distinction is made between voting and nonvoting shares in regard to a revocation. Thus, in a case similar to that of Ray and Charlie, a donee who owns more than 50% of *all* shares of S corporation stock has the ability to revoke the election of S status. The right to revoke is statutory and can presumably be exercised unilaterally without regard to the contrary wishes of a shareholder who has a majority interest in the voting stock. Of course, any shareholder who acts in a manner injurious to the financial welfare of the other shareholders or the corporation itself may incur liability if damage to the other shareholders or the corporation results from the revocation. Nonetheless, the stockholder controlling a majority of the voting shares may be overruled on the revocation issue and may be without legal recourse to overturn the revocation or may not be committed to the litigation required to prove that the revoking party caused financial loss. The best means of preventing a revocation by one shareholder is to include a provision in the shareholders' agreement that requires unanimous agreement of the shareholders, thereby binding the owners contractually and overriding the possibility that one owner might revoke the election.

The allocation of voting and nonvoting stock in the preceding example is somewhat a product of its particular facts. If Walbrook had been appraised at $1,500,000, for example, Ray might have elected to give Charlie $610,100 worth of voting stock and to avoid nonvoting stock, for the sake of simplicity. However, the use of nonvoting stock may enhance lifetime efforts to initiate business continuation planning. Gifts of nonvoting stock may be particularly appropriate in the following situations:

- The donor wants to give an equity interest to family members who are not active in the business.

- A transfer of voting stock will disturb the balance of voting power between or among the current shareholders, such as when two unrelated parties are 50% owners of a business.

- The donor is interested in shifting income, as well as equity, to other family members.

Theoretically, an S corporation could be recapitalized to leave a single share of voting stock with the senior generation while a large number of shares of nonvoting stock would be transferred to the younger generation. If the transfer exceeds $610,100, for example, a part gift, part sale transaction could be arranged so that the excess amount would be sold to avoid out-of- pocket liability to the donor for the gift tax. Naturally, in that case, as well as in many others, having a substantiated valuation is critical to refuting a challenge by the IRS as to the value of the gift (or subsequent estate tax valuation). A professional appraisal may be well worth its cost when the potential tax liability of a wrong guess is considered.

It should also be noted that a C corporation can be recapitalized to have voting and nonvoting common stock. Many of the features of a gift of nonvoting stock described above in the S corporation context also apply if a C corporation is the subject of planning, except that the prospect of having dividends paid by a C corporation is less likely than for an S corporation, and other aspects peculiar to S status, such as a revocation of the election, do not apply. Therefore, the income shifting effect that a gift of S corporation nonvoting stock may produce is an additional variable that must be factored into an S corporation owner's planning.

SHAREHOLDERS' AGREEMENT FOR S CORPORATION OWNERS

Every S corporation owned by more than one shareholder should have a shareholders' agreement that will incorporate all of the buy-sell provisions that typically apply to any closely held corporation. A buy-sell agreement can ensure that an orderly continuation of the business will occur in the event of a shareholder's death, disability, retirement or other event that would trigger its operation.

One Class of Stock Requirement. The final regulations under Section 1361 pertaining to the one class of stock requirement specifically address buy-sell and redemption agreements.[8] The focus of the regulations is to determine whether buy-sell and redemption agreements confer identical distribution and liquidation rights. In general, such agreements may restrict the transferability of stock and are not considered in determining whether an S corporation's shares have identical distribution and liquidation rights unless:

   (1)   A principal purpose of the agreement is to circumvent the one class of stock requirement, and

(2)   The agreement establishes a purchase price that, at the time the agreement is entered into, is significantly in excess of or below the fair market value of the stock.

How much more or less than fair market value may the buy-sell price be? The regulations state that a price established at book value or "...between fair market value and book value..." is permissible.[9] For this purpose, the regulations provide that a good faith determination of fair market value will be respected unless it can be shown that the value was substantially in error and the determination of the value was not performed with reasonable diligence.

Book value may be determined in accordance with generally accepted accounting principles (including permitted optional adjustments) or may be that which is used for any substantial nontax purpose.

OBSERVATION. The latter statement suggests that the Service is willing to permit a fair amount of latitude to S corporation shareholders in determining stock values without undue concern about violating the one class of stock requirement. The language of the regulations seems to imply that S corporation shareholders who are at least mindful of their corporation's book value can agree to a value in a buy-sell agreement that will not create a second class of stock even if it is not exactly fair market value.

As a matter of comparison, the need to pinpoint a fair market value in this context is not as rigorous as when the determination of value controls the tax consequences of a transaction, such as determining whether a given value reflects fair market value or accompanies a disguised gift, for estate and gift tax purposes. Thus, for the sake of satisfying the one class of stock requirement, S corporation shareholders will not typically require a professional appraisal, assuming that they are mindful of book value and have a general sense of the fair market value of their stock. The "reasonable diligence/not substantially in error" test leaves room for an ample range of values that shareholders can use in the design of their buy-sell agreements.

The regulations also furnish a reminder that, although fair market value is a hurdle easily cleared for the one class of stock test, other tax aspects must still be separately satisfied. While an agreement may be disregarded in determining whether shares of stock confer identical distribution and liquidation rights, payments pursuant to the agreement may have other income or transfer tax consequences.

In general, the regulations governing the one class of stock requirement, as they pertain to buy-sell agreements, are intended to prevent the manipulation of share values or creation of artificial differences among share values that are not tied to events of independent legal significance. The regulations expressly provide that bona fide agreements to redeem or purchase stock at the time of death, divorce, disability or termination of employment are disregarded in determining whether a corporation's shares of stock confer identical rights. Naturally, the typical shareholders' agreement for an S corporation is drawn to address those events and unless such agreements are deemed to be sham agreements not conducted in good faith, they will be respected on their own merits and not viewed as circumventing the one class of stock rule.

EXAMPLE. Dan and Seneca are shareholders of The Beachworks, an S corporation. Dan is also an employee, but his shares were not issued to him in connection with the performance of services. The Beachworks and Dan enter into a redemption agreement that provides the corporation will redeem Dan's shares for an amount significantly below their fair market value if Dan terminates employment or if the corporation's sales fall below certain levels.[10]

Under the regulations, the provision authorizing redemption in the event that Dan's employment is terminated would be disregarded for purposes of the one class of stock rule. A redemption triggered by a termination of employment is an exception because it has an independent legal significance that is not relevant to whether the shareholders have identical rights as to distribution and liquidation proceeds.

The provision that triggers a redemption of Dan's shares in the event the corporation's sales fall below certain levels is treated differently under the regulations than the termination of employment, which is an outright exception. The redemption triggered by a drop in sales levels would be disregarded *unless* a principal purpose of that portion of the agreement is to circumvent the one class of stock requirement.

General Purpose of Shareholders' Agreements

Certain types of businesses, whether organized as S or C corporations, may be strengthened in their relationships with banks and bonding companies, for example, if a buy-sell agreement is in effect. Other aspects of a lifetime stock transfer are discussed below in the income tax analysis of stock redemption and cross purchase agreements. The concerns of an S corporation owner in regard to the need to plan for a buyout in the event of disability are largely similar to those affecting the shareholder of a C corporation. A shareholders' agreement for an S corporation should contain provisions that address the unique features of an S corporation. The following are typical provisions that are designed to protect the S corporation election or the interests of the shareholders and their families.

Restriction on Transfers. *Shareholders shall Transfer Stock only in accordance with the provisions of this Agreement. Notwithstanding any other provisions of this Agreement, Shareholders shall not Transfer any share of Stock to any Person if such Transfer would cause, directly or indirectly, Corporation's Subchapter S election to terminate. Transfers prohibited under this Section include, without limitation, Transfers (a) to any Person which would cause Corporation to have more than thirty-five shareholders, (b) to any nonresident alien, (c) to any Person other than an individual, estate, or certain trusts which are permitted shareholders of Subchapter S corporations under the Internal Revenue Code, or (d) to any Person which would in any other way cause a termination of Corporation's Subchapter S election. Notwithstanding any other provision of this Agreement, no Transfer permitted by this Agreement shall be effective to vest any right, title or ownership of Stock unless (i) the transferor delivers to the Corporation an opinion of counsel, satisfactory to the Board of Directors of the Corporation in its sole discretion, indicating that such Transfer will not cause, directly or indirectly, a termination of the Corporation's Subchapter S election and (ii) the Board of Directors of the Corporation approves the Transfer, having knowledge of the prospective transferee. Without limiting the foregoing, a transferee, by accepting any Stock, shall be deemed to have become a party to this Agreement to the same extent as if that transferee had joined in its execution.*

Revocation or Termination of Subchapter S Election. *The Shareholders agree that the continuation of the Subchapter S election is of material economic importance to the corporation and the Shareholders. Accordingly, the Shareholders agree not to commit any act which may result in the revocation or the termination of the Subchapter S election and also agree to perform any act required for the continuation of such election. Provided, however, that the Subchapter S election may be revoked or terminated if all of the Shareholders agree to such revocation or termination and, in such event, the rights and obligations of the Shareholders to this Agreement that are independent of such election shall not be affected.*

Effect of Prohibited Transfers. *Any Transfer in violation of any provision of this Agreement, or any other action, direct or indirect, taken by any Person that would cause a revocation or a termination of the Corporation's Subchapter S election is void as of the time of such Transfer or other action. Any purported Transfer in violation of any provision of this Agreement will not affect the beneficial ownership of Stock. Thus, the Shareholder making a purported Transfer will retain the right to vote and the right to receive dividends and liquidation proceeds. Despite any purported Transfer in violation of this Agreement, the Shareholder making the purported Transfer shall continue to report the share of income or loss allocated to him by Corporation in accordance with the provisions of the Internal Revenue Code.*

(The capitalized terms, such as "Transfer," are specifically defined in the Agreement. "Transfer," for example, includes "...any sale, exchange, gift, bequest, pledge, hypothecation, encumbrance, descent or distribution pursuant to any intestacy laws or other operation of law...").

In general, a principal purpose of a shareholders' agreement is to restrict the transferability of stock in order to protect the interests of the owners and the corporation itself. A right of first refusal provision, for example, is used to prevent transfers to those who are not shareholders without first permitting existing shareholders to have the option to purchase the shares of one who would sell his or her stock. A right of first refusal applies to planning for both S and C corporations. In addition, if a transfer to an "outside" party is made, it is critical that the new owner be eligible to own S corporation stock. A transfer of S corporation stock to an ineligible shareholder can terminate the S corporation election. If a termination occurs, the S corporation would become a C corporation and its shareholders might incur additional tax liability. In addition, as discussed above, the S corporation election may also be terminated by the revocation of a majority shareholder. The following provisions deal with the possibility that the S corporation election could be terminated and specifies the measure of indemnification that would result from a termination.

Representations. *(a) Each Shareholder represents and warrants to the other Shareholder that his or her Will and other estate planning documents and techniques do not and shall not provide for any Transfer of Stock in violation of Section or any other provision of this Agreement;*

(b) Each Shareholder represents and warrants to the other Shareholder (i) that such Shareholder is a permitted shareholder of a Subchapter S corporation, and is a legal resident of the United States, (ii) that the Shareholder owns, legally or beneficially, the full amount of the shares of Stock described on Exhibit A as being owned by that Shareholder; and (iii) that the Shareholder has not made, or caused to be made, a Transfer of all or any portion of the shares of Stock described on Exhibit A as being owned by that Shareholder.

Indemnification for Breach. *If a Shareholder's breach of any provision of this Agreement causes Corporation's Subchapter S election to terminate, then such Shareholder shall indemnify the other Shareholder (a) for his or her loss, during the period in which Corporation is ineligible to make a Subchapter S election, of any Federal, state and local income tax benefits resulting from the termination, including all items of income, loss, deduction, and credit ("Tax Items") which would have been passed to such other Shareholder but for the termination, and (b) for any distribution not made by Corporation to such other Shareholder as a result of the termination. For the purposes of this Section, Federal, state and local income tax benefits mean the excess of (1) Shareholder's share of Federal, state and local income taxes imposed on Corporation as a C corporation (as described in the Internal Revenue Code), plus Shareholder's Federal, state and local income taxes on Corporation's dividend distributions, assuming such distributions are made by Corporation, over (2) Shareholder's share of Federal, state and local income taxes that would have been imposed on Corporation as a Subchapter S*

corporation if it had the same Tax Items that it had as a C corporation,
plus the amount of Federal, state and local income taxes that Share-
holders would have paid on the Tax Items which would have been
passed through to them had Corporation been a Subchapter S
corporation.

Another provision that is commonly employed in a shareholders'
agreement is a statement regarding the dividend payments that the S
corporation expects to make. The following provision does not address
continuation planning, but it is often found in shareholders' agreements
covering S corporations.

Dividend Payments. *The Board of Directors of Corporation shall*
declare dividends from time to time in order to enable Shareholders
to pay all Federal, state and local taxes on their shares of Corporation's
taxable income. Such dividends shall be declared in amounts suffi-
cient to enable Shareholders to pay such taxes as if Shareholders were
subject to tax at the highest marginal income tax rates then in effect
and shall be paid in proportion to their shareholdings in Corporation.

As discussed above, the one class of stock requirement has become
an issue of increased significance. While it is unlikely in most situations
that a second class of stock would be issued without the consent of all
shareholders, the following provision could be useful to protect an S
corporation from the careless action of a controlling shareholder:

Without the unanimous written consent of the Shareholders, the
Corporation shall not make any amendments to its Articles of Incor-
poration to authorize any additional class of Stock, other than
common stock differing only with respect to voting rights, and shall
not issue any other security of any other nature whatsoever, whether
classified as debt or as equity, which may result in the Corporation
being deemed to have more than one class of Stock under the Internal
Revenue Code, including, but not limited to, warrants, options or
other rights to subscribe for or purchase additional shares, any
instruments or rights convertible into any Stock of the Corporation or
any shadow or phantom stock rights the value of which is related to
or measured by the value or income of the Corporation or any Stock
of the Corporation.

The provisions cited above are fairly standard methods of dealing with the need to protect the S corporation election. In certain circumstances, it may be advisable to add provisions that are designed to protect a shareholder's interest in a manner that is peculiar to an S corporation.

EXAMPLE. Fred and Wilma are joint owners of a 50% interest in Bedrock, Inc., an S corporation; the other 50% is owned by Barney. Wilma is not employed by Bedrock and Fred is concerned that Barney might take advantage of Wilma financially, if she were to become a 50% owner with Barney in the event of Fred's death. Bedrock has been in business for 20 years and became an S corporation three years ago. During its incarnation as a C corporation, it never paid dividends, but in the past three years the shareholders have received substantial dividend payments.

Fred is concerned that Barney might withdraw an overly generous amount of compensation for himself if he and Wilma become co-owners after Fred's death. After discussing the issue with Barney and Bedrock's attorney, Fred and Barney agree to limit the annual increases in compensation that can be paid to a surviving shareholder-employee following the death of a shareholder. The purpose of the limitation is to prevent a shareholder-employee from withdrawing excessive amounts of compensation that otherwise would have been dividend income for both active and passive shareholders. The following provision is inserted into their shareholders' agreement:

> *The cash compensation which the Corporation may pay to a Shareholder who is a party to this Agreement and also an officer-employee of the Corporation for any corporate fiscal year shall be limited to an increase of not more than 10% more than the cash compensation paid to such officer-employee during the immediately preceding corporate fiscal year.*

Other provisions may need to be adopted to accommodate particular circumstances. For the most part, the areas that require attention beyond the usual C corporation situations are concerned with maintaining the S corporation election by preventing transfers to ineligible shareholders or by ensuring that a proper balance between compensation and shareholder income is maintained. As discussed below, other specific issues, such as adjustments requiring an allocation of AAA, may also need to be considered.

BUY-SELL PLANNING IN EVENT OF DEATH

Buy-sell planning for the death of an S corporation shareholder covers many of the same issues that apply to the death of a C corporation shareholder. However, the unique tax attributes of the S corporation naturally influence the income tax treatment of the shareholders in several respects that are significantly different from C corporation planning. While life insurance funding serves the same purposes for an S as for a C corporation, its effect on the tax planning of the shareholders has implications that require independent consideration.

Whether death or lifetime concerns dictate the terms of an agreement between or among S corporation shareholders, the agreement represents the product of how business continuation planning decisions are made. In the following discussion of planning for the death of a shareholder, it will be assumed that lifetime planning issues are moot and that planning for death is the driving force that shapes the terms of the shareholders' agreement.

When more than one shareholder is involved, the form of the shareholders' agreement may be a stock redemption, a cross purchase by individual shareholders, or a hybrid version that offers the option of either approach, often called a "wait and see" agreement. Sole shareholder agreements involving a sale to a nonowner are discussed below in this chapter. The wait and see format permits the corporation and the shareholders to have successive options to purchase a decedent's stock, with the obligation to purchase ultimately assumed by either the entity or the surviving shareholders. While the wait and see approach offers planning flexibility, it usually results in a purchase by either the corporation or the other shareholders, rather than some form of divided purchase. For purposes of analysis, the following discussion will generally be based on the premise that the shareholders must choose either a cross purchase or a stock redemption agreement.

Cross Purchase Agreement

Compared to C Corporation. A cross purchase agreement operates in a very similar manner whether an S corporation or a C corporation is involved. Many of the same factors are at work with regard to the shareholders' rights and obligations, income tax treatment of the shareholders and the corporation, valuation and funding. The following comparison focuses on the areas of similarity and difference between a cross purchase plan for an S corporation and a C corporation, and also contrasts the cross purchase plan to the stock redemption plan in certain respects.

Sale by Estate. Following the death of a shareholder, the basis of the stock owned by the shareholder's estate is stepped up to its fair market value for estate tax purposes under Section 1014. The step-up in basis occurs without regard to whether the decedent had owned shares of an S or a C corporation. Typically, the stock is sold for its fair market value and the estate has no gain or loss for income tax purposes.

Purchaser's Perspective. A cross purchase agreement can be designed to maintain the same proportion of ownership among the surviving shareholders, or to provide for a restructuring of ownership among the survivors of either an S or a C corporation. A cross purchase plan permits flexibility in allocating stock ownership and control that is not possible with a stock redemption agreement.

EXAMPLE. Spike owns 60% and Rip and Biff each own 20% of Fullflex Corporation. They "grew up" in the business together, but Spike and Rip agree that Biff doesn't have the "right stuff" to be a 50% owner, in the event that Spike's shares were redeemed by the corporation upon his death. Spike and Rip decide to enter into a cross purchase agreement in which each will purchase the other's shares upon death. Biff will remain a 20% shareholder for life.

As discussed below, in certain instances, a stock redemption plan funded by life insurance can offer advantages to an S corporation that are not available to a C corporation. However, the inherent flexibility of a cross purchase agreement may rule the day because of "people reasons" and other planning factors.

The individual purchaser obtains a basis in either S or C corporation stock that is equal to the purchase price of the stock. In order to fund the purchase of stock, the buyer may carry a life insurance policy on the seller's life, or may arrange financing after the seller's death.

Financing the Purchase: Income Tax Aspects. The income tax aspects of a financed purchase should be taken into account. First, if no interest rate is specified or the interest rate is "below market" with regard to the purchase of the stock, an interest rate will be imputed for income tax purposes.[11] Prior to the elimination of the long term capital gains deduction, a buyer might seek a price reduction from a seller if the deal were "sweetened" by specifying a low interest rate. The seller would benefit because a greater portion of the total price would be allocated to principal, and therefore taxed at favorable capital gains rates. The incentive to control the tax consequences by manipulating interest rates has generally been eliminated because of the narrow difference between ordinary income and capital gains rates (apart from the effect of the imputed interest rules). If the purchase of stock between or among family members involves a "below-market loan," income and gift tax considerations because of "foregone interest" under Section 7872 may be triggered, as well.

In evaluating the overall cost of a financed purchase of S corporation stock, it may be important to determine whether the purchaser's interest expense is deductible for income tax purposes. Prior to the Tax Reform Act of 1986 (TRA '86), interest expense incurred by the purchaser of a business might have been classified as an expense for either a "trade or business" or an "investment." Generally without regard to whether an S or a C corporation was involved, the classification of the interest expense seemed to be determined according to whether the dominant motive of the purchaser was of an "investment" or a "business" character.[12] TRA '86 made significant changes to the rules governing the deductibility of interest expense to individuals.

Since the TRA '86 amendments were made, it appears that the purchase of C corporation stock is likely to be subject to the same "dominant motive" test that had emerged under the case law. If an individual purchases stock in a C corporation and does not "materially participate" in the business, it appears that the purchase falls within the category of a "property held for investment," which is defined under Section 163(d)(5)(A) to include:

(i) Any property which produces income of a type described in section 469(e)(1), and

(ii) Any interest held by a taxpayer in an activity involving the conduct of a trade or business —

(I) which is not a passive activity, and

(II) with respect to which the taxpayer does not materially participate.

Subsection (i) includes "portfolio income" such as dividends, interest, etc.

In most cases, it appears that C corporation stock will fall into the category of "property held for investment." It may be possible for the interest expense to fall under the "trade or business" category provided that the interest is paid on debt properly allocable to a trade or business (other than the trade or business of performing services as an employee).

If an individual incurs debt to finance the purchase of S corporation stock, the interest expense might be classified as interest allocable to (1) an investment; (2) a passive activity; or (3) a trade or business.

Interest expense on debt incurred to purchase S corporation stock may be divided into two or three of the categories just described. The *General Explanation of the Tax Reform Act of 1986*, usually referred to as the "Blue Book," provides the following explanation in the context of defining what constitutes investment interest:

> ...it is intended that interest on indebtedness to acquire stock in an S corporation whose assets are used solely in conducting a trade or business, where the stock is not an interest in a passive activity because the taxpayer materially participates in the trade or business of the S corporation, is not investment interest, but rather is treated as interest incurred or continued in connection with a trade or business. In addition, interest treated as allocable to an interest in a partnership, or stock in an S corporation, that is treated as an interest in a passive activity under the passive loss rule ... is not subject to the investment interest limitation (except to the extent such interest expense is allocated to portfolio income under the passive loss rule.)[13]

Thus, it appears that interest paid or debt incurred to purchase stock of an S corporation, the assets of which are used *solely* in conducting a trade or business in which the taxpayer materially participates, will be treated as "trade or business" interest expense.[14] Apparently, if the S corporation is involved in a passive activity as defined in Section 469, and the purchaser does not "materially participate" in the passive activity, then the interest incurred in purchasing the S stock becomes part of the computation for determining the purchaser's income or loss from a passive activity. And, as the end of the cited passage states, to the extent that the S corporation has "portfolio income," a corresponding portion of the interest expense may be treated as investment interest.

Financed Purchase: Summary. What conclusions may be drawn from the discussion of interest expense classification in regard to the purchase of S corporation stock? The following practical points are worth considering:

(1)   Interest expense on debt incurred to purchase S corporation stock may be characterized differently than if C corporation stock is purchased. To the extent that the purchaser is a passive investor or the S corporation is involved in a passive activity or has substantial portfolio income, computing the after-tax cost of the purchase becomes correspondingly more complicated. The IRS has offered additional guidance regarding the proper allocation of interest expense.[15]

(2)   The classification of interest expense for income tax purposes determines its deductibility to the purchaser. If interest expense is attributable to a trade or business, its deductibility is limited only to the extent of the purchaser's taxable income. On the other hand, investment interest expense is deductible only to the extent of the purchaser's investment income and passive activity interest expense is considered within the computation of the purchaser's passive activity income or loss.

(3)   The deductibility of interest expense for income tax purposes has a direct bearing on the purchaser's overall cost. If interest expense is deductible, a 10% interest rate has an after-tax cost of seven percent to a purchaser who is in a 30% income tax bracket. In contrast, a nondeductible 10% rate is the equivalent of a deductible 14.3% rate to the same buyer. To the extent that a purchase of S corporation stock is financed, gauging the "bottom line" cost of the purchase becomes correspondingly more important.

(4)   For many of the same reasons applicable to a purchase of C
      corporation stock, the use of life insurance or disability
      buyout insurance to fund the purchase provides security and
      certainty to both buyer and seller. The purchase of insurance
      shifts the risk to the insurance company (other than the
      policyowner's dependence on the insurance company's divi-
      dend projections or other assumptions concerning the cost of
      the insurance). A financed purchase must balance the factors
      of interest expense, income tax cost and cash flow of the
      purchaser, together with the question of qualifying for a loan
      in the future if outside financing is required.

Life Insurance Funding. If life insurance is used to fund the purchase
of the stock under a cross purchase agreement, each shareholder will be
the owner and beneficiary of a policy on the other shareholder's life. The
premiums can be paid out of the policyowner's compensation as a Section
162 bonus plan that is deductible to the S corporation. (See Chapter 2 for
more on bonus plans.) Premiums could also be paid from the dividend
income received by the shareholder from the S corporation. Unless
multiple policies are involved (which could be avoided through a trusteed
arrangement), a cross purchase plan funded by life insurance is a simple
and convenient method of buyout.

A split dollar plan could also be installed in which the purchaser
would be the beneficiary of the death proceeds in excess of the cash value
or aggregate premiums paid by the corporation. Unless the S corporation
has an independent need to own the cash value or to receive a death benefit,
the bonus plan approach policy may be just as effective and easier to
explain than split dollar. (See Chapter 4 for more about split dollar plans.)

Purchase of AAA. A shareholder's basis in his or her stock is personal
to the shareholder and reflects the shareholder's financial experience with
the corporation. On the other hand, the accumulated adjustments account
(AAA) is not personal and is allocated directly to the stock of the
corporation. Its principal function is to keep track of income that has been
taxed to the shareholders but not distributed to them, for S corporations
that have earnings and profits (E&P). In the case of an S corporation
having no E&P, income that is retained by the business, but taxed to the
shareholders, results in a higher basis being maintained by the shareholders than if the income were distributed. Therefore, the amount of each

shareholder's stock basis reflects the retention by the corporation of income that has been taxed to the shareholders. On the other hand, in the case of an S corporation with E&P, income that is taxed to the shareholders, but not distributed, is reflected by the maintenance of AAA, which is a corporate account (and not personal to the shareholder, as basis is). Consequently, if one shareholder purchases the stock of another shareholder, the purchaser also acquires the AAA of the selling shareholder. By obtaining the AAA that was allocated to the stock of the other shareholder, the purchaser also deprives the estate of the selling shareholder of the ability to receive a distribution of income on which the decedent had already been taxed.

EXAMPLE. Julius and Brutus each own 50% of Idesmarch, Inc., an S corporation. Julius dies and Brutus buys the shares held by Julius' estate pursuant to their cross purchase agreement. For three years prior to Julius' death, the shareholders were taxed on substantial amounts of dividend income, of which they received only an amount sufficient to cover their income tax liability. At the time of Julius' death, the corporation had $400,000 in the accumulated adjustments account (AAA). When Brutus purchased the stock from Julius' estate, he also acquired the $200,000 of AAA attributable to the 50% interest that had been held by Julius. As a result, he also acquired income that otherwise might have been distributed tax free to Julius during his lifetime, or to his estate or its beneficiaries after his death.

A few points should be made in regard to the dimensions of the AAA "problem" and appropriate solutions. Since AAA, in general, represents income previously taxed to a shareholder, it seems only fair that the estate or beneficiary of a deceased shareholder should be able to receive a distribution equal to the decedent's share of AAA. It should be realized that a distribution of AAA is not necessarily tax free. Section 1368(c)(1) indicates that a distribution that reduces AAA follows the general pattern of distributions for an S corporation with no accumulated earnings and profits. The distribution first reduces basis and then, if it exceeds basis, the excess is treated as gain from the sale or exchange of property.

In most instances, a distribution that reduces AAA will be tax free to the shareholder and will reduce the shareholder's basis. Income received by the S corporation increases the shareholder's basis and basis remains increased until a distribution to the shareholder occurs (or, until it is otherwise lowered, such as by an expense or loss of the corporation). Therefore, if the purchaser of stock also acquires the right to AAA, a distribution that reduces AAA is not necessarily tax free. The usual rule of "basis first, then gain" still applies. The more important point in the context of buy-sell planning is that a proper adjustment should be made in order to be fair to the decedent's estate and its beneficiaries. Basically, three approaches can be employed:

1.   A distribution that eliminates AAA may be made to the estate prior to its transfer of the stock.

2.   The sale price of the stock may be adjusted to reflect "foregone AAA."

3.   The sale price may be flexible enough, that is, may have enough "cushion" to permit a transfer of AAA with the transfer of stock.

One Way Buyout. The sole shareholder of an S corporation may be unwilling or unable to share the ownership of stock with anyone else during the shareholder's lifetime. Leaving the stock to a spouse or family member by a bequest at death will not be practical if the beneficiary is unprepared to continue the business as an owner. Nonetheless, the owner of the business may be able to sell his or her stock at death to a key employee. The stock redemption alternative is not available if the S corporation is owned by a sole shareholder.

The features of a "one way buyout" are similar to those at the buyer's end of a cross purchase plan. The purchaser will be obligated to buy the owner's stock at death (and also upon certain lifetime events, such as disability). Typically, the purchaser will be the owner and beneficiary of an insurance policy on the life of the owner and the proceeds will fund a purchase upon death. Or, if the purchaser is a key employee, the policy may be owned under a contributory split dollar plan format in order to enable the corporation to control the cash value and to keep the shareholder's cost to a minimum. The other factors that apply to a cross purchase arrangement are equally applicable to a one way buyout. From the purchaser's perspective as a nonowner, it would be helpful to have an understanding of what it would mean to become the owner of an S corporation, rather than a C corporation or some other form of business entity.

Stock Redemption Plans and S Corporations

The owners of an S corporation may decide that a stock redemption agreement is preferable to a cross purchase plan. Or, if the buy-sell agreement is structured as a "wait and see" plan with the shareholders and the corporation each having an option to purchase stock, the corporation could be assigned the ultimate *obligation* to purchase the shares of a selling shareholder. In other circumstances, the stock redemption plan may simply be carried over from the corporation's prior existence as a C corporation. (In such a case, the prospect of redeeming shares from corporate distributions should be carefully examined, as discussed below.)

A stock redemption involves the corporation's purchase of its own shares from a shareholder in return for some form of consideration, whether it be cash or other property. All shares held by an owner may be redeemed in one transaction or a series of redemptions may be conducted over a period of time. Even if all of the shares are redeemed at once, the corporation may only pay a portion of the price with cash and the remainder may be financed with a note. Regardless of whether an S or a C corporation is involved, state law may prohibit a redemption that impairs the capital structure of the corporation.

Following the redemption, the remaining shareholders continue to hold their stock in the same proportion to each other as had been the case prior to the redemption.

EXAMPLE. McDuck Worldwide, an S corporation, is owned as follows:

Shareholder	Percentage
Scrooge	60%
Donald	25%
Huey	5%
Dewey	5%
Louie	5%

If McDuck Worldwide redeems all of Scrooge's shares, the resulting percentage of ownership will be:

Shareholder	Percentage
Donald	62.5%
Huey	12.5%
Dewey	12.5%
Louie	12.5%

As mentioned in the discussion of cross purchase agreements, it may not be a desirable outcome for the shareholders (and the corporation) to have the same ratio of ownership preserved. If Donald also dies, it may be better to have one of his nephews emerge as a leader and majority owner, rather than to subject McDuck to a triumvirate of young ducks mired in a deadlock on management issues.

Despite the lack of flexibility inherent in a stock redemption agreement, it may be preferred by the owners of an S corporation in several types of planning circumstances. S corporation shareholders might adopt a stock redemption plan for many of the same reasons as C corporation owners. In addition, some of the disadvantages associated with C corporation redemptions may not apply in the case of an S corporation redemption. And, as explained below in this chapter, the use of life insurance funding for an S corporation redemption offers an affirmative planning advantage that is not possible for a C corporation.

Regardless of whether a C or an S corporation is the object of buy-sell planning, if the business is owned by several shareholders, it may gravitate toward the stock redemption approach. The prospect of a sale of stock to a number of purchasers can be cumbersome for a variety of reasons. Having the obligation to purchase and the availability of funds for the buyout centered in the corporation rather than scattered among several shareholders promotes efficiency and a sense of security that the agreement will be completed.[16]

Another factor favoring a stock redemption is the use of the corporation as the source of funds for the purchase of stock. If the agreement is not fully funded by life insurance to cover a buyout upon death, the shareholder's family has recourse to the corporation for payment. The corporation may be more acceptable to the shareholders for advance funding through insurance or otherwise and for sustaining a series of payments after death.

In the case of life insurance funding, only one policy per shareholder is required, rather than the multiple policies that a cross purchase agreement would require. Having the ownership of the policies centered in the corporation permits a more convenient administration of the policies than does personal ownership.[17]

Stock Redemptions: Compare S and C Corporations

Alternative Minimum Tax. The Tax Reform Act of 1986 revised the corporate alternative minimum tax (AMT) and specified that certain items of "book income" or "adjusted current earnings" not otherwise subject to the regular corporate income tax are preference items that may trigger the application of the corporate AMT. Basically, the death proceeds in excess of the cash value of a corporate owned life insurance policy are a preference item. The receipt of proceeds by a corporation that ordinarily pays a modest amount of income tax could certainly expose the corporation to the AMT. Even if additional coverage for tax indemnification makes financial sense, the prospect of the AMT may simply chill the inclination to use corporate owned insurance. The corporate AMT simply does not apply to the S corporation because no alternative form of tax would be appropriate for an entity that is designed by law to be nontaxable.

Sale/Exchange or Dividend. Code section 302 specifies the requirements that must be met in order for a redemption to qualify as a distribution made in exchange for stock. If a distribution does not qualify as a redemption under Section 302, it is taxed under Section 301(c), which provides:

(c) AMOUNT TAXABLE. — In the case of a distribution to which subsection (a) applies —

(1) AMOUNT CONSTITUTING DIVIDEND. — That portion of the distribution which is a dividend (as defined in section 316) shall be included in gross income.

(2) AMOUNT APPLIED AGAINST BASIS. — That portion of the distribution which is not a dividend shall be applied against and reduce the adjusted basis of the stock.

(3) AMOUNT IN EXCESS OF BASIS. —

(A) IN GENERAL. — Except as provided in subparagraph (B), that portion of the distribution which is not a dividend, to the extent that it exceeds the adjusted basis of the stock, shall be treated as gain from the sale or exchange of property.

(B) DISTRIBUTIONS OUT OF INCREASE IN VALUE ACCRUED BEFORE MARCH 1, 1913. — That portion of the distribution which is not a dividend, to the extent that it exceeds the adjusted basis of the stock and to the extent that it is out of increase in value accrued before March 1, 1913, shall be exempt from tax.

For the sake of convenient reference, a distribution by a C corporation in payment for its own stock that does not qualify as a redemption under Section 302 is often called " a dividend." In many cases, such a payment *is* a dividend and is a distribution of the corporation's accumulated earnings and profits. However, as indicated above, if such a distribution exceeds the amount of a "dividend" (meaning, under Section 316, more than the total of accumulated or current earnings and profits), the excess reduces basis and, if basis is reduced to zero, the remainder of the distribution is treated as if it were gain from the sale of stock.

It is worth noting that the language of Section 1368(b)(1) and (2) is virtually identical to Section 301(c)(2) and (3)(A). In other words, distributions to a C corporation shareholder that exceed the portion treated as a dividend generate the same income tax treatment (reduce basis first, then gain) to that shareholder as distributions to the shareholder of an S corporation that has no earnings and profits. The importance of that tax treatment to the S corporation shareholder is analyzed below in greater detail.

The Tax Reform Act of 1986 repealed the long term capital gains deduction that effectively made 60% of long term capital gains exempt from tax.[18] Under the Revenue Reconciliation Act of 1990, the maximum tax rate applicable to long term capital gains is 28%, as compared to the tax rates applicable to ordinary income, which can be as high as 39.6%.[19] Other than instances in which a marginal dollar of net income resulting from a transaction makes a significant difference, the three percent difference in rates is generally inconsequential.

In recent years, the slight differential in tax rates between a transaction that results in capital gain and one that creates ordinary income has eased lifetime redemptions of stock for owners of C corporations having a low stock basis.

EXAMPLE. Amos owns 80% and his son Luke owns 20% of The Barnyard, a popular nightclub operating as a C corporation. Amos' basis in the business is $10,000 and the fair market value of his interest is estimated to be $1,000,000. The corporation pays $1,000,000 of cash to Amos in a complete redemption of his stock. However, Section 302(c) indicates that the constructive ownership rules of Section 318 apply in determining the ownership of stock in the context of a redemption. Specifically, Section 318(a)(1)(A)(ii) states that an individual is considered to own stock owned by his children. In other words, even though Amos no longer owns stock in the corporation, he is considered to own 20% of the stock indirectly because he is Luke's father. As a result, the distribution by the corporation is treated as a dividend, rather than a payment in exchange for stock that would otherwise qualify for capital gains treatment.

The difference between redemption and dividend treatment to Amos, however, does not amount to much because of his low basis. The $1,000,000 distribution is taxable as a dividend to Amos because of his son's ownership of stock in the corporation. On the other hand, if the redemption had been complete for Section 302 purposes, he would have a capital gain of $990,000, based on the difference between the $1,000,000 realized and the $10,000 basis in his stock.

Nonetheless, a redemption in the event of a shareholder's death can lead to significantly different income tax treatment than a lifetime redemption. Following a shareholder's death, Section 1014 provides that the basis of the stock held by the decedent's estate is stepped up to its fair market value for estate tax purposes. Consequently, a "qualifying" redemption (i.e., one that qualifies as a sale or exchange under Section 302) permits the decedent's estate to receive a nontaxable payment for its stock if it is sold at fair market value. In contrast, a distribution treated as a dividend is fully taxable to the estate.

WORKING WITH S CORPORATIONS

Thus, if Amos dies, a $1,000,000 distribution by the corporation to his estate for its stock would generate an income tax in the $400,000 range, if it is considered to be a dividend, rather than a payment in exchange for stock. (The payment would be classified as a dividend because Luke's ownership of shares would be attributed to the estate if he were an estate beneficiary, or if other rules of constructive ownership applied.) If Amos and Luke were unrelated and the attribution rules did not apply, the $1,000,000 distribution would be a complete redemption. In that case, his estate would receive $1,000,000 for stock in which its basis would be stepped up to $1,000,000 and no taxable gain would be realized.

What are the income tax consequences to the shareholder of an S corporation when a distribution is made to the shareholder in redemption of stock? In the same manner as for a C corporation, the S corporation's distribution either qualifies as being made in exchange for stock under Section 302 or it is classified as a dividend or other form of distribution. With a C corporation, a nonqualifying redemption is taxed as a distribution under Section 301. With an S corporation, Section 1368 applies to the taxation of distributions to a shareholder.

Section 1368 distinguishes between a distribution to the shareholder of an S corporation "having no earnings and profits" and one that is made to the shareholder of an S corporation "having earnings and profits." Typically, an S corporation having earnings and profits has carried E&P over from its former life as a C corporation. In comparing C corporation and S corporation redemptions, we will return to Amos and Luke and start with the assumption that the S corporation has no earnings and profits.

EXAMPLE. Suppose that the same facts apply as in the previous example, except that Amos has a basis of $400,000 in his 80% interest and that he would like to withdraw money from the corporation, but maintain a controlling stock interest. The corporation will redeem one half of his shares, which are worth $500,000 with a basis of $200,000, to Amos. The redemption does not qualify as an exchange under Section 302 and is therefore taxed as a distribution under Section 1368. Ironically, Amos pays less tax on the distribution than he would have paid if the redemption had qualified under Section 302. Compare the following:

Exchange under Section 302

Sale Price	$500,000
Minus Basis	$200,000
Gain	$300,000

Distribution Under Section 1368

Distribution	$500,000
Applied Against Basis	$400,000
Gain	$100,000

If C corporation stock were redeemed in the same circumstances, Amos would be taxed on the entire distribution of $500,000 (assuming the entire payment to be a dividend), rather than on gain of $300,000. With an S corporation, the distribution is taxed more favorably than an exchange because the shareholder's basis in *all* of his stock is taken into account for purposes of determining gain. If the redemption qualifies as an exchange, only the basis of the shares redeemed would be considered.

If Amos planned to die with 40% ownership of The Barnyard, he would be in better shape with a distribution rather than an exchange. On the other hand, if he expects to sell the rest of his stock during his lifetime, the greater reduction in basis resulting from the initial distribution works against him in the event of a subsequent sale of the stock. Following a distribution, his gain on a lifetime sale of the remaining shares would be greater than if the sale followed an exchange. Thus, in the case of a less than complete redemption, a distribution may provide a current benefit that an exchange cannot. Nonetheless, the reduction in basis will cause a greater amount of income to be realized upon a sale of the shareholder's remaining stock, unless he dies owning it so that his estate's basis is stepped up to the fair market value of the stock.

Redemptions for S Corporations with E&P. S corporations with accumulated earnings and profits are usually former C corporations that elected S status. In 1987, for example, many closely held businesses led a virtual stampede of S corporation elections that continued in succeeding years at the urging of business tax advisers. Some of the newly converted S corporations had been C corporations in which earnings had been retained to avoid paying a taxable dividend to the shareholders. In any event, Section 1368 dictates that a distribution of E&P to an S corporation shareholder remains taxable as a dividend to the shareholder. Thus, a shareholder who has his stock redeemed by an S corporation with E&P faces a "dividend versus exchange" tax risk similar to a C corporation shareholder, depending upon the amount of E&P that is involved.

If the amount of E&P in the S corporation is substantial, the same effort should be made to qualify a redemption as an exchange as for a C corporation. However, if the amount of E&P is relatively low, the potential tax cost to the shareholder because of a dividend is relatively low, as well. In the example above, if E&P of $20,000 were distributed to Amos for his stock as part of the overall $500,000 distribution, it would be allocated as follows:

Distribution under Section 1368

Distribution = $500,000

E&P - Dividend	$ 20,000
Applied Against Basis	$400,000
Gain	$ 80,000

In this instance, $20,000 of the distribution is taxed as a dividend, only a small portion of the overall distribution.

Redemption for S Corporations with AAA and E&P. Even if an S Corporation has E&P that have carried forward from its previous existence as a C corporation, a corporate distribution will not necessarily be taxed if AAA is sufficient to absorb the distribution.

EXAMPLE. Based upon the same facts used for the immediately preceding examples in this chapter, assume that The Barnyard had net income that resulted in Amos and Luke being taxed as shareholders. In a typical situation in which the shareholders wish to reinvest corporate earnings rather than receive a distribution, the shareholders might elect to receive a "tax dividend" sufficient to cover their personal income tax liability. In that case, the S corporation income that is taxable to the shareholders, but not received by them, is added to the accumulated adjustments account (AAA) maintained by the corporation.

Suppose that, in exchange for a portion of his shares, Amos receives a distribution of $100,000 from The Barnyard at a time when the corporation's AAA is $250,000, its E&P is $50,000, and his basis is $200,000. Furthermore, the redemption does not qualify as a sale or exchange. If The Barnyard were a C corporation, the distribution would be taxed under Code section 301(c). However, S corporation distributions are taxed under the rules prescribed by Code section 1368. Specifically, Section 1368(c) provides that a distribution by an S corporation that has accumulated E&P is treated, to the extent of AAA, so that it is tax free to the extent of the shareholder's basis, and any amount received in excess of basis is treated as capital gain from a sale or exchange. Therefore, in this example, the $100,000 distributed by The Barnyard to Amos is a tax-free distribution. The distribution received by Amos in exchange for his shares is nontaxable, but his basis in the remaining shares he owns is also reduced by the distribution. Since the distribution is less than AAA, earnings and profits are not reduced, as dictated by the rules of distribution for S corporations having E&P under Section 1368(c). (Earnings and profits could be reduced before reducing AAA, if the shareholders so elected under Section 1368(e).)

If the distribution to Amos had qualified as a sale or exchange, AAA would have been adjusted in proportion to the number of shares redeemed, as compared to the number of shares outstanding immediately before the redemption.[20] However, the distribution did not qualify, and Section 1368(e) does not provide a specific rule for adjusting AAA in the case of a redemption treated as a Section 301 distribution. Thus, in this case, AAA is directly reduced by the full amount of the distribution to Amos because the distribution did not qualify as a sale or exchange under Sections 302(a) or 303(a).[21]

Post-Death Redemptions: Relief From Attribution Rules. A redemption of stock following the death of a shareholder of a family owned business naturally creates concern that the attribution rules may cause a redemption to be treated as a dividend, rather than a payment in exchange for stock. A nonqualifying redemption may cause the entire distribution of a C corporation to be treated as a dividend. And, a similar concern exists for an S corporation that has substantial E&P. However, S corporations having no E&P or minimal E&P need not be concerned about whether the attribution rules apply.

EXAMPLE. Under the same ownership facts as in the preceding examples, following Amos' death, The Barnyard, now an S corporation, redeems his 80% interest from his estate. Luke is a beneficiary of his father's estate and continues to own the remaining stock outstanding. Amos' estate is considered to own Luke's shares because of the constructive ownership rules under Section 318. The redemption fails to qualify as a payment in exchange for stock under Section 302 and the income tax consequences to Amos' estate are governed instead by Section 1368.

The Barnyard distributes $1,000,000 to Amos' estate. That amount is applied to reduce the estate's basis under the distribution rules. The basis of the stock is stepped up to its $1,000,000 fair market value under Section 1014 and the entire payment is tax free to the estate. In this case, the same tax result is achieved for a distribution as for a redemption qualifying under Section 302.

The attribution rules under Section 318 frequently cast a shadow over the use of a stock redemption agreement by family owned businesses. The complexity of the rules permeates both the estate and business planning of the owners and may result in a cross purchase arrangement being established, by default. If an S corporation does not have E&P, a stock redemption plan for a family owned business can be arranged with considerably more ease than for a C corporation.

In the event that stock is redeemed at a loss to the shareholder, qualification under Section 302 would permit recognition of the loss, while a distribution that reduces basis would not recognize the loss. A redemption resulting in a loss to the shareholder may be more likely in the event of a lifetime transaction, rather than a redemption at death in which the value received is usually equal to the stepped up basis for income tax purposes. While planning to minimize income tax gain from a redemption is a more common scenario, it is worth noting the difference in the treatment of loss resulting from a distribution under Section 1368, rather than a redemption under Section 302.

It should also be mentioned that the Section 318 attribution rules contain a particular provision concerning S corporations. Section 318(a)(5)(E) states:

(5) OPERATING RULES. —

(E) S CORPORATION TREATED AS PARTNERSHIP. —
For purposes of this subsection —

(i) an S corporation shall be treated as a partnership,
and

(ii) any shareholder of the S corporation shall be treated
as a partner of such partnership.

The preceding sentence shall not apply for purposes of determining
whether stock in the S corporation is constructively owned by any
person.

The "operating rules" define and limit particular applications of the
constructive ownership rules. Specific rules apply to attribute the ownership of stock held by corporations to shareholders and shareholders to
corporations; these attribution rules apply to situations in which 50% or
more in value of the stock of a corporation is owned by a shareholder. In
the case of an S corporation, attribution will occur to and from the
shareholders even if they own less than 50% of the S corporation's stock.
However, the treatment of an S corporation "as a partnership" relates only
to the operating rules and not to determine otherwise whether S corporation stock is constructively owned.

Stock Redemptions and AAA. Section 1368(e)(1)(B) provides a
special rule pertaining to an adjustment to AAA in the case of a redemption
which is treated as an exchange under Section 302(a) or Section 303(a).
Before discussing that provision, it may be helpful to point out the role that
a Section 303 redemption might play in the planning of an S corporation
shareholder. Technically, a Section 303 redemption belongs within the
category of estate planning techniques. Nonetheless, its purpose — to
facilitate the withdrawal of money from a closely held corporation for the
payment of death taxes and other expenses by allowing favorable income
tax treatment — is equally applicable to the planning of an S or a C
corporation shareholder. Naturally, the particular provisions of the section, such as the requirement that the stock constitute more than 35% of
the shareholder's adjusted gross estate, must be met for both types of
corporations. And, the constructive ownership rules of Section 318 do not
apply to a Section 303 redemption, in any event.

If an S corporation has a balance of AAA, both Section 302 and 303 redemptions create an adjustment to AAA. Section 1368(e)(1)(B) provides:

(1) ACCUMULATED ADJUSTMENTS ACCOUNT. —

(B) AMOUNT OF ADJUSTMENT IN THE CASE OF REDEMPTIONS. — In the case of any redemption which is treated as an exchange under section 302(a) or 303(a), the adjustment in the accumulated adjustments account shall be an amount which bears the same ratio to the balance in such account as the number of shares redeemed in such redemption bears to the number of shares of stock in the corporation immediately before such redemption.

If a redemption of stock qualifies as an exchange under Section 302 or Section 303, AAA is proportionately reduced. Apparently the rationale for a proportionate reduction is that AAA is a function of stock ownership at the corporate level, as opposed to basis, which is personal to the shareholder. Therefore, only the portion of the AAA attributable to other shares remaining after the redemption should remain available to those shares. Without a proportionate reduction in AAA other shareholders remaining after a redemption would enjoy a potential windfall if the AAA attributable to the redeemed shares were allocated to their shares.

S Corporation Financing and "Straight Debt" Rules. An S corporation may not have sufficient funds to redeem a shareholder's stock, either during the shareholder's lifetime or following a shareholder's death, if insurance proceeds received by the corporation are not sufficient to complete the redemption. Generally, the S corporation will purchase the shares on a self-financed basis by issuing a promissory note payable to the shareholder or the shareholder's estate for the balance of the purchase price.

The S corporation and its shareholders should structure such debt as "straight debt" in order to avoid any challenge by the IRS with regard to the single class of stock requirement. Code section 1361(c)(5) provides:

(5) STRAIGHT DEBT SAFE HARBOR. —

(A) IN GENERAL. — For purposes of subsection (b)(1)(D), straight debt shall not be treated as a second class of stock.

(B) STRAIGHT DEBT DEFINED. — For purposes of this paragraph, the term "straight debt" means any written unconditional promise to pay on demand or on a specified date a sum certain in money if —

(i) the interest rate (and interest payment dates) are not contingent on profits, the borrower's discretion, or similar factors,

(ii) there is no convertibility (directly or indirectly) into stock, and

(iii) the creditor is an individual (other than a nonresident alien), an estate, a trust described in paragraph (2), or a person which is actively and regularly engaged in the business of lending money.

It is advisable for any note issued by the S corporation to pay its shareholder by an unconditional promise to pay, executed in writing, and in conformity with the straight debt requirements. The S corporation's obligation to repay should not vary according to its financial experience. For example, if repayment were conditioned upon maintaining a certain level of corporate income, or if interest payments could be deferred if corporate earnings decreased, the purported debt could be reclassified by the IRS as equity, possibly creating a prohibited second class of stock.

The regulations pertaining to straight debt provide that an obligation subordinated to other corporate debt does not prevent qualification as straight debt.[22] Furthermore, the S corporation need not be secured. The debt can be an unsecured general obligation of the corporation. Or, the debt may be secured by corporate assets, except for stock of the S corporation. This would avoid conversion of the debt into equity in the event of a corporate default, which would violate the straight debt rules.

The regulations that define straight debt also provide that a straight debt obligation will no longer qualify if it is transferred to a third party who is not an eligible shareholder (as defined under Regulation Section 1.1361-1(b)). Thus, in the event that an S corporation redeems stock from a shareholder by issuing a note intended to satisfy the straight debt rules, the terms of the note should prohibit its assignment or transfer to an ineligible shareholder. This situation could arise, for example, when a note is issued to a deceased shareholder's estate in conjunction with a redemption of shares. A subsequent transfer by the estate to a trust ineligible to hold S shares would disqualify the note as straight debt.[23] Naturally, it would be preferable to effect a redemption after a shareholder's death by using life insurance proceeds or other cash to avoid the complexity of complying with both the straight debt and eligible shareholder requirements.

It should be emphasized that the straight debt rules constitute a safe harbor for qualifying a note as a debt obligation and not a second class of stock. The regulations expressly provide that an obligation that satisfies the definition of straight debt is not considered a second class of stock even if it is considered equity under general principles of federal tax law.[24] If a straight debt obligation charges an unreasonably high interest rate, a portion of the interest may be recharacterized and treated as a payment that is not interest. Such recharacterization does not result in a second class of stock.

While it is prudent to follow the straight debt rules in order to avoid any concern as to the character of debt versus equity, a note could fail to satisfy the straight debt requirements and not necessarily be characterized as a second class of stock. However, if an S corporation issues a note or other obligation, regardless of how it is designated, it will be treated as a second class of stock if:

(1)   it constitutes equity or otherwise results in the holder being treated as the owner of stock under general principles of federal tax law; and

(2)   a principal purpose of its issuance is to circumvent the rights to distribution or liquidation proceeds conferred by outstanding shares of stock or to circumvent the limitation on eligible shareholders of S corporations.

Other Tax Aspects of Redemptions. In redeeming its stock, a corporation typically pays cash and/or a promissory note to the shareholder whose shares are redeemed. However, the payment for the stock may be made in the form of appreciated property. For example, if a closely held corporation purchases shares of publicly traded stock and distributes it to one of its shareholders in redemption of its own stock, the appreciation in the shares will be taxable gain to the corporation.[25] The publicly traded shares are taxed as if they were sold. The gain from such a distribution is taxable to the C corporation itself, or, if made by an S corporation, to the shareholders of the S corporation just as if the stock were transferred to a third party.

EXAMPLE. Amos owns 80% of The Barnyard, an S corporation. The Barnyard redeems Amos' shares in exchange for publicly traded stock worth $1,000,000. The transfer of the stock to a shareholder for the redemption payment is taxable to the corporation in the same manner as if it were sold to a third party. The corporation paid $600,000 for the stock; it realizes $400,000 of gain on its transfer of the stock valued at $1,000,000. The $400,000 is taxed to the shareholders according to the "per share, per day" rule. For instance, if the payment of the publicly traded stock occurred on July 1, Luke owns the other 20% of the shares, and The Barnyard reports its income on a calendar year, the income to the shareholders would be allocated as follows:

Shareholder	Ownership		Period/% of Year		Share of Income
Amos	80%	X	(6 mos.) 50%	=	40%
Luke	20%	X	(6 mos.) 50%	=	10%
					] 60%
	100%	X	(6 mos.) 50%	=	50%

Shareholder	Share of Income		Gain On Transfer		Shareholder's Income
Amos	40%	X	$400,000	=	$160,000
Luke	60%	X	$400,000	=	$240,000

Amos' share of the S corporation's income resulting from its invest-ment gain or the transfer of stock is taxed to him as a shareholder. Such income is independent of any income realized by him under Section 302 from *his gain* on the S corporation stock redeemed (or as a distribution under Section 1368, if the redemption did not qualify as a payment in exchange for stock). Amos is taxed on both ends of the transaction — as a shareholder because of the S corporation's gain in the transfer and on the distribution from the corporation to him as a shareholder. His only consolation may be that if he decides to sell the publicly traded stock, his basis will be its fair market value at the time of receipt from the S corporation.

If the shareholders of an S corporation have set up a sinking fund or developed an investment portfolio to meet the cost of a stock redemption, the tax upon appreciated property may be a rude surprise. A redemption paid by cash and/or a note would be far more efficient from an income tax standpoint. If the redemption is to take place following a shareholder's death, life insurance funding would be the most appropriate method of meeting the contingency of death and avoiding income tax liability to the shareholders. Insurance funding would be equally applicable without regard to whether the shares were redeemed by an S or a C corporation. As indicated in the following discussion, corporate owned life insurance offers a unique advantage for funding a stock redemption by an S corporation that is not available to a C corporation.

Life Insurance in S Corporation Stock Redemptions. Chapter 3 discusses the tax implications of life insurance policies owned by S corporations. Both C and S corporations frequently purchase life insurance policies to fund stock redemption agreements. Unlike the case with a C corporation, life insurance owned by an S corporation can provide an income tax advantage to the surviving shareholders in the event of a shareholder's death.

EXAMPLE. Murphy and O'Malley each own 50% of a C corporation worth $2,000,000. Each shareholder has a $100,000 basis in the business. A stock redemption agreement is in effect and the corporation has purchased a $1,000,000 policy on each shareholder. Murphy dies and the corporation redeems his shares so that O'Malley owns 100% of the stock. If O'Malley decides to sell the business he will realize $1,900,000 of gain from the sale, based on the difference between the $2,000,000 value of the corporation and his $100,000 basis in the stock. When the corporation redeems Murphy's shares, O'Malley's basis in the stock is not increased because it is purchased by the corporation and not by him, personally.

Suppose, instead, that Murphy and O'Malley own an S corporation in the same circumstances. Following Murphy's death, the corporation receives $1,000,000 of life insurance proceeds. Although the proceeds are tax exempt income to the corporation, the surviving shareholder's stock basis is increased proportionately, that is, by $500,000. The basis of Murphy's estate in the stock is increased to its fair market value under the step-up rule of Section 1014. The insurance proceeds do not affect the estate's basis (although it is possible that the estate's basis will be increased if the fair market value of the stock is increased because of the corporation's receipt of the insurance proceeds).

If the corporation owns a term insurance policy on Murphy's life, O'Malley's basis would be increased by $500,000, which is his pro rata share of the proceeds paid to the corporation. On the other hand, if the corporation owns a whole life policy, O'Malley's basis is increased only to the extent of his pro rata share of the "book income," that is, the proceeds minus cash value. The increase in basis would be limited to the extent that the cash value had been taken into account in permitting a basis reduction during the shareholder's lifetime. If, in any year, the cash value increase exceeded the premium, the "excess" amount may not have been taken into account in reducing basis. Such "excess" would also be added to the difference between the proceeds and the cash value in the year of death. (See Chapter 3 for a detailed explanation.)

For ease of explanation, the income in the year of death will be referred to as resulting from the "proceeds" of the policy.

In the example, O'Malley's basis is increased by the portion of the proceeds reflecting his stock ownership. It should be emphasized that the basis increase results from the receipt of proceeds by the S corporation. The increased basis that is available to an S corporation, but not a C corporation, is a function of the income generated by the proceeds. Thus, the surviving shareholder's basis would be increased in proportion to his stock ownership even if the decedent's stock were not redeemed.

Full Increase In Basis: Election to Terminate Tax Year. In the example above, if O'Malley contemplates a sale of the business after Murphy's death, he is in a better position to limit his exposure to income taxation because his basis has been partially increased by the corporation's receipt of the insurance proceeds. Thus, an increased basis can be obtained if life insurance is used to fund an S corporation redemption, in contrast to the unchanged basis that results if the S corporation redemption is completed without insurance or if a C corporation redeems its stock, with or without insurance funding. If a *fully* increased basis were of paramount importance to the surviving shareholder, a cross purchase plan would be preferable. In that case, the surviving owner could apply insurance proceeds received on the other shareholder's life to a purchase of stock from the decedent's estate.

If buy-sell planning is in its initial stages, a cross purchase agreement could be established. In many cases, however, that option may be foreclosed because an existing stock redemption agreement is in effect. A stock redemption agreement could be amended to become a cross purchase agreement easily enough, but the possible transfer of life insurance policies must also be considered. The prospective transfer of a policy held under a buy sell arrangement may trigger the application of the transfer for value rule. If a policy is transferred "for value" within the meaning of Section 101, the income tax exemption normally available to the beneficiary in receipt of the death proceeds might be lost. The transfer for value rule may be avoided if the transfer qualifies under an exception, such as a transfer to the insured. However, a transfer to a co-shareholder otherwise unprotected by an exception[26] is subject to the rule. It does not matter whether the transfer "for value" involves an actual payment of cash or property. The fact that each shareholder agrees to the change of ownership in mutual consideration of the other's obligation under the buy-sell agreement is sufficient to invoke the application of the rule.[27]

Suppose that a funded stock redemption agreement is in place when the shareholders make the S corporation election. The transfer of a policy to the respective insured shareholder would avoid the transfer for value rule, but would not direct the funds to where they are needed. A transfer to a shareholder who is not the insured would be a transfer for value without other relief from the rule. If the corporation had purchased term insurance to fund the stock redemption agreement, each shareholder could purchase a policy on the other's life upon the expiration of the coverage. Alternatively, the shareholders could consider allowing the stock redemption agreement to remain intact if they were willing and able to engage in further planning.

If the shareholders agree to terminate the tax year pursuant to Code section 1377(a)(2), it is possible for the surviving shareholder to increase basis in the S corporation's stock by the full amount of the proceeds, rather than by a pro rata portion of the proceeds. Section 1377(a)(2) states:

> (2) ELECTION TO TERMINATE YEAR. —
>
> > (A) IN GENERAL. — Under regulations prescribed by the Secretary, if any shareholder terminates the shareholder's interest in the corporation during the taxable year and all affected shareholders and the corporation agree to the application of this paragraph, paragraph (1) shall be applied to the affected shareholders as if the taxable year consisted of 2 taxable years the first of which ends on the date of the termination.
> >
> > (B) AFFECTED SHAREHOLDERS. — For purposes of subparagraph (A), the term "affected shareholders" means the shareholder whose interest is terminated and all shareholders to whom such shareholder has transferred shares during the taxable year. If such shareholder has transferred shares to the corporation, the term "affected shareholders" shall include all persons who are shareholders during the taxable year.

Most S corporations operate on a calendar year basis for income tax purposes. An election to terminate the taxable year affects the allocation of income, deductions, etc., for "affected shareholders" only for the year in which it is made. In other words, the taxable year that is otherwise applicable (typically the calendar year) continues to apply in subsequent years following the election. If the election is not made, the "per share, per day" rule of Section 1377(a)(1) applies to all tax items of the corporation and the shareholders for the full calendar year. If the Section 1377(a)(2) election *is* made, the affected shareholders are treated as if the S corporation's taxable year is divided into two short years and all income, deductions, etc., are allocated to each short year as if the short year were a full year.

Two conditions of Section 1377(a)(2) must be fulfilled in order for the election to be made:

1. *A shareholder must terminate his entire interest in the S corporation.* A shareholder's entire interest can be termi-

nated as the result of several different events, including a sale or redemption during the shareholder's lifetime or after his death.[28] If a shareholder's interest is terminated by a redemption, apparently no rules of attribution apply under Section 1377(a)(2) with regard to the meaning of "terminated." Thus, following the death of a shareholder, the termination of interest caused by an S corporation's redemption of shares from the decedent's estate ends the first short taxable year.

2. *"All affected shareholders and the corporation agree..."* In order to satisfy this requirement, it is advisable for the shareholders of the S corporation to specify their agreement to the Section 1377(a)(2) election in the stock redemption agreement. Section 1377(a)(2)(B) provides that the term "affected shareholder" means the shareholder whose interest is terminated and all shareholders to whom such shareholder has transferred shares during the taxable year. Furthermore, if the terminating shareholder transfers shares to the corporation, all shareholders during the taxable year are affected shareholders. Therefore, it is prudent for the shareholders to specify their unanimous agreement in the buy-sell agreement (and to bind successors in interest, such as an executor), in order to assure the agreement of all affected shareholders and the corporation, in any event. The termination of the shareholder's interest is likely to occur as the result of an event covered by the terms of the buy-sell agreement executed by the shareholders.

The IRS has provided regulatory guidance for S corporation shareholders with regard to the time and manner of making the election to terminate the taxable year.[29]

If an S corporation is on the cash basis method, a stock redemption agreement funded by corporate owned life insurance may be coordinated with a Section 1377(a)(2) election to permit a surviving shareholder to obtain a full, rather than partial, increase in stock basis.

EXAMPLE. Murphy and O'Malley each own 50% of an S corporation worth $2,000,000, which owns $1,000,000 of term insurance on each shareholder's life. The following events occur:

Event	Date
Murphy dies	April 15
S Corporation redeems Murphy's shares by transferring promissory note to his estate.	April 30
S Corporation receives $1,000,000 of life insurance proceeds.	May 15
S Corporation transfers cash to estate in cancellation of promissory note.	June 1

The redemption that terminates the interest of the shareholder (Murphy's estate) also terminates the taxable year. The (tax exempt) income of the S corporation attributable to the insurance proceeds is allocated to O'Malley as the sole shareholder. Consequently, O'Malley's basis in the stock is increased by the full amount of the proceeds since he owns all of the stock in the taxable year when the income is received by the corporation. The basis of Murphy's stock remains stepped up to its fair market value at death under the general rule of Section 1014 without regard to whether O'Malley receives a partial or full increase in basis.

A few points should be noted in regard to the viability of permitting a full increase in the basis of the surviving shareholders:

(1)   It is unlikely that an S corporation on the accrual basis would be able to defer the realization of income from the insurance proceeds until after a redemption by note. An accrual basis taxpayer is considered to be in receipt of income when it is earned, that is, when the right to receive occurs, not when actual receipt occurs.[30] Presumably, that right is established upon the death of the insured, subject to divestment if the insurer's death claim procedure cannot be satisfied. (It is assumed that the filing of a death claim by the beneficiary and payment by the insurer amounts to ministerial action that completes the processing of a death claim. Such action confirms, rather than establishes, the beneficiary's right to receive death proceeds, unless the circumstances require more than a verification of coverage and proof of death to process the claim. In some cases, the corporation's right to receive may not accrue until the actual payment of the claim

is made by the insurer. Nonetheless, that possibility does not provide certainty in the planning process for an S corporation on the accrual basis.)

(2)   If an S corporation on the cash basis delays the redemption and the submission of the death claim, the IRS might assert that the corporation is in constructive receipt of the proceeds prior to the redemption. It would be difficult to pinpoint the moment when constructive receipt occurs, but even a cash basis taxpayer should not procrastinate the submission of the claim (although a prompt redemption within the period shown in the example above should be successful).

(3)   In the example, the distribution of cash by the S corporation on June 1 to the estate is a payment to cancel the promissory note. The payment of the debt has no effect on the basis of the surviving shareholder in the S corporation's stock. The corporation has simply reduced an asset (cash) in exchange for the removal of a liability (the note).

In deciding whether the election to terminate the tax year is a feasible planning strategy, the "affected shareholders" should be mindful of the fact that the election also determines that their income, deductions, etc., apart from the redemption and insurance proceeds, will be treated as occurring in two separate taxable years. However, any shareholder who is not an "affected shareholder" has income, deductions, etc., in one taxable year.

Election to Terminate Tax Year Through a "Qualifying Disposition." In addition to the election under Section 1377(a)(2), when a shareholder terminates his interest he may terminate the taxable year when a "qualifying disposition" of stock occurs. Under the regulations to Section 1368, a qualifying disposition is:[31]

1.   A disposition by a shareholder of 20% or more of the outstanding stock of the corporation in one or more transactions during any 30-day period during the corporation's taxable year;

2.   A redemption treated as an exchange under Section 302(a) or Section 303(a) of 20% or more of the outstanding stock of the

corporation from a shareholder in one or more transactions during any 30-day period during the corporation's taxable year; or

3.   An issuance of an amount of stock equal to or greater than 25% of the previously outstanding stock to one or more new shareholders during any 30-day period during the corporation's taxable year.

An election may be made upon the occurrence of any qualifying disposition. The effect of making the election is that an S corporation must divide the taxable year into separate taxable years for purposes of allocating items of income and loss; making adjustments to AAA, E&P, and basis; and determining the tax effect of distributions by the corporation.

An election is made by attaching a statement to the S corporation's income tax return. The statement must set forth facts relating to the qualifying disposition, such as whether it is a sale, gift, redemption, or issuance of stock. The statement must also specify that each shareholder who holds stock in the taxable year must consent to the election. The election is irrevocable.

However, under the regulations to Section 1368, if the shareholders of an S corporation elect to terminate the taxable year under Section 1377(a)(2), and the event resulting in the termination of a shareholder's entire interest also constitutes a qualifying disposition, the Section 1377 termination election rules control and a qualifying disposition election cannot be made. (Presumably, the same result occurs even after the 1996 amendment to Section 1377(a)(2), which requires an election by all affected shareholders and the corporation.)

Comparison of Premium Cost: Stock Redemption or Cross Purchase Plan. The allocation of premiums between or among the shareholders may determine whether a buy-sell agreement is structured as a stock redemption or cross purchase plan. The decision to follow one format or the other may be driven by a variety of factors, including the effect on the survivor's basis, as described above, and other aspects of planning that are independent of life insurance coverage. When life insurance funding is considered, the question of whether the S corporation or the shareholders should pay the premiums is also taken into account.

A comparison of income tax brackets is frequently made in the case of C corporation planning. If the C corporation is in a low tax bracket, a stock redemption plan may be preferred because a nondeductible premium is acceptable to the corporation. In contrast, a C corporation in a higher tax bracket will attach more importance to a corporate tax deduction and will tend to favor a cross purchase plan, rather than the stock redemption (or split dollar) approach. Of course, in most closely held corporations, the insured is usually both stockholder and employee; the effect of the plan on the corporation's cost will be experienced at least indirectly according to the extent of the insured's stock ownership. In addition, it may be that the tax cost of the premiums to the corporation will be less important than the tax cost to the individual shareholder.

Naturally, a tax bracket comparison is not possible when an S corporation is the subject of buy-sell planning. The passthrough feature causes the corporate cost to be borne directly by the shareholder. Determining the allocation of premium expense to the shareholders calls into play many of the same factors as for a C corporation (differences in age, percentage of ownership, etc.), but the impact of the cost is more dramatic without the cushion of a corporate tax bracket.

EXAMPLE. Harry, Larry and Barry are the owners of HLB, Inc., an S corporation. Harry owns 60% of the company and is more than 20 years older than Larry and Barry, who own 30% and 10% of the company, respectively. The three owners are engaged in buy-sell planning and have obtained premium quotes for the life insurance coverage needed to fund the buyout. Based upon their ages and the policies required, they are informed that the premiums would be:

Shareholder	Premium
Harry	$12,000
Larry	$ 3,000
Barry	$ 1,000

They are interested in knowing the allocation of premium expense if they establish a stock redemption or a cross purchase agreement. If a stock redemption plan is adopted, HLB will be the owner and beneficiary of the policy and it will pay the premiums as a nondeductible expense. As such,

the premiums will be paid from the corporation's income that is taxable
to the shareholders and allocated in the following manner:

Harry's Premium = $12,000

Shareholder	Taxable Income
Harry	$7,200
Larry	$3,600
Barry	$1,200

Larry's Premium = $3,000

Shareholder	Taxable Income
Harry	$1,800
Larry	$ 900
Barry	$ 300

Barry's Premium = $1,000

Shareholder	Taxable Income
Harry	$ 600
Larry	$ 300
Barry	$ 100

Total Premium Expense = $16,000

Shareholder	Taxable Income
Harry	$9,600
Larry	$4,800
Barry	$1,600

The allocation of the premium expense to the taxable income of HLB
chargeable to the shareholders is made in direct proportion to their stock
ownership. It therefore follows that Harry, as the majority shareholder,
bears the greatest portion of the premium expense. Larry is next, and
Barry, as a 10% shareholder, has the lightest burden.

Rather than a stock redemption plan, the shareholders might enter
into a cross purchase agreement. In that case, each shareholder would be
the owner and beneficiary of policies on the lives of the other shareholders.
The source of the premium would be compensation paid to each of them
as employees, rather than corporate income charged to them *as sharehold-*

ers. Assuming that the surviving shareholders would continue to own stock in the same proportion to each other in the event of any shareholder's death, the premium allocation would be as follows:

Harry's Premium = $12,000

Policyowner	Compensation
Larry	$9,000
Barry	$3,000

Larry's Premium = $3,000

Policyowner	Compensation
Harry	$2,571
Barry	$ 429

Barry's Premium = $1,000

Policyowner	Compensation
Harry	$ 667
Larry	$ 333

Total Premium Expense = $16,000

Compensation Summary

Harry	$3,238
Larry	$9,333
Barry	$3,429

As the oldest shareholder holding the largest percentage of stock, Harry carries the greatest portion of the cost under a stock redemption plan. Consequently, he is relieved of a large portion of the premium expense when the cost of the coverage is shifted more directly to the purchasers of stock under a cross purchase plan. Conversely, the cross purchase plan imposes a greater premium expense upon Larry and Barry. The cost of paying the premiums from their compensation is approximately twice as expensive to them than if HLB paid the premiums for corporate owned policies under a stock redemption plan.

If there is tension among the shareholders on money matters generally, the difference in allocation of cost between the two approaches can add fuel to the fire. However, if the relationship is harmonious and the business is financially healthy enough to make adjustments in compensation, the cost difference should not be an obstacle. The decision to follow either format may be made for reasons that are independent of premium allocation. Any perceived imbalance can be rectified through the payment of more (or less) bonus compensation to the affected shareholder. Reconciling the allocation of cost will be a function of how the shareholders perceive the relative benefits of the buy-sell agreement to each of them, as well as their overall sense of how each of them has contributed to the prosperity of the business.

VALUATION OF S CORPORATION STOCK

The valuation of S corporation stock may be conducted according to many of the same principles that govern the valuation of C corporation stock.[32] The features of S corporations that influence a valuation are the lack of a taxable entity and particular S requirements, such as the shareholder eligibility rules and the one class of stock restriction. Stock appraisals that involve a capitalization of C corporation earnings on an after-tax basis are not necessarily susceptible to the same approach when an S corporation is valued. Many closely held C corporations limit taxable income in order to avoid a "double tax" on the shareholders' income. In contrast, the "dividend policy" of an S corporation may run the gamut from no dividends to substantial amounts that are paid to shareholders.

For purposes of this chapter, the valuation of an S corporation is concerned with its federal estate and gift tax implications. In pertinent part, Regulation Section 20.2031-3 states:

Valuation of Interests in Businesses: The fair market value of any interest of a decedent in a business, whether a partnership or a proprietorship, is the net amount which a willing purchaser, whether an individual or a corporation, would pay for the interest to a willing seller, neither being under any compulsion to buy or to sell and both having reasonable knowledge of relevant facts. The net value is determined on the basis of all relevant factors including —

(a) A fair appraisal as of the applicable valuation date of all the assets of the business, tangible and intangible, including good will;

(b) The demonstrated earning capacity of the business; and

(c) The other factors set forth in paragraphs (f) and (h) of §20.2031-2 relating to the valuation of corporate stock, to the extent applicable.

While the "willing buyer-willing seller" test also applies to S corporations, the prospective purchaser of a business must take the S corporation election into account. In general, the ownership and one class of stock restrictions may limit the marketability of the stock, although those factors may be of no importance in a particular case.

The potential purchaser's assessment of shareholder income is likely to be colored by whether the purchaser can obtain a controlling interest in the corporation. If a shareholder has a majority interest in an S corporation, dividend policy, among other items, can be suited to the shareholder's needs. On the other hand, the purchaser of a minority interest may be forced to accept the dividend policy of the corporation beyond the negotiation of a compensation arrangement if he or she will also be an employee of the corporation.

Establish Value for Federal Estate Tax Purposes. Traditionally, a buy-sell agreement that meets the following requirements has been effective in establishing the value of a business interest for federal estate tax purposes:

1.   The estate must be obligated to sell at death (under either a mandatory purchase agreement or an option held by the business or survivors);

2.   The price must be fixed by the terms of the agreement or the agreement must contain a formula or method for determining the price;

3.   The agreement must prohibit the owner from disposing of his interest during life without first offering it to the other party or parties at no more than the contract price;

4.   The price must be fair and adequate when the agreement is made.[33]

Those requirements have been equally applicable to S or C corporation stock (and other forms of business ownership). If the four requirements were satisfied, the price established at the time when the agreement was made could be effective to "fix" the value for estate tax purposes until the owner's death. Even at that, the price specified in the agreement was not deemed to be controlling for estate tax purposes if it was merely a scheme for avoiding estate taxes.[34]

Section 2703, which was introduced into the law as part of Chapter 14 of the Code, provides the following:

SEC. 2703. CERTAIN RIGHTS AND RESTRICTIONS DISRE-GARDED.

(a) GENERAL RULE. — For purposes of this subtitle, the value of any property shall be determined without regard to —

(1) any option, agreement, or other right to acquire or use the property at a price less than the fair market value of the property (without regard to such option, agreement, or right), or

(2) any restriction on the right to sell or use such property.

(b) EXCEPTIONS. — Subsection (a) shall not apply to any option, agreement, right, or restriction which meets each of the following requirements:

(1) It is a bona fide business arrangement.

(2) It is not a device to transfer such property to members of the decedent's family for less than full and adequate consideration in money or money's worth.

(3) Its terms are comparable to similar arrangements entered into by persons in an arms' length transaction.

A buy-sell agreement which is entered into or substantially modified after October 8, 1990, must satisfy the three requirements stated above or it will not have any weight for estate, gift and generation-skipping tax purposes with regard to the value of the business interest subject to its terms. The legislative history accompanying the enactment of Section 2703 states:

Buy-sell agreements. — The bill provides that the value of property for transfer tax purposes is determined without regard to any option, agreement or other right to acquire or use the property at less than fair market value or any restriction on the right to sell or use such property, unless the option, agreement, right or restriction meets three requirements. These requirements apply to any restriction, however created. For example, they apply to restrictions implicit in the capital structure of the partnership or contained in a partnership agreement, articles of incorporation, or corporate bylaws or a shareholder's agreement.

The first two requirements are that the option, agreement, right or restriction (1) be a bona fide business arrangement, and (2) not be a device to transfer such property to members of the decedent's family for less than full and adequate consideration in money or money's worth. These requirements are similar to those contained in the present Treasury regulations, except that the bill clarifies that the business arrangement and device requirements are independent tests. The mere showing that the agreement is a bona fide business arrangement would not give the agreement estate tax effect if other facts indicate that the agreement is a device to transfer property to members of the decedents [decedent's] family for less than full and adequate consideration. In making this clarification, it adopts the reasoning of *Saint Louis County Bank* and rejects the suggestion of other cases that the maintenance of family control standing alone assures the absence of a device to transfer wealth.

In addition, the bill adds a third requirement, not found in present law, that the terms of the option, agreement, right or restrictions be comparable to similar arrangements entered into by persons in an arm's length transaction. This requires that the taxpayer show that the agreement was one that could have been obtained in an arm's length bargain. Such determination would entail consideration of such factors as the expected term of the agreement, the present value of the property, its expected value at the time of exercise, and consideration offered for the option. It is not met simply by showing isolated comparables but requires a demonstration of the general practice of unrelated parties. Expert testimony would be evidence of such practice. In unusual cases where comparables [are] difficult to find because the taxpayer owns a unique business, the taxpayer can use the comparables from similar businesses.

The bill does not otherwise alter the requirements for giving weight to a buy-sell agreement. For example, it leaves intact present law rules requiring that an agreement have lifetime restrictions in order to be binding on death.[35]

Establishing the value of a closely held business has always been a critical element of business continuation planning. In the future, the determination of a proper value for C or S corporation stock has been rendered even more significant for estate, gift and generation-skipping tax purposes because of the "comparable to similar arrangements" provision. The full meaning of that provision will become clearer with time and experience; with the proliferation of S corporations in the current business environment, the meaning of "similar businesses" may include the tax and ownership structure of a corporation (S or C) as well as the particular industry or other category in which it fits.

FOOTNOTE REFERENCES

1. IRC Sec. 1014(a).
2. *General Utilities and Operating Company v. Helvering*, 296 U.S. 200 (1935); Secs. 631, 632, 633 of P.L. 99-514, Tax Reform Act of 1986, amending IRC Secs. 336, 337 and 1374.
3. IRC Sec. 1015(a).
4. IRC Secs. 2701-04, added to the Code by Sec. 11602(a) of P.L. 101-508, the Revenue Reconciliation Act of 1990.
5. IRC Sec. 2701(a)(2)(C) and Reg. §25.2701-1(c)(3).
6. However, it should be noted that the IRS may revalue a gift for estate tax purposes after the gift tax statute of limitations has expired. See *Estate of Frederick R. Smith v. Comm.*, 94 TC 872 (1990), acq. 1990-2 CB 1.
7. Revenue Ruling 93-12, 1993-1 CB 202, provides an additional measure of comfort to Ray, Charlie and their appraiser with respect to the discounts permitted for the gifts of stock to a family member. While it was possible for an individual to make a discounted gift of closely held stock or other property to a family member prior to the publication of Revenue Ruling 93-12, the likelihood of challenge to such discounts by the IRS was greater before the ruling was issued. Revenue Ruling 93-12 states that, in the case of a corporation with a single class of stock, notwithstanding the family relationship of the donor, the donee and other shareholders, the shares of other family members will not be aggregated with transferred shares to determine whether the transferred shares should be valued as part of a controlling interest. Thus, the family

relationship does not, per se, prevent a discount from being available when a gift is made by a donor to a donee who is a related party. However, apart from the family relationship, a gift of a minority interest in a family owned business must independently qualify for a discount based upon lack of marketability or lack of control.

8. Reg. §1.1361-1(l)(2)(iii). See also Letter Rulings 9308606 and 9410010, both of which featured buy-sell agreements approved by the IRS as not creating a second class of stock. In each ruling, the principal purpose of the agreement was not to circumvent the single class of stock requirement and the purchase price at the time when the agreement was entered into, was not significantly in excess of or below the fair market value of the stock. See also Letter Rulings 9425023, 9425027 and 9433024, which reach the same conclusion. In Letter Ruling 9413023, the Service ruled that the minority discount does not establish a price that is significantly in excess of or below the fair market value of the stock when the purchase price under a buy-sell agreement was the result of arm's length negotiations and therefore no second class of stock was established.

9. Reg. §1.1361-1(l)(2)(iii).

10. Reg. §1.1361-1(l)(2)(v), Ex. 9.

11. See IRC Secs. 483 and 1274.

12. See., e.g. *Miller v. Comm.* 70 TC 448 (1978); GCM 39529.

13. *General Explanation of the Tax Reform Act of 1986*, p. 265, footnote 57.

14. In fact, the Service ruled in Letter Ruling 9040066 that investment interest expense (subject to the limitations of Section 163(d)) that had been incurred to purchase a C corporation may be transformed into trade or business interest that is deductible without limitation by the corporation's S election, to the extent that the S corporation engages in an active trade or business.

15. See IRS Announcement 87-4, 1987-3 IRB 17; Temp. Regs. §1.163-8T; T.D. 8145, 1987-2 CB 47; and IRS Notice 88-20, 1988-1 CB 487, which provide guidance concerning how debt will be characterized by a tracing of the use of debt proceeds.

16. In any event, the 75 shareholder limitation applicable to S corporations should be kept in mind in multi-shareholder situations.

17. Having only one policy per insured is a classic reason favoring a stock redemption, but a cross purchase plan could be administered by having a trustee hold legal title to one policy on each shareholder. Upon a shareholder's death, the proceeds would be received by the trustee and applied to purchase the decedent's stock. The shares received by the trustee would then be distributed on a pro rata basis to the surviving shareholders.

18. Secs. 301, 302 of P.L. 99-514, Tax Reform Act of 1986.

19. Sec. 11101(c) of P.L. 101-508, Revenue Reconciliation Act of 1990.

20. IRC Sec. 1368(e)(1)(B). See "Yolanda and Zeke" example at the end of Chapter 1.

21. See Rev. Rul. 95-14, 1995-1 CB 169.

22. Reg. §1.1361-1(l)(5)(ii).

23. Reg. §1.1361-1(l)(5)(iii)(B).

24. Reg. §1.1361-1(l)(5)(iv).

25. IRC Sec. 311(b).

26. If the transferee is a partner of the insured in a bona fide partnership, then the transfer should be exempt, even if the transferee is also a co-shareholder. See Let. Rul. 9045004.

27. See *Monroe v. Patterson*, 197 F. Supp. 146 (N.D. Ala. 1961); Let. Rul. 7734048.

28. On July 11, 1995, the Treasury Department and the IRS issued Proposed Regulations [PS-268-82; 60 Fed. Reg. 35882 (7/12/95)] that address methods for computing an S corporation shareholder's pro rata share of the corporation's items of income, loss, deduction and credit. These regulations apply to S corporation taxable years that

begin after the date when the final regulations are published, but can be relied upon in the meantime, pending the publication of final regulations. Prop. Reg. §1.1377-1(b)(3).

29. Prop. Reg. §1.1377-1(b)(4).
30. *Helvering v. Enright*, 312 U.S. 636, (1941).
31. Reg. §1.1368-1(g)(2).
32. See Rev. Rul. 59-60, 1959-1 CB 237; Reg. §20.2031-2(f) and (h); Reg. §20.2031-3.
33. *May v. McGowan*, 194 F.2d 396; *Estate of Bruno Bischoff v. Comm.*, 69 TC 32 (1977); *Estate of Mabel G. Seltzer v. Comm.*, TC Memo 1985-519; TAMs 8541005, 8710004.
34. *Slocum v. U.S.*, 256 F. Supp. 753 (S.D.N.Y. 1966). Also, see *St. Louis County Bank v. U.S.*, 49 AFTR 2d ¶148,515 (8th Cir. 1982).
35. Senate Committee Report for Sec. 2703 in P.L. 101-508, Revenue Reconciliation Act of 1990.

Chapter 6

ESTATE PLANNING CONSIDERATIONS

The owner of any closely held business has particular concerns that must be addressed as part of his or her estate planning. Whether the business operates as a sole proprietorship, a partnership, an S corporation or a C corporation, the owner faces estate planning issues that differ from those of the individual who does not own a significant share in an operating business. These estate planning issues often intermesh with business continuation planning needs. Business continuation aspects of S corporation planning are covered in Chapter 5.

Any closely held business owner who engages in estate planning is typically confronted with both personal and tax planning dilemmas. If the owner dies, can the spouse manage the business? If the spouse is not active and other shareholders are involved, should the spouse inherit stock or sell to the other owners? Are the owner's children interested in the business? If interested, do they show the right level of ability and motivation to participate in its future management? Are they likely to work compatibly with the other owners and *their* children in the future? Are they compatible with each other? What should be done when one child is interested in the business and the others are not? Questions like these are frequently difficult to answer, and even more difficult to resolve by a plan that works in action over time, as well as on paper.

The owners of both S and C corporations must struggle with the problems inherent in finding answers to these questions. On occasion, emotional issues — jealousies, unresolved sibling rivalries, a struggle for control — dominate the agenda. Naturally, the estate, gift and income tax implications weigh heavily in the development of a suitable estate plan. Volumes have been written about both the tax and nontax consequences of estate planning for closely held businesses. In addition to the general variety of planning issues that a C corporation owner faces, the S corporation owner must be attentive to the eligibility requirements for the ownership of S stock.

Specifically, Section 1361(c)(2) contains rules for determining whether certain trusts are permitted to be S corporation shareholders, including an "electing small business trust," as introduced by the Small Business Job Protection Act of 1996. In addition, Section 1361(d) provides a special rule for a "qualified subchapter S trust" (QSST), a statutory creation designed to permit the ownership of S corporation stock. Our focus in this chapter will be to consider how these rules influence the estate planning decisions of S corporation owners and how familiar estate planning techniques are applied or modified when S corporation stock is involved.

ESTATE OWNERSHIP OF S CORPORATION STOCK

Rather than jump straight into the technical thicket of rules governing trust ownership, we will wade into the estate planning area by assuming that an S corporation shareholder dies without having established a lifetime or testamentary trust. Suppose, for example, that the shareholder leaves his entire estate under his will, including all of his S corporation stock, to his wife, or outright to his adult children, if he is not survived by his wife. Immediately following his death, the S corporation stock is owned by his estate. The executor holds the stock, pending distribution to the beneficiaries named in the decedent's will.

Code section 1361 indicates its approval of S corporation stock ownership by an estate, in typical tax law style, by backing an estate out of an excluded category. Specifically, Section 1361(b)(1)(B) states, in pertinent part:

(b) SMALL BUSINESS CORPORATION. —

(1) IN GENERAL. — For purposes of this subchapter, the term "small business corporation" means a domestic corporation which is not an ineligible corporation and which does not —

(B) have as a shareholder a person (other than an estate, a trust described in subsection (c)(2), or an organization described in subsection (c)(7)) who is not an individual,

In addition, for purposes of the 75 shareholder limit, Section 1361(c)(1) states that a husband and wife (and their estates) are treated as one shareholder. Furthermore, an estate is apparently deemed to be a single shareholder, that is, no rules directing the beneficiaries to be counted as shareholders are applicable.

If S corporation stock is left to a beneficiary as an outright bequest under the terms of a will, it is held by the decedent's executor, pending distribution to the beneficiaries named in the will. In order to permit a smooth continuation of the business, the executor may be granted powers under the will to continue its operation. For the most part, these powers would be identical to those granted to an executor in a situation in which a C corporation would continue its business operation after an owner's death. However, it may be worthwhile to include a clause that enables the executor to take action in order to protect the corporation's S election, without preventing the executor from terminating the S election, if termination is warranted. In addition, it may be advisable for the executor to have other specific powers necessary to serve the interests of beneficiaries who are differently situated. For example, the executor may be authorized to recapitalize the S stock so that voting common stock will be held by beneficiaries who are active in the business and nonvoting common stock will be held by beneficiaries who are not active.

While an estate is a permissible owner of S corporation stock without a time limitation of the type applicable to certain trusts, an estate may be classified as a de facto trust, or a "resulting trust." In other words, if estate administration is unduly prolonged and the executor effectively assumes the functions of a trustee, the IRS might claim that the estate is actually a testamentary trust.[1] As such, it becomes subject to the trust ownership eligibility rules under Sections 1361(c), (d), and (e).

If the same parties serve as executors and trustees, the line differentiating an estate from a trust may be blurred if ordinary formalities are not observed. In one case involving the same parties serving in both fiduciary roles, a court determined that an estate had become a testamentary trust.[2] As a result, the trust was held to be an ineligible shareholder (although the case predated the rules permitting certain trusts to own S corporation stock). Nonetheless, the principle of the case still applies under current law — if an estate is determined to be a de facto trust, it may become an ineligible shareholder of an S corporation if the time limitation applicable to testamentary trusts (discussed below) is exceeded.

EXAMPLE. How might the "resulting trust" doctrine be applied? Suppose that Jeff, the sole shareholder of an S corporation, leaves his entire estate to his wife, or, if she does not survive him, to their minor children. Jeff and his wife die in a common disaster and Jeff's brother, Lincoln, as contingent executor, holds the S corporation stock on behalf of the children for an extended period of time. If Lincoln does not distribute the assets of the estate within a reasonable period of time, a resulting trust may be deemed to arise. In such a case, it may be unclear when the estate will be deemed to be a trust and Lincoln will be regarded as a trustee, rather than as an executor. In order to avoid having the estate characterized as a trust, Lincoln may pursue one of the following alternatives if the administration of the estate is extended.

• He may distribute the stock to the guardian of the children, as custodian of a Uniform Gifts to Minors Account (UGMA) or a Uniform Transfers to Minors Account (UTMA).[3] Stock transferred to a minor under an UGMA or UTMA is considered to be owned by an individual under a fiduciary relationship, rather than owned by a trust. However, if stock is owned by two or more minors, but held in the name of a guardian or custodian, each minor is counted as a shareholder.[4]

• If Jeff's will contains a provision permitting the establishment of a contingent trust, he may transfer the shares to himself as trustee of a trust for the benefit of the minor children until age 21, for example. A transfer to such a trust should comply with the requirements necessary for the trust to be classified as a QSST (discussed below) or another type of trust eligible to own S corporation stock.

The Service has ruled that the estate of a deceased shareholder that holds S corporation stock solely to facilitate the payment of federal estate tax for the period during which the estate complies with the provisions of Section 6166 (installment payments of estate tax) will continue to be an eligible shareholder.[5]

Finally, as used in Section 1361(b)(1)(B), the term estate means a decedent's estate or the estate of an individual in a bankruptcy case.[6] The term "estate" does not include the estate of an infant, an incompetent or other person under a disability. For purposes of applying the ownership rules, S corporation stock held by an individual, an incompetent or an individual under a disability is considered to be owned by the individual, rather than by his or her estate.[7]

TRUST OWNERSHIP OF S CORPORATION STOCK

Code section 1361(c)(2) indicates that certain trusts are permitted to own S corporation stock. For tax years beginning prior to January 1, 1997, eligible trusts include the following:

1. A trust, all of which is treated as owned by the trust grantor or a beneficiary under Sections 671-679 (a "grantor trust" or "Section 678 trust"). The trust grantor or beneficiary who is the deemed owner of the stock must be a U.S. citizen or resident.

2. A trust of the type described in number 1 above may continue to own S corporation stock following the death of the deemed owner, but only for 60 days following the deemed owner's death, *unless* the entire corpus of the trust is included in the deemed owner's estate, in which case the trust can remain a shareholder for as long as two years. The estate of the deemed owner is treated as the shareholder.

3. A trust that acquires S corporation stock pursuant to the terms of a will may hold the stock for no longer than 60 days, starting from the day on which the trust acquires the stock. The estate of the testator is treated as the deemed owner.

4. A trust created primarily to exercise the voting power of stock transferred to it. Each beneficiary of a voting trust is treated as a shareholder.

The Small Business Job Protection Act of 1996 amendments to the Code changed numbers 2 and 3 above as follows:

2. A trust which is of the type described above in number 1 immediately before the death of the deemed owner and which continues in the existence after such death, but only for the two year period beginning on the day of the deemed owner's death.[8]

3. A trust with respect to stock transferred to it pursuant to the terms of a will, but only for the two year period beginning on the day on which such stock is transferred to it.[9]

The effect of these changes is to provide relief from the potential time pressure of the 60-day rule by permitting a grantor trust or Section 678 trust to own S corporation stock for a two year period.

OBSERVATION. At first glance, the rules governing the eligibility of trusts to be S corporation shareholders may not seem to follow any discernible pattern or rationale. However, upon more careful consideration, it seems clear that the rules are designed to avoid allowing a trust to be able to shelter an individual grantor or beneficiary from being taxed on S corporation income. The S corporation itself is a conduit; the net income of the corporation is passed through to the shareholders. Those trusts in which income is taxed to the trust owner or beneficiary, that is, in which the trusts effectively function as a conduit between the S corporation's income and the trust owner or beneficiary, are permitted to own S stock.

As in many other areas of the tax law, a page of history is worth a volume of logic, in Justice Holmes' phrase. Originally, the Code had prohibited the ownership of S corporation stock by any person or entity other than an individual or an estate. Over a period of time, after litigation between taxpayers and the IRS, Congress loosened its prohibition against trust ownership, in order to permit more flexibility in planning to the owners of an S corporation. Thus, while the rules governing trust ownership of S corporation stock operate restrictively in regard to certain trust arrangements, they actually constitute a liberalization compared to the former complete disallowance of trust ownership.

In addition to the trusts described above that are permitted to own S corporation stock under Section 1361(c), the Code authorizes S stock to be owned by a "qualified subchapter S trust" (QSST) under Section 1361(d). A QSST is a statutory creation and requires that a beneficiary or the beneficiary's legal representative make an election to have a trust become a QSST.

If the election is made, the QSST is treated as a trust subject to Code sections 671-79 (often called the "grantor trust" rules) and, for purposes of Section 678(a), the beneficiary of the trust is treated as the owner of that portion of the trust that consists of the S corporation stock with respect to which the election is made. (Section 678(a) describes a general rule of trust ownership for a case in which a person *other than* the grantor is treated as the substantial owner of the trust.[10])

A few points should be noted with regard to the QSST election requirements:

1.   The stock of each S corporation requires a separate election.[11] If the stock of more than one S corporation is involved, a separate election must be made for each corporation, even if the stock of two or more corporations is held by the same trust.

2.   If a QSST election is made by any beneficiary, it will be treated as made by each successive beneficiary unless a successive beneficiary refuses to consent to it.[12] As a result, a QSST will not be inadvertently terminated because of a beneficiary's inaction. Once the election is made, QSST status continues as long as the trust remains qualified unless the beneficiary takes affirmative action to revoke the election by refusing to consent to it.

3.   In general, the QSST election must be filed by the later of the following two dates:

   a. Within the 16-day-and-2-month period beginning on the date on which the S corporation stock is initially transferred to the QSST; or

   b. Within the 16-day-and-2-month period beginning on the first day of the first taxable year for which the S corporation is effective.[13]

   The election may be made retroactive for a period of up to two months and 15 days.[14]

4.   The QSST election is revocable only with the consent of the IRS.[15]

If the current income beneficiary is a minor and a legal representative has not been appointed, the natural or adopted parent may make the election on the minor's behalf. It should be realized that the QSST election is not a substitute for the election to be an S corporation under Section 1362(a). It may be necessary to coordinate the two elections, such as in a case in which a trust holds stock of a corporation that plans to make an S corporation election. In that case, the S corporation election should be made prior to the QSST election. Although the trust is not an eligible shareholder, when the S corporation election is made, it can file its QSST election to be retroactive to the date of the S election. In that manner, both the QSST and S corporation elections can be made, assuming that the trust otherwise complies with the QSST requirements.

Section 1361(d)(3) sets forth the following definition of a QSST:

(3) QUALIFIED SUBCHAPTER S TRUST. — For purposes of this subsection, the term "qualified subchapter S trust" means a trust —

(A) the terms of which require that —

(i) during the life of the current income beneficiary, there shall be only 1 income beneficiary of the trust,

(ii) any corpus distributed during the life of the current income beneficiary may be distributed only to such beneficiary,

(iii) the income interest of the current income beneficiary in the trust shall terminate on the earlier of such beneficiary's death or the termination of the trust, and

(iv) upon the termination of the trust during the life of the current income beneficiary, the trust shall distribute all of its assets to such beneficiary, and

(B) all of the income (within the meaning of section 643(b)) of which is distributed (or required to be distributed) currently to 1 individual who is a citizen or resident of the United States.

A substantially separate and independent share of a trust within the meaning of 663(c) shall be treated as a separate trust for purposes of this subsection and subsection (c).

In effect, a QSST is a one beneficiary trust. While successive income beneficiaries are permitted, only the current income beneficiary may receive income or corpus during the beneficiary's lifetime.[16] While only the current income beneficiary may receive corpus distributions during that beneficiary's lifetime, distributions of corpus are not mandatory. For that matter, income distributions are not mandatory either. QSST income may be distributed or accumulated, provided that income distributions are made to the income beneficiary of the trust. However, it is advisable to require that income be distributed to the current income beneficiary of a QSST in order to ensure compliance with the QSST requirements.

A trust designed to operate as a QSST may permit the trustee to accumulate trust income *in the event* that it does not hold shares of S corporation stock, without losing its qualification as a QSST.[17] With respect to the income distribution requirement, income earned after the last distribution date prior to a beneficiary's death may be distributed to either the estate of the deceased beneficiary or to the successor beneficiary.[18]

Revenue Ruling 93-31 illustrates the need to comply with the QSST requirements.[19] In that ruling, the trust instrument provided for the income of a trust to be paid in equal shares to two individuals. While the trust was designed to provide "separate shares" for the two beneficiaries, it also authorized the trustee to distribute all or a portion of the trust corpus to "B," one of the beneficiaries. Under the facts of the ruling, B had substantial income and it was unlikely that a distribution of corpus would be made to him. Under the regulations to Code section 663 governing separate shares, a trust may be treated as having separate shares even if an amount of corpus in excess of the beneficiary's proportionate share may be paid, if the possibility of payment is remote. However, the standards of Section 1361(d)(3) are more stringent. Revenue Ruling 93-31 states that in order for a QSST to qualify as such, its terms must provide that it has only one income beneficiary and any corpus distributed during the life of that beneficiary may be distributed *only* to that beneficiary (emphasis added). The single beneficiary requirement of a QSST was strictly applied, even if the possibility of a distribution of corpus was remote.

Once again, a QSST is a statutory creation and failure to maintain continuing qualification under its requirements can result in disqualification. If the QSST no longer qualifies, then the trust is not an eligible shareholder and the S corporation election may be lost (subject to possible relief under the inadvertent termination rules of Section 1362(f)).

If a QSST fails to meet any of the requirements of Section 1361(d)(3)(A) (payment only to current income beneficiary, etc.), the trust no longer qualifies as a QSST on the date when it ceases to satisfy any of the QSST requirements. On the other hand, if the trust satisfies the Section 1361(d)(3)(A) requirements, but ceases to meet the Section 1361(d)(3)(B) requirements (all income required to be distributed currently to one individual, etc.), its failure as a QSST is effective as of the first day of the first taxable year beginning after the first taxable year for which it failed to meet the (3)(B) requirements. Thus, the difference between the two types of disqualification largely amounts to a difference in the date on which the QSST disqualification is effective.

Electing Small Business Trust

The Small Business Job Protection Act of 1996 added a new type of trust eligible to own S corporation stock. This is an "electing small business trust," which will be referred to below as a "small business trust." The purpose of this new provision is to liberalize the trust ownership rules for estate planning purposes. A small business trust generally requires all of its beneficiaries to be individuals or estates eligible to hold S corporation stock. However, charitable organizations are permitted to hold contingent remainder interests. An interest in a small business trust must be acquired through a gift, bequest or form of acquisition other than a purchase.

Section 1361(e), which was added to the Code by the Small Business Job Protection Act of 1996, provides:

(e) ELECTING SMALL BUSINESS TRUST DEFINED —

(1) ELECTING SMALL BUSINESS TRUST. — For purposes of this section —

(A) IN GENERAL. — Except as provided in subparagraph (B), the term "electing small business trust" means any trust if —

(i) such trust does not have as a beneficiary any person other than (I) an individual, (II) an estate, or (III) an organization described in paragraph (2), (3), (4), or (5) of section 170(c),

(ii) no interest in such trust was acquired by purchase, and

(iii) an election under this subsection applies to such trust.

(B) CERTAIN TRUSTS NOT ELIGIBLE. — The term "electing small business trust" shall not include —

(i) any qualified subchapter S trust (as defined in subsection (d)(3)) if an election under subsection (d)(2) applies to any corporation the stock of which is held by such trust, and

(ii) any trust exempt from tax under this subtitle.

(C) PURCHASE. — For purposes of subparagraph (A), the term "purchase" means any acquisition if the basis of the property acquired is determined under section 1012.

(2) POTENTIAL CURRENT BENEFICIARY. — For purposes of this section, the term "potential current beneficiary" means, with respect to any period, any person who at any time during such period is entitled to, or at the discretion of any person may receive, a distribution from the principal or income of the trust. If the trust disposes of all of the stock which it holds in an S corporation, then, with respect to such corporation, the term "potential current beneficiary" does not include any person who first met the requirements of the preceding sentence during the 60-day period ending on the date of such disposition.

(3) ELECTION. — An election under this subsection shall be made by the trustee. Any such election shall apply to the taxable year of the trust for which made and all subsequent taxable years of such trust unless revoked with the consent of the Secretary.

(4) CROSS REFERENCE. — For special treatment of electing small business trusts, see section 641(d).

As indicated above, for tax years beginning in 1997, Section 1361(e)(A)(i) permits certain charitable organizations to be beneficiaries, if the charity "holds a contingent interest and is not a potential current beneficiary." However, for tax years beginning on or after January 1, 1998, certain charitable organizations are allowed to be beneficiaries of small business trusts, without regard to the condition that they hold contingent interests and are not potential current income beneficiaries.

It is worth noting that a QSST cannot elect to be a small business trust. In addition, a trust that is exempt from tax under the income tax provisions of the Code cannot make the election. Among other types of tax exempt entities, this includes qualified pension and profit-sharing plans and certain charitable organizations to which the Small Business Job Protection Act of 1996 otherwise granted the ability to own S corporation stock.

After the election to be a small business trust is made, income taxation of such trust is determined under Code section 641(d), which provides as follows, for tax years beginning after December 31, 1996:

SPECIAL RULES FOR TAXATION OF ELECTING SMALL BUSINESS TRUSTS. —

(1) IN GENERAL. — For purposes of this chapter —

(A) the portion of any electing small business trust which consists of stock in 1 or more S corporations shall be treated as a separate trust, and

(B) the amount of the tax imposed by this chapter on such separate trust shall be determined with the modifications of paragraph (2).

(2) MODIFICATIONS. — For purposes of paragraph (1), the modifications of this paragraph are the following:

(A) Except as provided in section 1(h), the amount of the tax imposed by section 1(e) shall be determined by using the highest rate of tax set forth in section 1(e).

(B) The exemption amount under section 55(d) shall be zero.

(C) The only items of income, loss, deduction, or credit to be taken into account are the following:

(i) The items required to be taken into account under section 1366.

(ii) Any gain or loss from the disposition of stock in an S corporation.

(iii) To the extent provided in regulations, State or local income taxes or administrative expenses to the extent allocable to items described in clauses (i) and (ii).

No deduction or credit shall be allowed for any amount not described in this paragraph, and no item described in this paragraph shall be apportioned to any beneficiary.

(D) No amount shall be allowed under paragraph (1) or (2) of section 1211(b).

(3) TREATMENT OF REMAINDER OF TRUST AND DISTRIBUTIONS. — For purposes of determining —

(A) the amount of the tax imposed by this chapter on the portion of any electing small business trust not treated as a separate trust under paragraph (1), and

(B) the distributable net income of the entire trust,

the items referred to in paragraph (2)(C) shall be excluded. Except as provided in the preceding sentence, this subsection shall not affect the taxation of any distribution from the trust.

(4) TREATMENT OF UNUSED DEDUCTIONS WHERE TERMINATION OF SEPARATE TRUST. — If a portion of an electing small business trust ceases to be treated as a separate trust under paragraph (1), any carryover or excess deduction of the separate trust which is referred to in section 642(h) shall be taken into account by the entire trust.

(5) ELECTING SMALL BUSINESS TRUST. — For purposes of this subsection, the term "electing small business trust" has the meaning given such term by section 1361(e)(1).

As discussed above in this chapter, the rules governing trust ownership of S corporation stock (prior to the Small Business Job Protection Act of 1996) were designed to ensure that a trust could not be used to shelter S corporation shareholders from income taxation. The small business trust rules are crafted to achieve the same outcome. Section 641(d) dictates that income tax liability is imposed upon the trust itself. However, the *rate of tax* is the highest rate imposed by Section 1(e), which governs income taxation of estates and trusts.

OBSERVATION. As a result of the rules provided under Section 641(d), not only is the small business trust prevented from sheltering S corporation income, it is subjected to the highest income tax rate applicable to estates and trusts. If the trust were qualified to own S corporation stock other than as a small business trust (such as a QSST or a grantor trust, generally), the individual trust beneficiary, rather than the trust itself, would be taxed. However, the beneficiary would be taxed according to his particular tax bracket. In contrast, a small business trust is subject to income taxation at the highest applicable rate for estates and trusts. Therefore, as a matter of income tax planning, the election to be a small business trust generally will be sensible only for those trust beneficiaries who will be in the highest income tax bracket.

APPLICATION OF THE TRUST OWNERSHIP RULES

The Tax Reform Act of 1976 permitted S corporation stock to be owned by certain types of trusts, including grantor trusts, voting trusts and testamentary trusts subject to the 60-day limitation. The rules governing trust ownership of S corporation stock were expanded further by the Economic Recovery Tax Act of 1981 ("ERTA"), which added provisions permitting ownership by a QSST and a Section 678 trust. For the most part, the rules pertaining to trust ownership have evolved as a function of the income tax features of the trusts within the broader backdrop of the S corporation tax provisions. The Small Business Job Protection Act of 1996 represents a significant step in the evolution of the trust ownership rules.

Our concern in this chapter is directed to how the trust ownership rules affect the estate planning decisions of S corporation shareholders. Lifetime gifts of S corporation stock to eligible trusts are discussed later in this chapter. First, the application of the trust ownership rules will be examined with regard to typical estate planning situations through the following series of examples.

EXAMPLE. Norm, an S corporation shareholder, establishes a trust under his will that will hold all of the assets of his estate except his tangible personal property. Norm's wife, Vera, and their children are the beneficiaries of the trust. Norm is not particularly concerned about estate planning at this time because the total assets held by Vera and him are worth less than the exemption equivalent amount of $600,000.

The trust established under Norm's will falls within the category described in Section 1361(c)(2)(A)(iii). As such, for tax years beginning prior to January 1, 1997, Norm's trustee may hold S corporation stock only for the 60-day period beginning on the day on which the trustee receives the stock. For tax years beginning on or after January 1, 1997, the trustee's holding period is two years from the date the stock is received, rather than 60 days. Norm might want to consider revising his trust to comply with the requirements of a QSST or Section 678 trust, which are described more fully in the following examples.

EXAMPLE. Norm attends an estate planning seminar and decides to set up a "living trust." He transfers his S corporation stock and other assets to a revocable trust, under which the trustee has the discretion to pay income and principal to Norm, his wife or their children as the trustee may deem appropriate for their comfort and living needs. Following Norm's death, the trust will continue according to similar terms for the benefit of his wife and children.

The revocable trust is a grantor trust for income tax purposes and its assets are included in Norm's gross estate. Therefore, for tax years beginning prior to January 1, 1997, the 60-day period following Norm's death is extended to two years.[20] For tax years beginning on or after January 1, 1997, the holding period is two years, in any event. While other alternatives are still available to Norm during his lifetime, at least his trustee has additional time to hold the S stock until it is distributed to a beneficiary or to a trust eligible to hold S corporation stock. Besides an outright distribution of S stock to an individual, under the facts of this example or the preceding one, the trustee could distribute the stock to the custodian of a UGMA or a UTMA or to the trustee of a trust established by Vera that is an eligible shareholder.

EXAMPLE. Norm's S corporation prospers over time and grows to a value of $1,000,000 within a total estate valued at $2,500,000. He decides to establish "A/B trusts" under his will. The "B" or "credit shelter trust" will utilize the unified credit (and any other credits available under the federal estate tax law), thereby absorbing the $600,000 exemption equivalent permitted to Norm's estate. Under the terms of the trust, the trustee must pay all of the income to Vera during her lifetime. In addition, the trustee may distribute principal for the health, education, maintenance or support of Vera and their children during Vera's lifetime, if she survives Norm. Vera has a noncumulative power to withdraw the greater of $5,000 or five percent of the value of the trust principal in any year. She also has a power to appoint any part or all of the trust principal to any of the children during her lifetime. The B trust is designed to provide flexibility and maximum protection for Vera while excluding its value from her gross estate for federal estate tax purposes. After Vera's death, the principal will be divided outright between their two children or held in a separate trust for a child who has not attained 30 years of age.

The "A" trust will be a marital trust that will pay all of its income to Vera on a quarterly basis during her lifetime. The trustee may pay principal to Vera for her health, maintenance and support. In addition, Vera has an unrestricted right to withdraw any part or all of the principal of the trust at any time during her life. Upon her death, she may appoint the principal to any beneficiary she names under the terms of her will.

Norm plans to allocate his S corporation stock to both trusts.

Before the small business trust election became effective, Norm would have needed to modify the structure of the credit shelter trust in order for it to have been eligible to hold S corporation stock. Before discussing trust design, it is worth pointing out planning alternatives that may be simpler and more acceptable to a client such as Norm.

Unless there is a reason not to distribute all of the stock to Vera or the marital trust, the problem may be avoided by using other assets to fund the "B" trust. This solution presumes that other appropriate assets are available, and that they can be designated to fund the B trust. It is important to avoid having the S stock pass to the B trust by default because jointly held assets were not retitled or beneficiary designations for life insurance policies not completed. It has been the author's experience that many business owners with A/B trusts in place prior to an S corporation election have not considered whether the terms of their estate plan accommodate the ownership of S corporation stock by their trusts. As a result, a transfer of their stock to a trust that is not eligible to be an S corporation shareholder may terminate the S corporation election.[21] The need for shareholders to act with diligence in coordinating their estate planning is discussed below.

Another method of dealing with the trust ownership problem is to allocate the S stock exclusively to the marital trust. The B trust may be funded by the proceeds of an insurance policy on the shareholder's life or by investment assets titled in his name. The marital trust can easily qualify as a QSST (see marital trust analysis below).

Separate Share Trust

[The following discussion applies to S corporations with tax years beginning before January 1, 1997, or, if an election to be a small business trust is not made, in any tax year.] Norm's credit shelter trust is a typical example of a trust designed to absorb the grantor's unified credit and provide for family members while excluding the value of its assets from the gross estate of the surviving spouse at her subsequent death. The trustee has the ability to "sprinkle or spray" income and principal among the beneficiaries (within the confines of an ascertainable standard applicable to principal payments). The sprinkle or spray provision prevents the trust from qualifying as a QSST because it violates the requirement that income and principal must be payable only to the current income beneficiary of the trust.

TRA '86 added the "separate and independent share" provision to the QSST definition found in Section 1361(d)(3). Section 663(c) specifies that substantially separate and independent shares of different beneficiaries of a trust are to be treated as separate trusts. Norm's B trust may be modified to accommodate the ownership of S corporation stock by dividing it into separate shares. Rather than have the trust managed as a single fund which can "spray" or "sprinkle" principal and income to his wife and children, the trust could be divided into separate shares, each of which would exclusively benefit a single beneficiary. In this way, the B trust could be divided to permit each share to function as a separate trust, thereby qualifying under the separate share rule applicable to a QSST. Each trust would be required to distribute all of its income to one beneficiary and any distributions of principal would also be made to the income beneficiary. Thus, if Norm and Vera have two children, $600,000 worth of S stock allocated to the B trust could be equally divided among three separate shares, with each share having all of its income and principal payable for the exclusive benefit of Vera or either of their children as the respective beneficiary of the share.[22] In that manner, each trust would qualify as a QSST, provided that it otherwise conformed to the statutory requirements of a QSST.

In order to ensure compliance with the QSST standards, the three separate share trusts might be revised in the following manner. The trusts for the children would direct that income be paid to each child and that principal could be distributed to each child according to the trustee's discretion until the child's attainment of age 30, for example. Vera's trust could provide that all income be paid to her and that principal could be distributed to her according to the terms of an ascertainable standard (payments for health, maintenance and support). She could retain the five percent/$5,000 annual noncumulative power of withdrawal, but her ability to appoint trust principal to the children should be eliminated. A limited power of appointment is a *beneficiary* power, rather than a *trustee* power. Nonetheless, in order to avoid running afoul of the QSST requirement that corpus must be distributed only to a current income beneficiary, it would be advisable to delete her power of appointment.

Each beneficiary would still be required to make the QSST election under the statutory procedure described above. Provisions should also be made for the continuing qualification of the QSST in the event of a beneficiary's death if it is expected that the trust would maintain ownership of the stock rather than distribute it to a succeeding beneficiary. In any event, the three separate share trusts should still be excluded from Vera's estate for federal estate tax purposes upon her subsequent death.

Dividing the credit shelter trust into separate share QSSTs is probably the most feasible planning solution for Norm and Vera. However, it is also possible that a client such as Norm could establish a "Section 678 trust." Section 678 describes a trust in which a person other than the grantor is treated as the substantial owner of the trust. If an individual has a power solely exercisable by himself to vest corpus or income of the trust solely in himself, then that individual is considered to be the owner of the trust (or a portion of the trust, as the case may be).

A Section 678 trust is not subject to the restrictions of a QSST — no election is required and it need not be designed as a single beneficiary trust. In some circumstances, it offers greater flexibility in planning than a QSST. However, it would not be appropriate in Norm's situation. To qualify as an S corporation shareholder, a Section 678 trust must meet the test of being a trust "all of which is treated [under Sections 671-679] as owned by an individual..."[23] That apparently means that the individual must own all of the income and the principal of a trust under the grantor trust rules.[24] If a beneficiary can demand all of the income and principal of a trust, that would interfere with Norm's trust both with respect to Vera and the children. Enabling the children to have unfettered access to principal would be contrary to Norm's wishes; allowing Vera to withdraw all of the principal would cause the value of the trust to be includable in her estate for federal estate tax purposes.

Thus, a separate share QSST seems the best route available for Norm to transfer S stock after his death to an eligible shareholder while keeping the value of the trust out of Vera's estate and having the trust managed according to his objectives for Vera and the children.

Marital Trust as Owner of S Corporation Stock. A marital trust for the benefit of a surviving spouse is frequently designed in the manner described in the preceding example. The surviving spouse is entitled to all of the income of the trust and has the right to withdraw all of the trust principal during her lifetime and may appoint the principal at death under the terms of her will. This form of marital trust is usually referred to as a life estate/power of appointment trust.[25] While the trustee may be authorized to make principal distributions to the spouse according to the trustee's discretion or within the terms of an ascertainable standard, the spouse's access and control over both income and principal amounts to virtual ownership of the entire trust. As such, the spouse's rights and interest in a marital trust are very similar to those of a beneficiary in a QSST.[26]

A QSST and a marital trust are both essentially trusts designed exclusively for one beneficiary. The following points of comparison should be considered.

Identity of Beneficiary. By definition, a marital trust is established for the benefit of a surviving spouse. A QSST may be established for a spousal or nonspousal beneficiary, provided that the beneficiary is a citizen or resident of the United States. Thus, a marital trust established for a spouse who is a citizen or resident of the United States can qualify as a QSST and own S corporation stock with no time limitation.[27]

Income Requirements. Under a life estate/power of appointment marital trust, the surviving spouse must be entitled "...for life to all of the income...payable annually or at more frequent intervals..."[28] A QSST requires that all its income must be distributed to the current income beneficiary during the beneficiary's lifetime. "Income," for QSST purposes, is defined in Section 1361(d)(3)(B) as being income within the meaning of Section 643(b).

Section 643(b) states:

SEC. 643. DEFINITIONS APPLICABLE TO SUBPARTS A, B, C, AND D.

(b) INCOME. — For purposes of this subpart and subparts B, C, and D, the term "income", when not preceded by the words "taxable", "distributable net", "undistributed net", or "gross", means the amount of income of the estate or trust for the taxable year determined under the terms of the governing instrument and applicable local law. Items of gross income constituting extraordinary dividends or taxable stock dividends which the fiduciary, acting in good faith, determines to be allocable to corpus under the terms of the governing instrument and applicable local law shall not be considered income.

The terms of a QSST should make it clear that "income" does not include capital gains in order to clarify that the beneficiary is entitled to all accounting income within the Section 643(b) definition. Once again, it is advisable to have all QSST income actually distributed to a beneficiary in order to avoid any question concerning its qualification under the income requirement.[29]

Principal. Under both a marital trust and a QSST, principal may be distributed to a beneficiary or may be accumulated, but it must be distributed only to the income beneficiary of the trust. Variations in regard to the distribution of the principal are more likely to occur when a marital trust is designed to be a QTIP trust, as discussed immediately below.

EXAMPLE. Norm is the sole shareholder of an S corporation worth $1,000,000 and his gross estate is valued at $3,000,000. Norm and Vera are married and have two children. Norm divorces Vera and marries Diane. Pursuant to a prenuptial agreement and a revised estate plan, Norm's new will transfers his S corporation stock to a qualified terminable interest property (QTIP) trust. In the event of his death, he wants Diane to receive income from the S corporation stock held in trust, but he also wants to retain the right to pass the stock to his children after Diane's death.

The QTIP trust can qualify as a QSST. Before discussing how the respective governing provisions of a QTIP trust and a QSST intermesh within one trust, it may be helpful to turn to Section 2056(b)(7), which authorizes and defines qualified terminable interest property. In pertinent part, that subsection states:

(b) LIMITATION IN THE CASE OF LIFE ESTATE OR OTHER TERMINABLE INTEREST. —

(7) ELECTION WITH RESPECT TO LIFE ESTATE FOR SURVIVING SPOUSE. —

(B) QUALIFIED TERMINABLE INTEREST PROPERTY DEFINED. — For purposes of this paragraph —

(i) IN GENERAL. — The term "qualified terminable interest property" means property —

(I) which passes from the decedent,

(II) in which the surviving spouse has a qualifying income interest for life, and

(III) to which an election under this paragraph applies.

(ii) QUALIFYING INCOME INTEREST FOR LIFE. — The surviving spouse has a qualifying income interest for life if —

(I) the surviving spouse is entitled to all the income from the property, payable annually or at more frequent intervals, or has a usufruct interest for life in the property, and

(II) no person has a power to appoint any part of the property to any person other than the surviving spouse.

* * * * * * * *

(v) ELECTION. — An election under this paragraph with respect to any property shall be made by the executor on the return of tax imposed by section 2001. Such an election, once made, shall be irrevocable.

In matching the QTIP and QSST provisions, the income must be paid only to the spouse (QTIP) or current income beneficiary (QSST). Just as for the life estate/power of appointment marital trust, the spouse must be entitled to receive all of the property's income at least annually. The other prong of the "qualifying income interest" definition — that the trust property may not be appointed to anyone other than the surviving spouse — makes the QTIP a closer relative to the QSST than the conventional marital trust permitting a power of appointment. Under the latter form of marital trust, it is possible for the surviving spouse to appoint property from the trust to another person. A QTIP trust, on the other hand, permits no one, including the surviving spouse, to appoint its property to anyone other than the spouse. Similarly, the QSST provisions allow corpus to be distributed only to the current income beneficiary during the beneficiary's lifetime, unless the trust terminates on an earlier date.

While a QTIP trust is frequently drawn to limit the surviving spouse's access to the trust corpus (as with Norm and Diane), the spouse may be allowed to withdraw principal from the QTIP, if the trust grantor so desires. The QSST definition indicates that only corpus may be distributed to the income beneficiary, but does not expressly address a *withdrawal* by the beneficiary.[30]

Election. In order for the trust to qualify as a QTIP, the decedent's executor must make an irrevocable election on the federal estate tax return. The election is a requirement for QTIP status and must be made within nine months after the decedent's death, when the federal estate tax return is due. At the same time, the surviving spouse must be mindful of the filing deadline described above that is applicable to a QSST.

The Electing Small Business Trust

For tax years beginning after December 31, 1996, the trustee of a credit shelter trust or a marital trust may elect to have either trust treated as a small business trust. Code section 1361(e) defines an electing small business trust and specifies its requirements. The following analysis covers the interaction of the small business trust rules and the terms of typical credit shelter trusts and marital trusts.

Credit Shelter Trusts

The discussion on the preceding pages of this chapter addresses the inability of the typical spray trust involving several beneficiaries to qualify as an S corporation shareholder. Thus, a credit shelter trust that would hold S corporation shares is often required to satisfy the separate share trust rules. In that case, the trust is dedicated to the needs of one beneficiary and it is not possible to distribute income and principal to both surviving spouse and children.

No such obstacle exists with a small business trust, which is not specifically limited to the number of beneficiaries it may have. In fact, the qualification rules for a small business trust and a QSST are mutually exclusive, as indicated under Section 1361(e)(1)(B)(i). Consequently, the owner of S corporation stock may have any type of credit shelter trust he wishes, so long as the trustee is prepared to elect small business trust status.

Marital Trust

The trustee of a marital trust can elect small business trust status with no qualification concerns. The election is equally available whether the marital trust is a QTIP, a life estate/power of appointment trust, or any other trust that satisfies the marital deduction requirements.

Following the death of an S corporation shareholder, the trustee of a marital trust established by the shareholder may contemplate electing either QSST or small business trust status. As discussed above, the significant overlap between the marital trust requirements and the QSST rules often facilitates the trustee's decision to elect QSST status. On the other hand, the small business trust election may not be preferable for a marital trust. A small business trust is treated as a separate trust and would require administration and tax reporting that would be separate from a marital trust holding assets other than S stock. Thus, a surviving spouse who is the beneficiary of a marital trust may have S corporation stock held by the trustee under a small business trust election, with other assets held in a separate marital trust. The complication of having separate marital trusts becomes more pronounced when income tax consequences to the spouse are considered.

The marital trust requirements generally provide that all trust income must be distributed to the surviving spouse. The QSST rules are similar in this respect. Consequently, a marital trust funded with S corporation stock, subject to a QSST election, has all of its income distributed and taxed to the surviving spouse. Under the small business trust rules, the trust itself, rather than its beneficiary, is taxed even if all of its income is paid to its beneficiary, as would be the case with a marital trust. Thus, a surviving spouse who is not in the highest income tax bracket might receive less net income from a marital trust if the trustee elects to have it treated as a small business trust, rather than as a QSST.

Marital Trust: Spouse's Right to Income

A closely held business interest frequently comprises a significant portion of the value of a decedent's estate, regardless of whether it is organized as a C corporation or as an S corporation. The stock of a decedent may be left to a surviving spouse outright or in one form or another of marital trust. The spouse may be active in the management of the business; if not active in daily operations, the spouse may nonetheless have the "last word" in regard to major decisions and overall direction. In either case, the spouse may retain ownership and control until the children have completed their education or a period of training before they can assume managerial roles.

In any event, a business interest represents not only a significant asset, but is usually the primary source of income during the shareholder's lifetime. The income generated by the business may be eliminated or sharply reduced if a surviving spouse is not active as an employee following the shareholder's death. As a rule, closely held C corporations avoid paying dividends to shareholders, primarily because dividends are nondeductible to the corporation. The fact that an S corporation is not a separate taxable entity and the "double taxation" issue is avoided, gener- ally means that dividends paid to S corporation owners are far more acceptable than dividends paid to C corporation shareholders. Thus, if S corporation stock will be transferred to a marital trust for the benefit of a surviving spouse following a shareholder's death, the prospect that the corporation may consistently pay income to the trust is enhanced because of its S election.

In addition to the financial reality that income can be more readily directed to a surviving spouse when S corporation stock is held by a marital trust, it is important to recognize the "income producing" requirement of the regulations under Section 2056. Specifically, Regulation Section 20.2056(b)-5(f)(1) states that the surviving spouse's right to income is met:

> (f) *Right to income.* (1)...if the effect of the trust is to give her substantially that degree of beneficial enjoyment of the trust property during her life which the principles of the law of trusts accord to a person who is unqualifiedly designated as the life beneficiary of a trust. Such degree of enjoyment is given only if it was the decedent's intention, as manifested by the terms of the trust instrument and the surrounding circumstances, that the trust should produce for the surviving spouse during her life such an income, or that the spouse should have such use of the trust property as is consistent with the value of the trust corpus and with its preservation. The designation of the spouse as sole income beneficiary for life of the entire interest or a specific portion of the entire interest will be sufficient to qualify the trust unless the terms of the trust and the surrounding circumstances considered as a whole evidence an intention to deprive the spouse of the requisite degree of enjoyment. In determining whether a trust evidences that intention, the treatment required or permitted with respect to individual items must be considered in relation to the entire system provided for the administration of the trust.

Regulation Section 20.2056(b)-5(f)(4) elaborates on the spouse's right to income:

> (4) Provisions granting administrative powers to the trustee will not have the effect of disqualifying an interest passing in trust unless the grant of powers evidences the intention to deprive the surviving spouse of the beneficial enjoyment required by the statute. Such an intention will not be considered to exist if the entire terms of the

instrument are such that the local courts will impose reasonable limitations upon the exercise of the powers. ... For example, a power to retain trust assets which consist substantially of unproductive property will not disqualify the interest if the applicable rules for the administration of the trust require, or permit the spouse to require, that the trustee either make the property productive or convert it within a reasonable time.

And, finally, Regulation Section 20.2056(b)-5(f)(5) states:

An interest passing in trust will not satisfy the condition set forth in paragraph (a)(1) of this section that the surviving spouse be entitled to all the income if the primary purpose of the trust is to safeguard property without providing the spouse with the required beneficial enjoyment. Such trusts include not only trusts which expressly provide for the accumulation of the income but also trusts which indirectly accomplish a similar purpose. For example, assume that the corpus of a trust consists substantially of property which is not likely to be income producing during the life of the surviving spouse and that the spouse cannot compel the trustee to convert or otherwise deal with the property as described in subparagraph (4) of this paragraph. An interest passing to such a trust will not qualify unless the applicable rules for the administration require, or permit the spouse to require, that the trustee provide the required beneficial enjoyment such as by payments to the spouse out of other assets of the trust.

The purpose of the cited regulations is to define the nature and character of the spouse's income interest in respect to qualification for the marital deduction. Qualification turns, generally, on the unfettered right of the spouse to receive income from the trust property without restriction by the terms of the trust, or otherwise, so that the spouse's right to income is not compromised. The spouse need not actually receive income from the marital trust property, but must have the *right* to compel the trustee to convert the property to be income producing.

In funding a marital trust, the trustee should be mindful of the requirement that the spouse's right to income must be fulfilled. More to the point in the planning context, the estate planner should anticipate the allocation of property to marital and credit shelter trusts that will be established after the client's death. Closely held stock may be used to fund a marital trust, whether the corporation is a C or an S corporation. The stock of either type of corporation need not pay dividends to the trust at any prescribed level or with any particular regularity. If closely held stock is expected to fund a marital trust, the surviving spouse's need for income should be taken into account and some thought should be given as to whether the spouse's income needs will be satisfied from the stock or other property. An S corporation is more likely than a C corporation to pay dividends because the nondeductibility issue is not a factor for an S corporation. Of course, the S corporation must be financially healthy enough to pay dividends and the payment of dividends must make sense within its overall business operation.

Naturally, in planning for both the S corporation and the spouse, the percentage of stock that will be held by the surviving spouse is an important factor. For example, if the spouse is a minority shareholder, and is not related to the controlling shareholders, the spouse may be at the financial mercy of those holding voting control with respect to dividends. Or, if one of two equal shareholders dies, and leaves his or her stock to a surviving spouse, the level of corporate distributions may not be fairly handled because the employed shareholder has the "upper hand" in managing the business. Or, a deadlock situation may develop between the spouse and the other owner.[31] In short, many of the usual factors that accompany business continuation planning may come into play in determining whether dividends from the S stock can and will be paid on a regular basis.[32]

In regard to both estate and business continuation planning, it may be just as effective, and considerably easier, to transfer stock outright to a surviving spouse, rather than to a marital trust. The transfer of the S stock and other assets may be divided among an outright bequest, a marital trust that may or may not be a QTIP trust, or a credit shelter trust. Many variations in the allocation of these assets are possible and may be determined according to personal circumstances, business strategy or other considerations independent of tax planning.

For married S corporation shareholders who have substantial estates, the disposition of property qualifying for the marital deduction assumes greater importance as their assets grow in value. As an estate grows larger, the amount of its value that is absorbed by the unified credit becomes proportionately smaller. Conversely, the amount of its value that will be transferred to the marital share becomes proportionally greater (assuming a standard credit shelter/marital trust allocation) as the total value of the estate increases. For instance, the $600,000 exemption equivalent of the unified credit is 40% of an adjusted gross estate worth $1,500,000, but only 20% of a $3,000,000 estate, 10% of a $6,000,000 estate, and so forth. In situations involving larger estates, assets other than S corporation stock may be available to fund the credit shelter trust. In such cases, transfers of S corporation stock to marital trusts may be easily effected within the rules governing trust ownership of S stock, such as the QSST requirements. Other issues related to the spouse's interest in holding the stock (versus giving it to family members or selling it to others) may emerge as more critical as the shareholder establishes an overall business continuation plan that will also provide income security for the surviving spouse.

Other Marital Trust Planning for Transfers of S Corporation Stock

A marital trust that will hold S corporation stock may be designed as a Section 678 trust, rather than as a QSST, or a small business trust. Any of these trusts can hold S corporation stock without any time limitation. As described above in the discussion of a credit shelter trust, a Section 678 trust is one in which a person other than the grantor is treated as the substantial owner of a trust. A surviving spouse who is the beneficiary of a life estate/power of appointment marital trust is the owner of the trust for purposes of Section 678 and Section 1361(c)(2)(A)(i). However, if the spouse's access to principal is restricted by the terms of a QTIP trust, it is unclear whether the spouse's ownership would qualify under the "all of which" provision of Section 1361(c)(2)(A)(i).

Following the death of the surviving spouse, if outright distribution of the S corporation stock does not occur, the marital trust may be divided into one or more QSSTs that are eligible to own S corporation stock, or may become a small business trust (or possibly, by one or more Section 678 trusts, although that may provide too much access to principal if younger children are the succeeding beneficiaries). If the Section 678 trust holding stock for the surviving spouse's benefit is a life estate/power of appointment trust, it can continue to hold S corporation stock for up to two years after the death of the surviving spouse, even if a succeeding trust for the benefit of children is not otherwise eligible to own S corporation stock.[33] However, if the Section 678 trust were structured as a QTIP trust, the problem with the "all of which" provision mentioned above would prevent both the two year and sixty day extension periods[34] from being available, without further qualification of the trust as being independently eligible to own S corporation stock. Thus, it seems generally preferable for a marital trust to be structured as a QSST in order to ensure current and continuing eligibility for the ownership of stock. As discussed above, income tax planning and reporting is also facilitated if a QSST, rather than a small business trust election is made.

Estate Trust

Another type of marital trust is an estate trust, in which income may be accumulated for the benefit of the surviving spouse. An estate trust is not frequently employed and would not qualify to hold S corporation stock if income were permitted to accumulate because such accumulation would not be in compliance with the requirements of a QSST or a Section 678 trust. (However, an estate trust could qualify as a QSST if the accumulation feature is disregarded and all of its income is, in fact, currently distributed to the spouse, thus satisfying the terms of Section 1361(d)(3)(B).) Generally it is advisable for S corporation stock to be transferred to another form of marital trust or outright to the spouse. If the estate trust must remain in place because of a shareholder's overall estate plan, it should be funded with property other than S corporation stock.

Irrevocable Trust Planning

[The following discussion applies to S corporations with tax years beginning before January 1, 1997, or, if an election to be a small business trust is not made, in any tax year.] The S corporation shareholder may decide to transfer S corporation stock to an irrevocable trust established during the shareholder's lifetime. Transfers of S corporation stock to a grantor retained annuity trust (GRAT) or an intentionally defective irrevocable trust (IDIT) are discussed below.

As part of the broader estate planning process, an S corporation shareholder is more likely to transfer a life insurance policy, or cash for the payment of premiums, to an irrevocable trust that is the owner of a policy. However, the terms of the irrevocable trust should take into account the prospect that S corporation stock will be owned after the grantor's death even though the only asset of the trust during the owner's lifetime will be an insurance policy and cash held primarily for the payment of premiums.

EXAMPLE. Stanley and Walter each own 50% of an S corporation. In the event that Walter dies, Stanley will buy his stock. On the other hand, Stanley hopes that his two sons, Stosh and Josh, will succeed him in the business after his death. Stanley plans to allow Stosh and Josh to inherit his stock by providing that the stock will be left to them, in trust, until each attains age 35, when final distribution will be made.

Stanley has also established an irrevocable trust funded by a life insurance policy. He has three concerns: (1) that his sons will inherit his stock and continue the business with Walter; (2) that his estate will have sufficient liquidity to pay estate taxes (he is widowed); and (3) that the business will be able to retain S corporation status.

In this situation, it is quite possible that the trustee of Stanley's irrevocable trust will use the proceeds of life insurance to purchase assets from his estate. The transfer of cash to the estate will enable Stanley's executor to pay estate settlement costs without being forced to sell personal assets or liquidate business property. The trustee should have the right to purchase assets from, or loan money to, the estate. However, the trustee must not be obligated to do so in order to enable the proceeds to steer clear of estate taxation under Code section 2042. Depending upon the composition of Stanley's estate and the needs of his sons at the time of his death, his executor may decide to sell his S stock, or other assets, to the trustee of his irrevocable trust.

If it is expected that the irrevocable trust may purchase the S stock from Stanley's estate, the trust should be designed to qualify as an eligible shareholder following Stanley's death. Typically, a QSST (rather than a Section 678 trust) offers the best method for providing planning flexibility to an eligible shareholder. However, if the trust is not an eligible shareholder, it should not receive S corporation stock through a purchase from the executor. (Alternatively, if the S stock is poured over to the irrevocable trust by the terms of the shareholder's will, the 60-day limitation will apply, which may effectively force the trustee to distribute stock to the beneficiaries in order to avoid terminating the S corporation election, assuming, of course, that the trust instrument would permit a distribution to be made.) In order for the irrevocable trust to qualify as a QSST after

Stanley's death, separate shares may be established for Stosh and Josh. It will be necessary for each of them, as beneficiaries, to elect QSST status. The provisions of each trust should comply with the QSST requirements and should function exclusively for the benefit of each son until the age of distribution.

Both the nature of the irrevocable trust and the circumstances that typically surround irrevocable trust planning call for particular diligence on the part of the estate planner who advises the S corporation owner. In many instances, the life underwriter generates action by the client when estate liquidity problems are reviewed. Life insurance provides cash at death to pay federal estate taxes and other settlement costs. In order to avoid compounding the estate tax problem the insurance is supposed to solve, ownership of the policy by an irrevocable trust is often recommended as a means of excluding the proceeds from the insured's estate. Beyond developing the point that a liquidity problem exists because of the character of the client's assets, the irrevocable trust planning usually concentrates on the life insurance policy funding the trust. While the irrevocable trust is typically coordinated with the terms of the will and other trusts of the client and the client's spouse, the prospect that S stock may be transferred to the irrevocable trust following the client's death should be taken into consideration *when the trust is established.* It is unwise to expect that future planning to facilitate the ownership of S stock will necessarily be available in the event that the stock is transferred to the trust by the executor in exchange for the proceeds of insurance. The trust should specify the power of the trustee to take whatever action may be necessary to preserve the S corporation election if S stock becomes a trust asset. Coordinating the estate and business planning objectives of the shareholder becomes especially important in a situation in which the terms of the trust cannot be changed and the asset composition of the estate owner may change substantially over time.

COORDINATION OF ESTATE AND BUSINESS CONTINUATION PLANNING

The qualification rules under Code section 1361 defining eligible owners of S corporation stock make it imperative that both *succeeding* and *surviving* owners pass muster in regard to eligibility, following the death of an S corporation shareholder. The prospect of shareholder ineligibility becomes a greater concern in situations involving two or more unrelated shareholders. If the shareholders execute a buy-sell agreement in which the estate of each owner is required to sell the deceased shareholder's stock at death, the prospect of a transfer to an ineligible shareholder is eliminated. On the other hand, if no buy-sell agreement exists, or if a shareholder is not a party to a buy-sell agreement or is otherwise free to transfer S stock to an ineligible trust or other owner at death, planning measures should be adopted to avoid the risk of transfer to an ineligible shareholder. Chapter 5 contains a sample provision in which the shareholders of an S corporation represent to each other that their estate planning actions will not result in a termination of the S corporation election. While the shareholders need not be involved in each other's personal planning, maintenance of the S corporation election requires additional vigilance and more coordinated planning than generally followed for C corporations.

SMALL BUSINESS TRUST APPLICATION

In many instances, following the grantor's death, the terms of an irrevocable trust established to hold life insurance are substantially similar to the terms of a credit shelter trust. In fact, assets constituting the $600,000 exemption equivalent may be transferred from the decedent's estate directly to an irrevocable trust, to avoid administering two identical trusts. Thus, apart from other considerations discussed below, an irrevocable trust which is funded with S corporation stock following a shareholder's death, may elect to be a small business trust.

However, the "no purchase" rule of Section 1361(e)(1)(A)(ii) will come into play if the trustee of an irrevocable trust receives life insurance proceeds and plans to purchase assets from the estate of the deceased shareholder. A small business trust is not permitted to acquire S corporation shares by a purchase. While that rule should be noted to avoid disqualification of small business trust status, in many cases, other planning actions can be taken to avoid its application. For instance, the trustee may purchase assets, other than S corporation stock, from the executor in order to transfer cash to the estate. Also, rather than purchase assets from the estate, the trustee may lend all or a portion of the insurance proceeds to the executor for the payment of estate taxes. S corporation stock may be used to fund trusts in conjunction with the decedent's estate plan without constituting a purchase of stock.

As previously mentioned, the small business trust was formulated to facilitate estate planning. In certain situations, S corporation stock may be more easily transferred in the event of a shareholder's death because the requirements of a small business trust are less rigid than those of a QSST. For example, S stock may be distributed to a credit shelter trust with spray provisions if the trustee elects small business trust status. Nonetheless, the small business trust is only a solution, not a panacea. If an exchange of assets for purposes of furnishing estate liquidity is contemplated between an executor and the trustee of an irrevocable trust, it may be better to have the trust designed to satisfy the QSST rules, rather than the small business trust requirements. It is still critical to coordinate estate planning and S corporation planning, even though the small business trust may function as a bail out device in certain situations because of its flexibility.

SPECIALIZED TRUST PLANNING TECHNIQUES

The trusts and examples discussed above are popular estate planning techniques. Other types of trusts may also be considered for the ownership of S corporation stock in particular circumstances. The following discussion evaluates the possible ownership of S corporation stock by more specialized trust arrangements.

Voting Trust

A trust created primarily to exercise the voting power of stock transferred to it is permitted to be an S corporation shareholder.[35] A voting trust is usually established so that a trustee may vote on behalf of beneficiaries who are entitled to the benefits of stock ownership other than the right to vote. The beneficiaries may be prevented from voting because they are under a legal disability, (e.g., they may be minors) and the trust will be in effect until the beneficiaries reach a specified age. In other cases, the beneficiaries may be family members who are inactive in a closely held business. A voting trust may represent a middle ground between providing voting power to those not in a position to exercise it prudently and depriving them of any representation on voting matters through the issuance of nonvoting stock (apart from differences in value between voting and nonvoting stock).

Each beneficiary of a voting trust is counted as a shareholder of an S corporation.[36] Therefore, the trust beneficiaries are counted in determining whether the 75 shareholder limit is satisfied. In regard to the one class of stock requirement, a U.S. District Court has upheld the use of a voting trust to hold S corporation stock. In *The A. & N. Furniture & Appliance Company v. United States*, the shareholders (father, mother and their two children) entered into a voting trust agreement in which the father was designated trustee and given the irrevocable right for ten years to vote all the shares of each shareholder.[37] The court rejected the Service's assertion that two classes of stock resulted from the creation of the trust. It held that the change in voting power did not affect the rights of the shareholders with respect to distributions, income and losses. Therefore, the corporation continued to satisfy the one class of stock requirement. Furthermore, in *Parker Oil Company, Inc. v. Commissioner*, the Tax Court held that a second class of stock did not result because of the execution of an irrevocable proxy in which a nonshareholder was permitted to vote on behalf of the shareholders in order to resolve a dispute among the shareholders.[38]

The Service has provided guidance under its regulations in regard to the requirements that a "qualified voting trust" must meet. Specifically, the beneficial owners must be treated as the owners of their respective portions of the trust under subpart E and the trust must have been created pursuant to a written trust agreement entered into by the shareholders, that: (1) delegates the right to vote to one or more trustees; (2) requires all distributions with respect to the stock of the corporation to be paid to, or on behalf of, the beneficial owners of the stock; (3) requires title and possession of the stock to be delivered to the beneficial owners upon termination of the trust; and (4), must terminate, under its own terms or under state law, on or before a specific date or event.[39]

TRANSFER OF S CORPORATION STOCK TO A GRAT

Chapter 14 of the Internal Revenue Code prescribes rules for valuing certain types of gifts in which a donor has a retained interest. Specifically, Code section 2702 governs transfers by a donor in trust for the benefit of a "family member." Family members include the transferor's spouse; any ancestor or descendant of the donor or the donor's spouse; any sibling of the transferor; and the spouse of any ancestor, descendant, or sibling. Under Section 2702, if a donor transfers an interest held in trust for the benefit of a family member and retains a term interest, the value of the gift is the entire value of the transferred property, unless the donor's retained interest is a "qualified" annuity or unitrust interest.

A qualified annuity interest means that the donor transfers property in trust and retains the right to receive a fixed dollar or percentage amount based upon the value of the transferred property when the transfer is made [grantor retained annuity interest (GRAT)]. A grantor retained unitrust interest (GRUT) involves a transfer in trust in which the transferor is entitled to a fixed percentage of the value of the transferred property, determined on an annual basis. In general, the owner of an S corporation is more likely to utilize a GRAT than a GRUT to shift future asset appreciation to his children. A GRAT permits a "freeze" in the value of the stock at the time when it is established. This is different from the GRUT, which requires an annual revaluation of the trust principal. Without the need for future revaluation, the value of a gift made to a GRAT can be precisely determined when made. While a GRUT permits additional gifts to be made in the future, a GRAT allows only a single transfer to be made. However, a shareholder can set up successive GRATs with future transfers of stock dependent upon variables such as the actual appreciation of the S corporation, fluctuations in interest rates, and the shareholder's health.

The pros and cons of transferring S corporation stock to a GRAT will be discussed by reference to the following example.

EXAMPLE. Mr. Big, age 55, and Mrs. Big, age 50, each own 50% of the Big Company, a Pennsylvania corporation that has an S corporation election in effect. The company has grown steadily in value during the past several years. Mr. Big expects that it will continue to appreciate in value at a 10% to 15% annual rate for the foreseeable future. The Bigs have two children: Johnny Big, age 26, and Susie Big, age 24, both of whom are currently employed in the family business and expected to be active in the business in the future.

Mr. Big estimates the value of the Big Company to be $4,000,000 and the combined value of both spouses' estates to be approximately $8,000,000. He expects that the Big Company will grow substantially in value during the next several years. Mr. Big is appalled at the prospect that each additional dollar of value realized by the Big Company may be subject to an ultimate federal estate tax of 55% in the estate of the surviving spouse.

Mr. Big and Mrs. Big are considering the transfer of $1,000,000 of stock as a lifetime gift to their children. Mr. Big recognizes that such a gift would consume the bulk of the $600,000 exemption equivalent otherwise available to each spouse's estate. After reviewing his concerns with his attorney and his certified public accountant, Mr. Big engages the services of a business valuation specialist, who confirms that the fair market value of the Big Company is $4,000,000. In addition, the appraiser has included a 20% minority discount from the entity value for the proposed gift of stock. The tax attorney suggests to Mr. Big that the $1,000,000 gift of stock might be transferred to a grantor retained annuity trust (GRAT), rather than as an outright gift to the Big children.

The following terms are suggested for the GRAT:

Term:	10 years or grantor's death, if earlier
Value of Stock (Entity Value):	$1,000,000
Earnings rate for S Corporation shares:	12%
§ 7520 rate:	8%
Value of Stock (Minority Interest @ 20% Discount):	$800,000
Annuity Rate:	15%
Annuity Amount:	$120,000
Value of Annuity:	$779,340
Value of Remainder (Gift Tax Value):	$20,660

Mr. and Mrs. Big and their advisers need to review a number of issues before deciding whether a transfer of Big Company stock to a GRAT will achieve their objectives. A determination of whether S corporation stock should be transferred to a GRAT should consider both complex points of the law, as well as judgments about the future growth of a business and the likelihood of a given transferor's survival for a certain number of years. In actual practice, most clients are interested in knowing the major benefits and risks of any prospective transaction. However, while clients such as the Bigs may have a limited interest in the technical aspects of a transfer of S stock to a GRAT, as in many other areas of the tax law, the devil is in the details. Therefore, a prudent adviser may need to sift through certain fine points of a GRAT transfer in order to conclude whether a transfer to a GRAT is appropriate, and be able to describe it to clients on a "bottom line" basis. The following discussion of the factors to be weighed in transferring S stock to a GRAT will cover both tax law considerations and other key issues that are apt to be of concern to the shareholder interested in shifting value to the next generation.

All of the usual factors that dictate whether a gift of S corporation stock is advisable also pertain to a contemplated transfer to a GRAT. Specifically, from an estate and gift tax planning standpoint, it is essential that Mr. Big expects his company to grow in value in the future. By making an irrevocable transfer of stock, Mr. Big can remove future appreciation in value from his estate.

Estate Tax Consequences

If the grantor dies during the GRAT period, the value of the transferred property, or a similar measure of value, will be subject to federal estate taxation. The IRS has ruled that the amount includable in the grantor's gross estate under Section 2036 is the value of trust principal necessary to generate the annuity amount, based upon an annual rate of return equal to the Section 7520 rate in effect on the date of death.[40] However, the Service has also privately ruled that, under Section 2039, the full value of the transferred asset will be includable in the grantor's estate in the event of the grantor's death.[41] The annuity in the private letter ruling was structured to be in effect for the lesser of 15 years or the grantor's lifetime. The different measures of inclusion for estate tax purposes may depend upon whether the annuity is payable over a term certain, or whether a life contingency is involved. If based upon a life contingency, it is more likely that the full value of the trust corpus will be included than for a term certain annuity, which may cause the includable amount to be based upon the Section 7520 rate necessary to provide the annuity on the date of death.

The use of a life contingency in the design of the GRAT should also have the effect of making the gift of the remainder interest more valuable if the trust ends upon the grantor's death. However, the IRS has adopted the position in its final regulations under Section 2702 that the gift of the remainder interest must be valued as if it is contingent upon the grantor's survival, even if it is for a term certain.[42] The effect of the IRS position, in many instances, may be to cause the grantor to use a life contingency in specifying the terms of the annuity. Apart from the gift tax consequences, the life contingency avoids the obligation to have the annuity payments continue to the grantor's estate in the event of a premature death.

Other design features could be incorporated to adjust the estate or gift tax effect of the GRAT transaction. However, these variations are beyond the scope of our discussion. The more significant point to be made in this context concerns the need to communicate the downside risk of estate tax inclusion to a prospective grantor. Regardless of the exact measurement of the estate tax inclusion, it is critical for the S corporation shareholder to recognize the risk of premature death. For an older client, the best solution may be to utilize a shorter GRAT term, such as five years, instead of ten.

Naturally, the health of the client will be an important factor in evaluating the risk. In the case of a married couple, it is advisable to have the healthier spouse act as the grantor of the trust. In our example, we will assume that Mrs. Big is healthier and has a greater life expectancy than Mr. Big. However, even if Mrs. Big is more likely to survive the term of the GRAT than her husband, the Bigs should recognize the consequences of Mrs. Big's premature death. Either the entire value of the transferred stock or an amount sufficient to fund an annuity at the prevailing Section 7520 rate will be included in her estate for federal estate tax purposes.[43] In the event of Mrs. Big's death during the GRAT term, the transferred shares held by the GRAT will not qualify for the marital deduction, thereby causing estate taxation upon her death. The GRAT could be designed to have the shares qualify for the marital deduction by having a contingent marital trust included within the trust instrument to defer estate taxation. However, if the Bigs are comfortable in accepting the risk of Mrs. Big's premature death, it is probably preferable to allow the shares to be distributed outright to Johnny and Susie, or held in further trust for their benefit until each of them reaches a designated age, such as 35 years old.

Insurance on Mrs. Big's Life

In a situation in which the potential estate tax value of the asset transferred to the GRAT exceeds the transferor's $600,000 exemption equivalent, a substantial federal estate tax liability could be payable even if the transferor is survived by his or her spouse. If the Bigs are concerned about that possibility, an insurance policy could be purchased on Mrs. Big's life in order to provide cash for the payment of estate taxes. In order to exclude the proceeds from Mr. and Mrs. Big's estates, the policy should be owned by a third party, such as an irrevocable trust, or one or both of the Big children. A 10-year level term or low cost universal life policy might be appropriate if the coverage is obtained solely to meet the need for estate liquidity. At the same time, the Bigs should consider whether permanent insurance protection makes more sense should Mrs. Big establish an additional GRAT in the future, or for other reasons.

GRAT Requirements and Design Features

The gift tax value of the transferred shares is reduced by the present value of the qualified annuity interest that Mrs. Big will receive. The regulations under Section 2702 specify that the following requirements must be met in the governing instrument of the GRAT:

1. The annuity amount must be payable for each taxable year of the trust;

2. Only one contribution to that GRAT may be made;

3. The trust instrument must prohibit commutation of the annuity payments;

4. The trust instrument must prohibit annuity payments from being made to any person other than the annuitant during the GRAT period; and

5. The term of the annuity must be fixed in the trust and must be for

    a) the annuitant's life; or

    b) a fixed term of years; or

    c) the shorter of a) or b).

Other features of a GRAT permit considerable flexibility in its design. The GRAT period, for example, may be as short as two years or as long as the grantor desires. As a practical matter, in the author's experience, a typical GRAT term generally does not exceed 10 years. The value of the remainder interest gift to a GRAT is calculated by subtracting the present value of the retained annuity interest from the fair market value of the transferred shares. The gift of a remainder interest to the beneficiaries of the GRAT is determined at the time when the transfer of stock to the GRAT is completed. In general, the annuity interest is worth more, and the gift of the remainder interest is correspondingly worth less, as the annuity period is longer and/or the annuity rate of return is greater.

Three rates must be considered in the design of a GRAT: the annuity rate, the Section 7520 rate, and the actual return of the transferred asset. First, the stated annuity rate payable under the terms of a GRAT may be *any* rate agreed to by the grantor and the trustee. The annuity rate could be 20%, 30%, or higher if the grantor is intent upon reducing the value of the gift to a short-term GRAT and a rapidly appreciating asset is transferred. Practically speaking, the annuity rate of return should reflect the level of income that the transferred property can produce during the GRAT period. In the Big Company example, the annuity rate is 15%, which means that, based upon an $800,000 valuation of the transferred shares, the GRAT must make annual annuity payments of $120,000 to Mrs. Big.

The present value of the annuity is determined by multiplying the annuity amount ($120,000) by an annuity factor that is a function of the GRAT term (10 years) and the applicable Section 7520 rate (eight percent). The Section 7520 rate is published by the IRS on a monthly basis and is adjusted, generally, in response to the direction of interest rates in the economy. In determining the present value of the annuity, the Section 7520 rate operates as a discount factor, which means that a *higher* rate makes the present value of the annuity worth *less* than if a lower rate were in effect. Conversely, a *higher* Section 7520 rate means that the gift of the remainder interest is worth *more* than if a lower rate were in effect. To illustrate the point in the context of the Big Company example, if the Section 7520 rate were either 10% or six percent, rather than eight percent, the following values would be derived.

Section 7520 Rate	Present Value Of Annuity	Gift of Remainder Interest
6%	$800,000/$776,948	$0/$23,052[44]
8%	$779,340	$20,660
10%	$714,552	$85,448

In determining whether a transfer to a GRAT is feasible, the overall rate of return of the asset generally should be greater than the Section 7520 rate in order for the transaction to make economic sense. It is possible that an asset having a relatively low income yield could still be appropriate for a GRAT because of its expected growth in value.

In any event, the third rate in the operation of a GRAT is the *actual* return of the transferred asset during its term. During a given period of years, certain assets may provide a stream of income that is fairly predictable and reliable. When S corporation stock is transferred to a GRAT, the transferor should have a reasonably good idea of the likely level of future corporate income, that is, S corporation distributions that will fund the annuity payments by the GRAT to the grantor. The passthrough tax structure of the S corporation is the feature that makes S shares, rather than C corporation shares, especially suitable for a GRAT. A closely held C corporation rarely pays dividends of any substantial amount because of the shareholders' desire to minimize double taxation. Naturally, no such concern exists with an S corporation because corporate distributions are taxed directly to the shareholders. At the same time, however, the transferor of S stock to a GRAT must make a careful assessment of the future earnings that the S corporation is apt to realize.

If Mrs. Big transfers a 25% interest to a GRAT in exchange for an annual annuity payment of $120,000, the GRAT is obligated to make the payment to her whether or not the Big Company actually distributes that amount to the GRAT. The Bigs must be mindful of that obligation as they contemplate the transfer.

Obligation to Other Shareholders

In general, all of the shareholders of an S corporation must be equally entitled to distributions in order to satisfy the single class of stock requirement. If the Big Company distributes $120,000 to a GRAT that owns 25% of the stock, it should also distribute an equal amount to Mrs. Big, individually, as a 25% shareholder, and should distribute $240,000 to Mr. Big, as a 50% shareholder. The S stock held by the GRAT is its source of annuity payments required in the future. If *all* of the Bigs' S stock were transferred to the GRAT, there would be no further concern about other shareholders (but, of course, a major concern by the Bigs as to relinquishing control). In any event, distributions made by the S corporation to the GRAT must be in proportion to distributions made to other S corporation shareholders.[45] Therefore, in the Big Company situation, Mr. and Mrs. Big need to feel comfortable that the corporation can make distributions sufficient to support *both* the GRAT obligation *and* payments to each of them as individual shareholders.

S Corporation Earnings May be More or Less Than Needed to Cover Annuity Payments

If the Big Company distributions exceed the GRAT's proportionate share needed to meet the annuity obligation, the excess distribution can be held by the GRAT and added to its principal value. Alternatively, depending upon the respective needs of the corporation and its shareholders, the Big Company may retain the "excess" portion, even though the shareholders will be taxed upon the undistributed earnings. Further, as discussed below, Mrs. Big will be taxed on the GRAT's share of the earnings, as the owner of the trust for income tax purposes.

If, on the other hand, the earnings of the Big Company are insufficient to cover the annuity payments, the GRAT is nonetheless liable to Mrs. Big for the shortfall. The trustee could execute a promissory note in favor of Mrs. Big, and discharge its debt by future payments (as corporate earnings improve, or by a loan from the corporation to the GRAT.) As with any other debt obligation executed between related parties, a note executed by the GRAT in favor of Mrs. Big, or a loan by the corporation to the GRAT, should be conducted on an arm's length basis. It should contain provisions governing repayment, a market-level interest rate, appropriate security and other steps that would be followed by two unrelated parties in a business setting.[46]

In addition to a formally executed promise of future payment, the GRAT could take other measures to meet its obligation to Mrs. Big in a situation where current S corporation earnings are insufficient. Distributions could be made by the Big Company to the GRAT and to the Bigs from the corporation's accumulated adjustments account, if the account balance is sufficient and if that action is otherwise agreeable to the Bigs, as individual shareholders. The GRAT could also fulfill its annuity obligation by making principal payments to Mrs. Big. In other words, to the extent that corporate earnings are insufficient, the GRAT could transfer shares of the corporation to Mrs. Big to discharge its obligation. Of course, a re-transfer of shares to fund annuity payments defeats the original purpose of transferring shares from Mrs. Big's ownership.

In evaluating the feasibility of a transfer of S corporation stock to a GRAT, Mr. and Mrs. Big should also consider the broader picture of the corporation's income. The GRAT is necessarily dependent upon the corporation to make distributions sufficient to enable the annuity obligation to be met. If the Bigs can comfortably afford to reduce the employee compensation they receive — whether as salary or bonuses — and the corporation remains fairly prosperous otherwise, they may opt to cut their compensation so that the corporation can pay greater shareholder distributions. Those alternatives represent the familiar choices of an S corporation owner-employee who is either a sole owner or a co-owner with a spouse or other family members in a harmonious situation. Corporate earnings may be paid out as employee compensation, or as shareholder distributions, with a similar income tax result. Obviously, it is easy to assume that compensation can be reduced to permit shareholder distributions. Adjustments between employee compensation and shareholder distributions may not be so readily made if unrelated individuals are co-shareholders. Regardless of how the corporation allocates compensation and corporate distributions, there must be an expectation that corporate earnings will be financially consistent during the GRAT period in order to sustain distributions to the GRAT for annuity payments.

The Big Company example assumes that substantial stock value ($800,000) can be shifted for a relatively small gift ($20,660). If the Bigs believe that a 15% annuity is too expensive for the corporation, the annuity rate can be reduced. If the level of corporate profits cannot be projected with reasonable certainty over the next 10 years, a shorter GRAT period will reduce the present value of the annuity and will make the gift of the remainder interest correspondingly greater. A more modest shifting of value may be an acceptable tradeoff if the prospective grantor of a GRAT is concerned that the annuity rate cannot be sustained or that the GRAT period is too long.

Unique Aspects of Transferring S Corporation Stock to a GRAT

In the Big Company example, the annuity rate is based upon a 15% return. That rate of return is calculated by dividing the annual annuity amount by the fair market value of the transferred stock, including the 20% minority interest discount. When, as in the Big Company example, a minority interest discount applies, the earnings rate necessary for the corporation to provide distributions to the GRAT is lower than the annuity rate that is based on the discounted value of the gift. In effect, the minority discount provides gift tax leverage. A $120,000 payment that represents a 12% return based upon the $1,000,000 entity value equals a 15% annuity rate based upon the $800,000 gift tax value of the transferred shares.

The description of the annuity in the trust instrument constitutes another significant aspect of GRAT design for an S corporation stock transfer. Generally, when a hard to value asset such as S corporation stock is the subject of the GRAT, it is preferable to describe the annuity in percentage terms, rather than as a dollar amount. Even if an S stock transfer to a GRAT is supported by a professional appraisal, as in the Big Company example, it is possible that the IRS may revalue the stock for gift tax purposes. Specifically, suppose that the Big Company stock transferred to the GRAT is subsequently valued by the Service as being worth $1,000,000 rather than $800,000. In that case, the required annuity payments at a 15% rate would be $150,000. Consequently, the GRAT should make annual annuity payments of $150,000, rather than $120,000, and would owe Mrs. Big an additional $30,000 for each year in question. While the additional annuity payments may be financially disruptive to the Bigs' plans (and to the Big Company), increased annuity payments may be preferable to a subsequent adjustment in the gift tax value of the remainder.

However, under the particular facts of the Big Company example, a $200,000 valuation adjustment means that the revalued remainder interest gift would be $25,825. The Bigs' situation involves a high return annuity and a minimal gift. As a result, the increased cost of the annuity (and the need to make additional distributions to the Bigs, as individual shareholders) may be less appealing than an increased consumption of Mrs. Big's unified credit. In certain situations, the consequences of a gift tax valuation adjustment may be preferable to an increased annuity obligation. Nonetheless, in many instances, the annuity is more frequently described as a percentage return, rather than as a dollar amount, to minimize an adjustment in the amount of the taxable gift.

Grantor Trust Status

In order for the GRAT to qualify as an S corporation shareholder, it must fit within one of the categories described in Section 1361 as a grantor trust, a Section 678 trust, or a QSST. In most situations, a grantor trust offers the most likely means of qualification to own S corporation stock.

Apart from whether it holds S corporation stock, a GRAT is usually designed as a grantor trust, which means that the transferor will be considered as its owner for federal income tax purposes. Consequently, neither the grantor nor the trust recognizes any gain or loss upon the grantor's transfer of stock to fund the trust, which means that the annuity payments by the trustee, however made, are not taxable, per se, to the grantor. As the owner of the trust for income tax purposes, the grantor reports income or gain and enjoys the benefit of any deductions or losses experienced by the GRAT. When S stock is held in the GRAT, the grantor is taxed on the trust's proportionate share of the corporation's earnings, without regard to the annuity payments, and, as for any other S corporation situation, without regard to whether earnings are actually distributed.

If S corporation stock is transferred to a GRAT, it is imperative that the GRAT qualify as a grantor trust. Furthermore, such qualification should extend to both the income and the principal of the trust, that is, qualification as a grantor trust should be complete. It is therefore critical for the trust instrument to contain a provision that will expressly qualify the grantor trust requirement.

The power to substitute trust assets of an equivalent value has been a frequently used provision to achieve grantor trust status. Under Code section 675(4)(C), grantor trust status is realized if the grantor retains the power *in a nonfiduciary capacity*, without the approval or consent of any person in a fiduciary capacity, to reacquire the trust corpus by substituting other property of an equivalent value. The IRS has issued several private letter rulings citing the ability to substitute trust assets as an approved grantor trust provision.[47] The substitution power, by its terms, must expressly be held in a nonfiduciary capacity. However, the Service has also ruled that, even when the grantor holds the power but is not a trustee, the determination of whether the power is held in a nonfiduciary capacity is a question of fact that must be determined by the circumstances surrounding the creation and administration of the trust.[48]

The IRS has ruled that a GRAT provision to make annuity payments from income, and, if income is insufficient, from principal, enables a GRAT to be treated as a grantor trust under Section 677(a).[49] The power to add beneficiaries (other than after-born or after-adopted children) may also be included in a GRAT to secure grantor trust status. Typically, such a power would be held by an independent trustee and may be restrictive in its scope, confining the additional beneficiaries to a class, such as the descendants of the grantor.

Continuation/Termination of Trust After GRAT Period

If Mrs. Big survives for 10 years, Johnny and Susie Big will be 36 and 26 years old, respectively. At that time, the trustee will distribute their shares of the Big Company stock to each of them outright. However, if they were younger, or, if other circumstances warrant, the distribution by the trustee of the GRAT could be deferred. The trust instrument could operate in two stages: 1) as a GRAT for 10 years (or any other period) as described above; and 2) as a grantor trust, or other form of trust qualified to own S corporation stock, until the beneficiaries reach a specified age of distribution. In other words, after the obligation of the GRAT to make annuity payments is over, the trust may still continue to hold the S stock until the beneficiaries reach certain ages, or, in the discretion of the trustee, the S stock may be distributed to the beneficiaries.

Following the termination of the GRAT period, the trust must still qualify as an S corporation shareholder. It can do so by maintaining its status as a grantor trust, or it could become a Section 678 trust, or a QSST, depending upon the objectives and expectations of the grantor when the trust is established.

[The preceding discussion applies to S corporations with tax years beginning before January 1, 1997, or, if an election to be a small business trust is not made, in any tax year. The following discussion considers whether the trustee of a GRAT can elect small business trust status in tax years beginning after December 31, 1996.]

Electing Small Business Trust Status

If S stock is transferred to a GRAT, can the trustee of the GRAT elect small business trust status? It appears that the trustee could make the election so that the trust would continue to qualify as both a GRAT *and* as an S corporation shareholder. The transfer of stock to the GRAT is a *gift* by the grantor and is not a purchase by the GRAT.[50] However, the small business trust itself would be subject to income taxation, rather than the grantor under the grantor trust rules. If the grantor would otherwise be in the highest individual income tax bracket, the trust would pay the same income tax liability otherwise chargeable to the grantor. Nonetheless, it would be more difficult for the trust to make the annuity payments to the grantor because it would require S corporation income sufficient to make the annuity payment from the after tax income of the trust.

Furthermore, because the trust is subject to tax at the highest income tax bracket, its tax cost will be greater than that of the grantor who is not in the highest individual income tax bracket. In general, it would be more desirable for the GRAT to be a grantor trust, rather than a small business trust, for purposes of qualifying as an S corporation shareholder.

SALE OF S CORPORATION STOCK TO AN INTENTIONALLY DEFECTIVE IRREVOCABLE TRUST (IDIT)

Instead of giving shares to a GRAT, an S corporation owner such as Mrs. Big might consider selling shares to an intentionally defective irrevocable trust (IDIT), also known as an intentionally defective grantor trust. The trust is "defective" for income tax purposes because the grantor, or a beneficiary, is treated as its owner for income tax purposes under Code sections 671 through 679. The term "defective" might be misleading if one is not generally familiar with the income tax background of trusts. In the past, a grantor of a trust may have found it desirable to shift income taxation from himself to a trust. If, in attempting to achieve that objective, the grantor retained a right or power that made him the owner of the trust for income tax purposes, the trust was said to be "defective" in that it was not effective in transferring ownership of the trust for income tax purposes. Viewed in that manner, the various grantor trust provisions constituted traps, or impediments, that stood in the way of making the trust taxable for income tax purposes.

At the same time, even if an irrevocable trust is defective for income tax purposes, it can be effective to transfer ownership from the grantor for federal estate and gift tax purposes. The typical irrevocable trust that owns a life insurance policy is an example of this technique. An irrevocable life insurance trust has all incidents of ownership in the insurance policies it owns on the life of the grantor. The trust would generally be permitted to apply its income to purchase life insurance on the life of its grantor, which would make it defective for income tax purposes under Code section 677(a)(3), at least to the extent that income was so expended.

In recent years, the concept of using an irrevocable trust that is income tax defective, but effective for estate and gift tax purposes (i.e., excluded from the grantor's estate) has generated interest for planning with business or investment assets and life insurance policies. The concept is based upon a *sale*, rather than a gift, of an asset to the irrevocable trust. The sale of the asset to the IDIT is not a taxable event because the grantor is considered the owner of the trust for income tax purposes.[51] A client such a Mrs. Big, for example, might transfer $800,000 of S corporation stock to an IDIT in exchange for a promissory note. The note could be secured by the stock transferred to the trust and could specify that interest must be paid according to the applicable federal rate (AFR) in effect under Section 1274 on the date when the transaction occurs. Payments could include principal and interest amortized over a specified number of years, or could be interest only with a balloon payment at the end of the period.

Proper valuation of the asset to be transferred, whether S corporation stock or otherwise, is as critical for an IDIT as it is for a GRAT. An undervalued asset could create a taxable gift to the trust. For example, if Mrs. Big transfers stock valued at $800,000 to an IDIT for an $800,000 note and the stock is subsequently determined to be worth $1,000,000, the additional $200,000 would be considered a gift of a future interest to the trust. However, the risk of undervaluation for a sale to an IDIT is no greater than for any other transfer of a hard to value asset between related parties.

Comparing an IDIT Sale to a GRAT Gift

The sale of S corporation stock to an IDIT may offer certain advantages that would not be realized by the transfer of S stock to a GRAT. Unlike the GRAT, the IDIT transaction presents no risk that the transferred property will be included in the grantor's estate for federal estate tax purposes if the grantor dies during the trust period. Assuming that the S stock is properly valued, there is no retained interest held by the trust grantor because the transfer of stock is a sale. Therefore, assuming that the trust is properly drawn so that the grantor has no right or power over trust assets that would result in estate taxation, the assets are excluded from the grantor's estate. Of course, the present value of the note receivable is included in the grantor's estate if the note is not paid in full by the trust during the grantor's lifetime. While the determination of the period during which note payments will be made by the IDIT does not present the same mortality risk as for a GRAT, the grantor must still evaluate the ability of the S corporation to fund the note payments.

The regulations under Section 2702 restrict the extent to which annuity payments by a GRAT may be made on an "end-loaded" basis. Specifically, the annuity amount payable in any year may not exceed 120% of the amount paid during the preceding year.[52] A sale of stock to an IDIT, in contrast, has no particular restrictions governing the amount or timing of principal payments by the trust. Furthermore, the threshold rate of return necessary for a GRAT to be feasible is the Section 7520 rate. On the other hand, the pertinent rate for a transfer to an IDIT is the Section 1274 rate. The Section 7520 rate is 120% of the mid-term Section 1274 rate (applicable to notes between three and nine years in duration), and is generally also more than the long-term Section 1274 rate (more than nine years). In addition, the rules governing GRATs under Section 2702 do not apply to a sale to an IDIT.[53]

Naturally, an IDIT that would own S corporation stock must satisfy the trust ownership requirements under Section 1361. The same considerations discussed above pertaining to the qualification of a GRAT as a grantor trust or other type of trust eligible to own S stock also apply to the design of an IDIT. By definition, a small business trust is a taxable entity, rather than a defective trust for income tax purposes, thus eliminating it as an eligible trust for this purpose.

Caution: Subsequent Sale of S Corporation Stock by Beneficiary of GRAT or IDIT

The junior generation family member who receives S corporation stock distributed from a GRAT or an IDIT assumes the income tax basis of the transferor (plus, in the case of a GRAT, any gift taxes paid by the grantor, if applicable). Many family businesses operating as S corporations involve stock that has a low basis in the hands of the senior generation owner. If the business owner's son or daughter inherits a parent's shares, or acquired the stock by purchase under a buy-sell agreement funded by life insurance, the recipient has the advantage of a stepped up basis for income tax purposes. In that case, the child who eventually sells his stock may be subject to significantly less capital gains tax than the beneficiary of the GRAT or IDIT who assumes a much lower stock basis. As with any other situation that involves acquiring ownership with a stepped up basis (as for an inheritance) or a carryover basis (as for a gift), the prospective income tax cost must be weighed against the prospective estate and gift tax savings. In addition, the age and health of the transferor and the odds that the beneficiary will sell his stock in the future must also be taken into account.

IRS Assertion of Deemed "Gift" by Grantor

Both a GRAT and an IDIT are grantor trusts in which the grantor is deemed to be the owner of the trust for income tax purposes. Under both arrangements, a grantor may be subject to income taxation without receiving the benefit of the income on which he is taxed. For example, when S stock is transferred to a GRAT, the income earned by the shares held in the GRAT and taxed to the grantor may exceed the annuity payments made to the grantor. Similarly, a sale of S stock to an IDIT may result in interest payments made by the trust to the grantor that are less than the S stock income realized by the IDIT and taxed to the grantor. To the extent that the grantor *needs* the income for his support, the "phantom income" effect of the GRAT or IDIT would be unattractive. On the other hand, the client, such as Mrs. Big, who is interested in shifting maximum value to her children at a minimum gift tax cost, would not mind bearing the income tax cost created by the grantor trust rules. In the latter case, the grantor who pays income tax on an amount that will be enjoyed by her children can receive the tax payment (or, at least, the tax paid on income not received by the grantor) as a form of gift that is not subject to gift tax.

The problem is that the IRS also views the additional income tax burden of the grantor as bestowing value upon the trust beneficiaries. The argument of the Service is that the grantor should be reimbursed by the trust for the income tax liability incurred. Unless a grantor has a specific right to reimbursement under state law or the terms of the trust, it is difficult to follow the logic of the Service on this point. Some commentators have suggested that the trust instrument should contain a provision that specifically waives any reimbursement right.

The income taxation of the grantor under a GRAT or an IDIT is a direct product of the grantor trust rules. The "deemed gift" theory of the IRS seems misconceived because it ignores the legal obligation of the grantor to pay income taxes as a result of a group of statutory rules that place the burden on the grantor. Nonetheless, in several private letter rulings, the Service has required that a GRAT contain a tax reimbursement provision as a condition of issuing a favorable ruling as to the qualification of the trust under Section 2702.[54] In the case of a GRAT, it is critical for the grantor not to make any subsequent gifts to the trust because a GRAT, by definition, permits only a single contribution by the grantor. The outcome of this issue remains unclear.

In determining the design of a GRAT with regard to a tax reimbursement clause, it should be added that such a provision is not a governing instrument requirement necessary to satisfy the GRAT rules under Section 2702. The concern of the Service with regard to the reimbursement provision for a GRAT is generally directed to the tax paid by the grantor on trust income that exceeds the annuity amount. Moreover, the right to reimbursement of the grantor may be a question to be resolved under state law, and the answer under state law may not be clear. Therefore, rather than include a provision in the GRAT in which the grantor expressly waives a right to reimbursement, the best solution may be to include a provision authorizing, but not requiring, the trustee to reimburse the grantor for tax on undistributed trust income. A similar provision is probably also advisable for an IDIT.

PROHIBITED TECHNIQUES FOR TRANSFERS OF S CORPORATION STOCK

This chapter reviews the requirements of various trusts that may be successfully utilized to own S corporation stock, including specialized arrangements such as grantor retained annuity trusts, (GRATs), described herein as a particularly attractive form of trust for certain S corporation shareholders. Given the particularity of the rules governing ownership of S corporation stock, it may be especially useful for the practitioner to be aware of certain commonly employed planning arrangements that *cannot* be used to hold or transfer S corporation stock.

IRA

Revenue Ruling 92-73 provides that an individual retirement arrangement (IRA) is not permitted to own S corporation stock under Code section 1361.[55] Under Code section 408(a), an IRA is a trust created for the exclusive benefit of an individual or the individual's beneficiaries, only if the governing instrument creating the trust meets the requirements of Section 408(a). The rules governing the taxation of IRAs provide, generally, that any amounts paid or distributed from an IRA are included in the gross income of the recipient as specified under Section 72 (relating to the taxation of annuities).[56] Revenue Ruling 92-73 notes that a trust may be an S corporation shareholder if it is a grantor trust so that an individual (who is a U.S. citizen or resident) is taxed on its income; or, it may be a qualified subchapter S trust (QSST), so that under Section 678(a) the trust beneficiary is treated as the owner of that portion of the QSST that holds S corporation stock. The ruling concludes that an IRA cannot qualify as a grantor trust or a QSST because the trust ownership rules under Section 1361 are incompatible with the rules that apply to an IRA.

Family Limited Partnership

In recent years, many affluent individuals have established family limited partnerships (FLPs) as a means of transferring an ownership interest in assets to other family members in order to reduce the transferor's prospective estate tax liability. A transfer to an FLP is especially advantageous from a gift tax standpoint because it can be structured so that minority and marketability discounts are claimed by the transferor. Frequently, assets that are not liquid but are likely to appreciate in future value, such as real estate or closely held C corporation stock, are the subjects of transfers to FLPs. S corporation stock, however, is not an appropriate asset for transfer because a partnership cannot qualify as a permitted S corporation shareholder. The owner of a family business held as an S corporation who is interested in making gifts of stock on a tax favored basis is more likely to establish a grantor retained annuity trust (GRAT) to achieve benefits similar to those obtained by a C corporation shareholder who establishes an FLP.

Charitable Remainder Trust

An S corporation owner who is charitably inclined may contemplate the transfer of S stock to a charitable remainder trust. Typically, a charitable remainder trust involves the transfer of assets to a trust that will provide a lifetime income for a donor or the joint lifetimes of a donor and spouse, followed by the distribution of the trust assets to a charity. The charitable remainder trust can enable the donor to obtain significant income and estate tax planning benefits. A number of different types of assets may be appropriate for funding a charitable remainder trust. Appreciated property, such as real estate, publicly traded securities or closely held stock, is generally selected for transfer to the trust. The asset given to the trust must be income producing during the donor's lifetime in order to satisfy the charitable remainder trust requirements.

In Revenue Ruling 92-48, the IRS ruled that a charitable remainder unitrust could not qualify to own S corporation stock as a QSST.[57] The ruling dealt with the question of whether a proposed charitable remainder unitrust will qualify as a charitable remainder trust under Section 664 and as a QSST under Section 1361(d)(3). The Service ruled that a charitable remainder trust could not qualify as a QSST because the trust arrangements described in Sections 664 and 1361(d) are mutually exclusive. The ruling deserves further discussion because it is instructive in regard to the operation of the QSST rules.

In its analysis, the Service pointed out that the beneficiary of a QSST must elect to be treated under Section 678(a) as the owner of the portion of the trust consisting of S corporation stock. As a result of the QSST election, the beneficiary, rather than the trust, is treated as the owner of the stock. The Service noted that the QSST election ensures that the trust represents only one S corporation shareholder, and guarantees that all income earned by the trust relating to the stock is taxed to the trust's beneficiary.

Section 664(c) provides that, generally, a trust meeting the definition of a charitable remainder trust is exempt from federal income tax. A charitable remainder unitrust provides that a beneficiary may receive a percentage of the net fair market value of the trust assets, referred to as the "unitrust amount." The unitrust amount required to be distributed is taxable to the beneficiary under Section 664(b). Section 664(a) and the regulations thereunder specify the tax treatment for the beneficiary and the trust, notwithstanding the other provisions of subchapter J of the Code which governs the taxation of trusts, generally.

In the ruling, the Service stated that Section 1361 and Section 664 contemplate two distinct systems of taxation. The IRS stressed that Section 664 provides favorable tax treatment *in lieu of* other provisions governing the taxation of trusts. Section 664(a) governs the taxation of a charitable remainder trust, which would override the income tax treatment of a trust beneficiary resulting from a QSST election. Section 1361(d) is specifically designed to cause the beneficiary to be taxed on trust income (rather than the trust). The beneficiary of a charitable remainder trust is not exclusively subject to taxation, and therefore, the trust cannot qualify as an S corporation shareholder. After concluding that a charitable remainder trust cannot qualify as a QSST, the Service took the opposite approach to prove the statutory incompatibility of the two trusts. If the QSST election were permitted, and the trust beneficiary were taxed on the trust income, the trust would not function exclusively as a charitable remainder unitrust. As a result, the trust would not be tax exempt, transfers to the trust would not be tax deductible and permitting the grantor trust provisions to apply would frustrate the intent and effect of the charitable remainder trust provisions.

Incidentally, while Revenue Ruling 92-48 addressed a charitable remainder unitrust, the same conclusion should be reached if the charitable remainder trust were a annuity trust, rather than a unitrust, in form.

The Service concluded that the arrangements described in Section 664 and Section 1361(d) are mutually exclusive. A charitable remainder trust cannot qualify as a QSST and a QSST cannot qualify under the charitable remainder trust requirements.

Electing Small Business Trust

For tax years beginning after December 31, 1996, an electing small business trust is permitted to own S corporation stock. However, any trust that is income tax exempt under the Code is not permitted to be an electing small business trust.[58] Thus, a charitable remainder trust, which is income tax exempt under Section 664, remains unable to own S corporation stock even after the introduction of the small business trust pursuant to the Small Business Job Protection Act of 1996.

FOOTNOTE REFERENCES

1. Reg. §1.641(b)-3(a).
2. *Old Virginia Brick Co., Inc.*, 367 F.2d 276 (4th Cir. 1966).
3. In Letter Ruling 8343037, minors are deemed to be shareholders of S corporation stock held by custodians under the UGMA. See also Rev. Rul. 71-287, 1971-2 CB 317.
4. TIR No. 113, Nov. 26, 1958.
5. Rev. Rul. 76-23, 1976-1 CB 264.
6. IRC Sec. 1361(c)(3).
7. Rev. Rul. 66-266, 1966-2 CB 356.
8. IRC Sec. 1361(c)(2)(A)(ii).
9. IRC Sec. 1361(c)(2)(A)(iii).
10. While the term "grantor trust" is often used for convenient description of a trust subject to Sections 671-679, a "Section 678 trust" could be called a "beneficiary trust," since, by definition, a person other than the grantor is treated as the substantial owner and that person is typically a beneficiary. The effect of the QSST election is to treat a beneficiary as if the beneficiary is the owner of the portion of the trust in which the S corporation stock is held. Regulation Section 1.1361-1(j)(6)(iv) states that when a grantor is treated as the owner of S corporation stock held by a trust because of the application of Sections 671-679, the QSST election may not be made with respect to that corporation. Apparently, the QSST election is precluded if the trust holding S corporation stock is independently classified as a "grantor trust" or a Section 678 trust. The effect of the election is to treat the trust as being subject to the grantor trust rules, so that the beneficiary of the trust is treated as the owner of that portion of the trust holding S corporation stock.
11. IRC Sec. 1361(d)(2)(B)(i).
12. IRC Sec. 1361(d)(2)(B)(ii).
13. Prop. Reg. §1.1361-1A(i)(3).
14. IRC Sec. 1361(d)(2)(D).
15. IRC Sec. 1361(d)(2)(C).
16. The IRS has been strict in its interpretation of the single income beneficiary requirement. See Revenue Ruling 89-45, 1989-1 CB 267, in which the Service held that a trust did not qualify as a QSST because it was possible that a portion of its corpus could be used to fund a new trust for an after-born grandchild of the grantor. In Revenue Ruling 89-55, 1989-1 CB 268, QSST treatment was disallowed because of the possibility that the trust might terminate and distribute corpus to other persons during the life of the current income beneficiary if the trust no longer held any S corporation stock. However, in Letter Ruling 9014008, the Service distinguished Revenue Ruling 89-55 and held that income accumulated during periods when S corporation stock is not held by a trust does not violate the rule that all income be paid to the beneficiary currently. Nonetheless, the Service also ruled in Letter Ruling 9014008 that the payment of income to a QSST beneficiary's revocable living trust, rather than to the beneficiary directly, violates the requirement that a QSST must distribute all of its income to its beneficiary.
17. Rev. Rul. 92-20, 1992-2 CB 227.
18. Rev. Rul. 92-64, 1992-2 CB 64.
19. Rev. Rul. 93-31, 1993-1 CB 186.
20. IRC Sec. 1361(c)(2)(A)(ii).
21. However, it should be noted that an irrevocable trust that was reformed by a court decree was permitted to be a QSST. See Let. Rul. 9040031. If a trust can be reformed within the 60 day or two year periods of limitation, or if no time limit applies, the risk of termination of the S corporation election can be avoided.

22. However, a distribution in discharge of a parental support obligation, such as education or support of a minor child, may be treated as a distribution for the benefit of the parent who owes the support obligation. Thus, a distribution for the support of a minor beneficiary could be deemed to be a distribution to the parent, which could cause the trust to run afoul of the "sole beneficiary" requirement of a QSST. See Let. Rul. 9028013.

23. IRC Sec. 1361(c)(2)(A)(i).

24. The "all of which" requirement seems to mean that the beneficiary must own all of the income and corpus of the trust. Section 678 refers to an individual's power to vest corpus *or* income in himself, but the "all of which" language seems to require a power over *both* in order for the trust to qualify under Section 1361(c)(2)(A)(i). Also see Reg. §1.671-3(b)(3), which states that if a grantor or another person is treated under Sections 674 through 678 as an owner of a portion by reason of a power over ordinary income only, items of income are not included in that portion.

25. Its requirements are described in Code section 2056(b)(5).

26. However, it is worth noting that "income" under Section 1361(d)(3)(B) is defined as income within the meaning of Section 643(b), that is, trust accounting income. Thus, a reference to income under a marital trust holding S corporation stock should incorporate the Section 643(b) definition of income to ensure compliance with the QSST requirements.

27. Additional planning may be required if the S corporation shareholder is married to a spouse who is a resident, but not a citizen, of the United States. In order for the S stock or other property transferred to a trust for the benefit of a noncitizen to qualify for the marital deduction, the trust must satisfy the "qualified domestic trust" (QDT) requirements of Section 2056A.

28. IRC Sec. 2056(b)(5).

29. It is prudent to have the terms of the trust specify that all Section 643(b) income must be distributed. However, in Letter Ruling 8923007, the Service ruled that, even without a provision mandating the distribution of income, the income distribution requirement was satisfied because state law imposed a duty on the trustee to currently distribute the trust's income.

30. IRC Sec. 1361(d)(3)(A)(ii).

31. However, the leverage that an *active* equal shareholder may exert in relation to a surviving spouse who is *not* active in the business as an employee can be neutralized by a provision which limits the annual compensation increases for shareholder/ employees as discussed in Chapter 5. The "leverage" referred to is specifically concerned with setting the level of employee compensation, which, in turn, determines the amount available for dividend distributions. As the suggested provision indicates, the compensation increase provided to an employed shareholder can be limited in order to permit a reasonable amount to be available for dividend distributions.

32. If the spouse is a minority shareholder or otherwise lacks voting control of the S corporation stock, the right to compel the trustee of the marital trust to convert the stock to be income producing may not be meaningful. For example, the trustee may be compelled by the spouse to sell the stock if no dividends are paid to the marital trust, but the outcome of the sale will be a function of whether the stock is marketable, as would be the case for the sale of any type of "unproductive" property.

33. IRC Sec. 1361(c)(2)(A)(ii).

34. IRC Sec. 1361(c)(2)(A)(ii).

35. IRC Sec. 1361(c)(2)(A)(iv).

36. IRC Sec. 1361(c)(2)(B)(iv).

37. *The A. & N. Furniture & Appliance Co. v. U.S.*, 271 F. Supp. 40 (S.D. Ohio, 1967).
38. *Parker Oil Co., Inc. v. Comm.*, 58 TC 985 (1972).
39. Reg. §1.1361-1(h)(1)(v). See also Letter Rulings 8949035 and 9411010.
40. Rev. Rul. 82-105, 1982-1 CB 133.
41. See Let. Rul. 9345035.
42. See Reg. §25.2702-3(e), Ex. 5.
43. Revenue Ruling 82-105, 1982-1 CB 133 specifies that the value includable under Section 2036 is the amount of trust principal necessary to support an annuity based upon the annual rate of return equal to the applicable interest rate (now Section 7520 rate) in effect at the grantor's death. In contrast, Letter Ruling 9345035, which involved a GRAT that would be in effect for 15 years or the earlier death of the grantor, held that the full value of the GRAT principal would be includable under Section 2039.
44. If the annuity rate is set at a high level, the present value of the annuity may equal, or exceed, the fair market value of the transferred property, As a result, the value of the remainder interest would be zero, which would mean that the transfer would be made with no gift tax cost. However, in Revenue Ruling 77-454, 1977-2 CB 351, the IRS adopted a position that the value of an interest retained by a grantor is limited to the present value of a hypothetical amount that will be received by the grantor until the trust is exhausted. Naturally, Revenue Ruling 77-454 was issued prior to the enactment of Chapter 14 and Code section 2702, which, together with applicable regulations, sets forth the rules that define a "qualified interest" (as an annuity under a GRAT arrangement, for example). The Service has asserted that a GRAT cannot be "zeroed out" (structured so that the remainder interest has no value). The $23,052 figure shown in the text indicates the gift tax value that would result according to the position of the Service in Revenue Ruling 77-454. Let. Ruls. 9351005, 9345035, 9253031, 9248016 and 9239015. But see *Estate of Benjamin Shapiro*, 66 TC Memo 1067 (1993), in which the Tax Court refuted the position of the IRS.
45. While the regulations under Section 1361 require that all shares of an S corporation must have identical rights with regard to distributions, a certain degree of flexibility is permitted as to distributions that may differ in timing or amount. For example, Regulation §1.1361-1(l)(2) states:

> "Although a corporation is not treated as having more than one class of stock so long as the governing provisions provide for identical distribution and liquidation rights, any distributions (including actual, constructive, or deemed distributions) that differ in timing or amount are to be given appropriate tax effect in accordance with the facts and circumstances."

Furthermore, Example 2 of Regulation §1.1361-1(l)(2)(v) provides:

> "*Example 2.* Distributions that differ in timing. (i) S, a corporation, has two equal shareholders, A and B. Under S's bylaws, A and B are entitled to equal distributions. S distributes $50,000 to A in the current year, but does not distribute $50,000 to B until one year later. The circumstances indicate that the difference in timing did not occur by reason of a binding agreement relating to distribution or liquidation proceeds. (ii) Under paragraph (l)(2)(i) of this section, the difference in timing of the distributions to A and B does not cause S to be treated as having more than one class of stock. However, section 7872 or other recharacterization principles may apply to determine the appropriate tax consequences."

Thus, while the parties to a GRAT in a situation like the Bigs should not assume that distributions can be made systematically on a disproportionate basis, the regulations provide some latitude to the S corporation in the timing or amount of distributions to shareholders.

46. However, in Letter Ruling 9515039, the Service allowed promissory notes to be used by a GRAT for annuity payments *if* the remainderperson guaranteed the note payments and had sufficient assets to pay off the note. The ruling further provides that if payment of the notes was to be made only from trust assets, the notes would be regarded as a cumulative right of withdrawal of trust assets and would not be treated as a qualified annuity interest under Regulation Section 25.2702-3(b). In contemplating a transfer to a GRAT, the parties should structure the transaction with a sense of confidence that the annuity obligation can be met by the trust, and that the use of a note is a "last resort" measure to make payments.

47. See Let. Ruls. 9525032, 9446008, 9403020, 9352017, 9351005 and 9247024.

48. See Let. Ruls. 9504025, 9437023, 9437022, 9418024 and 9416009.

49. See Let. Ruls. 9504021, 9449013, 9449012 and 9444033.

50. Code section 1361(e)(1)(A)(ii) prohibits a small business trust from acquireing an interest"by purchase." Section 1361(e)(1)(C) provides that "purchase" means any acquisition if the basis of the property acquired is determined under Section 1012. The GRAT would carry over the basis in the grantor's S stock under Section 1015 and, therefore, would not violate the "no purchase" rule.

51. Rev. Rul. 85-13, 1985-1 CB 184.

52. Reg. §25.2702-3(b)(l)(ii).

53. See Letter Rulings 9436006 and 9535026, in which the Service held that neither Section 2701 nor 2702 applied to IDIT asset sales.

54. See Let. Ruls. 9519029, 9504021, 9444033 and 9416009. But, see Letter Ruling 9543049, which modifies the position of the Service in Letter Ruling 9444033.

55. 1992-2 CB 224.

56. IRC Sec. 408(d)(1).

57. 1992-1 CB 301. See also Let. Rul. 8922014.

58. IRC Sec. 1361(e)(1)(B)(ii).

Chapter 7

BENEFIT PLANNING FOR SHAREHOLDERS OF S CORPORATIONS

Ownership of a closely held corporation provides shareholders with a degree of control and responsibility that is far different from that experienced by those who are solely employees. A corporate executive, for example, is wholly dependent upon his employer for the enjoyment of various types of insurance and other fringe benefits. Shareholder-employees of closely held corporations have the ability to design benefit programs that are favorable to themselves and to nonowner employees. The control available to shareholder-employees is recognized in the structure of Code provisions, regulations and rulings that impose restrictions on employees who also have an ownership interest in a business. Additional references to such limitations and restrictions are also discussed in Chapter 1.

A shareholder-employee of an S corporation must also take into account the effect of Section 1372 on the corporation's benefit planning. Section 1372 was introduced to the Code by the Subchapter S Revision Act of 1982 ("SSRA"). Its provisions and effect are the reference point for the discussions in the first half of this chapter. It states:

SEC. 1372. PARTNERSHIP RULES TO APPLY FOR FRINGE BENEFIT PURPOSES.

    (a) GENERAL RULE. — For purposes of applying the provisions of this subtitle which relate to employee fringe benefits —

        (1) the S corporation shall be treated as a partnership, and

        (2) any two-percent shareholder of the S corporation shall be treated as a partner of such partnership.

(b) TWO-PERCENT SHAREHOLDER DEFINED. — For purposes of this section, the term "two-percent shareholder" means any person who owns (or is considered as owning within the meaning of section 318) on any day during the taxable year of the S corporation more than two percent of the outstanding stock of such corporation or stock possessing more than two percent of the total combined voting power of all stock of such corporation.

EMPLOYEE FRINGE BENEFITS

Our starting point in an analysis of Section 1372 is the term "employee fringe benefits." The term is not defined in the statute and regulations pertaining to Section 1372 have not been issued by the IRS. The legislative history of Section 1372 refers to "statutory exemptions for fringe benefits" and enumerates the following benefits (sometimes referred to hereafter as "fringe benefits"):

1. The $5,000 death benefit exclusion (IRC Sec. 101(b)). However, note that the Small Business Job Protection Act of 1996 repeals this provision for decedents dying after August 20, 1996.

2. The exclusion from income of amounts paid for an accident and health plan (IRC Sec. 105(b),(c),(d)).

3. The exclusion from income of amounts paid by an employer to an accident and health plan (IRC Sec. 106).

4. The exclusion of the cost of up to $50,000 of group term life insurance on an employee's life (IRC Sec. 79).

5. The exclusion from income of meals or lodging furnished for the convenience of the employer (IRC Sec. 119).[1]

The analysis in this chapter will focus on the benefits encompassed within items 2, 3 and 4. The types of benefits falling within those categories are discussed below in greater depth and their role in the planning process is examined.

TWO-PERCENT SHAREHOLDER

As Section 1372(b) indicates, a "two-percent shareholder" is actually one who owns *more than* two-percent of the outstanding stock or the voting stock of the corporation. Many S corporations are owned by a sole shareholder or a majority shareholder together with one or more minority shareholders. Even if stock ownership is diluted among a wide group of shareholders, it is likely that at least one will be a two-percent shareholder (i.e., will own more than two percent), given that no more than 75 shareholders may own all of the corporation's stock. Unless an S corporation is owned by a sole shareholder who is not an employee, shareholder-employees of S corporations will generally be affected by Section 1372 treatment of employee fringe benefits. Even if some members of a shareholder group are employees and others are not, the interest that both groups have in the corporation's "bottom line" will be reflected in their approach to the cost allocation of employee benefits. Following the enactment of Section 1372, the tax consequences of a two-percent shareholder being treated "as a partner" were not entirely clear. The Senate Report accompanying the legislative history of the SSRA contains the following statement:

Explanation of Provision (sec. 1372)

Under the bill, the treatment of fringe benefits of any person owning more than two percent of the stock of the corporation will be treated in the same manner as a partner in a partnership. Thus, for example, amounts paid for the medical care of a shareholder-employee will not be deductible by the corporation (by reason of secs. 1363(b)(2) and 703(a)(2)(E)), will be deductible by that individual only to the extent personal medical expenses will be allowed as an itemized deduction under section 213. However, similar amounts paid by the corporation on behalf of shareholders owning two percent or less of the corporation may be deducted as a business expense.[2]

The Senate Report refers to Section 1363(b)(2), which states that the taxable income of an S corporation shall be computed in the same manner as in the case of an individual, *except* that "...the deductions referred to in section 703(a)(2) shall not be allowed to the corporation." Section 703 deals with the computation of partnership income and deductions. It specifies that deductions for such items as personal exemptions, real estate taxes, charitable contributions and other *individual* itemized deductions are not allowed to a partnership in computing its taxable income. Such deductions are not relevant to a determination of partnership income, which is carried over to individual returns according to the partnership interest of the respective partner. A partner's distributive share of income is added to other income on the partner's individual tax returns and personal deductions, exemptions, etc., are computed in order to determine the partner's taxable income.

The legislative intent reflected in the cited passage suggests a similar treatment for the enumerated benefits. For example, if an S corporation pays for a two-percent shareholder's premium for medical insurance under an accident and health plan, the legislative history suggests that such an expense should be nondeductible to the corporation. The premium is paid out of the corporation's taxable income, which means that its cost is effectively charged to the shareholders. The insured shareholder-employee receiving the benefit of the coverage would not be charged with income apart from the corresponding portion of shareholder income. In other words, the income exclusion permitted under Section 105(b) would be available to the employee. Also, the two-percent shareholder would be permitted to take an itemized deduction to the extent applicable under Section 213.

On the other hand, an expense for medical insurance or other benefits covered by the items listed in the legislative history would be deductible if paid by the S corporation on behalf of an employee who is not a shareholder or who owns two percent or less of the stock.

Following the enactment of the SSRA, some tax planning practitioners questioned whether the treatment suggested by the legislative history led to the proper result for the two-percent shareholder-employee. The controversy regarding the income tax treatment dealt with the question of whether the corporation's payment should be deductible or nondeductible. If allowed as a deduction, should a corresponding adjustment be made from the two-percent shareholder's standpoint? Despite the statement in the Senate Report, it was not entirely clear that treating the S corporation as a partnership and the two-percent shareholder as a partner necessarily resulted in the cited benefits becoming nondeductible to the corporation. In fact, the statutory exemptions cited in the Senate Report are income tax *exclusions* available to individuals. If the intent of Section 1372 is to deny those income exclusions to two-percent shareholders, then its effect should be to make the benefits taxable to individuals, rather than nondeductible to the corporation. If the benefit were deemed to be deductible by the S corporation and includable to the two-percent shareholder receiving it, the allocation of its cost from a tax standpoint would be shifted to the recipient, rather than borne by the shareholders.

EXAMPLE. Frankie owns 80% and Johnny owns 20% of F&J Inc., an S corporation in which they are also full-time employees. F&J pays premiums for individual disability insurance policies for each of them. The premium for Frankie's policy is $4,000 and Johnny's premium is $2,000. If F&J were a C corporation, the premiums would be deductible by the corporation under Section 162 and excluded from compensation under Section 106. According to the Senate Report accompanying the enactment of Section 1372, the premiums paid by an S corporation would be nondeductible because they are contributions to an accident and health plan under Section 106 provided for the benefit of a two-percent shareholder. If treated as nondeductible, the cost of the coverage would be allocated from the corporate income taxable to the shareholders, as follows:

$4,000 Premium for Frankie

Shareholder	Percentage	Cost Allocation
Frankie	80%	$3,200
Johnny	20%	$ 800

$2,000 Premium for Johnny

Shareholder	Percentage	Cost Allocation
Frankie	80%	$1,600
Johnny	20%	$ 400

Total Premiums: $6,000

Shareholder	Percentage	Cost Allocation
Frankie	80%	$4,800
Johnny	20%	$1,200

If premiums are treated as nondeductible, the brunt of the expense would be allocated to Frankie because of her stock ownership. Frankie and Johnny could both exclude the premiums from income by virtue of Section 106.

However, the results shown above for Frankie and Johnny are not, in fact, correct. The controversy caused by the statements in the Senate Report has been resolved by Revenue Ruling 91-26[3] in which the Service has provided definitive guidance in regard to the treatment of fringe benefits to a two-percent shareholder. See Appendix B for the full text of Revenue Ruling 91-26.

REVENUE RULING 91-26: THE DEFINITIVE WORD

Revenue Ruling 91-26 poses the following two issues:

1. If a partner performs services in the capacity of a partner and the partnership pays accident and health insurance premiums for current year coverage on behalf of such partner without regard to partnership income, what is the federal income tax treatment of the premium payments?

2. If an S corporation pays accident and health insurance premiums for current year coverage on behalf of a two-percent shareholder-employee, what is the federal income tax treatment of the premium payments?

Our focus in this chapter is on the second issue. However, given the analysis of the Service, it is necessary to discuss the partnership issue in order to discuss the proper income tax treatment to be accorded an S corporation and its two-percent shareholder-employee who receives one or more of the enumerated benefits.[4]

In its analysis of the second issue in the ruling, the Service noted that Section 1372 provides that, for purposes of applying the income tax provisions of the Code relating to employee fringe benefits, an S corporation is treated as a partnership and a two-percent shareholder who is also an employee of an S corporation is treated as a partner of a partnership. Payments to a partner of a partnership may be made as part of a partner's distributive share of income or loss from the partnership. However, payments to a partner may also be classified as "guaranteed payments" under Section 707(c).

Guaranteed payments, to the extent they are determined without regard to the income of a partnership, are payments made to a partner for services (or the use of capital), and are considered as made to a person who is not a member of a partnership, but *only* for the purpose of including the payment in gross income under Section 61 and allowing a trade or business deduction under Section 162, subject to the rules governing capital expenditures under Section 263. Both payments in kind and in cash are deductible by the partnership. In order for a guaranteed payment to be deductible by a partnership, it must meet the same tests (ordinary and necessary business expense, etc.) as if it were made to someone who is not a member of the partnership. Correspondingly, the cash payment or value of the benefit is included in the partner's income. It may not be excluded from gross income under the general fringe benefit rules because the benefit is treated as a distributive share of partnership income for purposes of all Code sections other than Section 61 and Section 162. No exclusion from gross income under the fringe benefit rules is permitted except to the extent a Code provision allowing exclusion of a fringe benefit specifically provides that it applies to partners.

In addressing the second issue, Revenue Ruling 91-26 states that employee fringe benefits paid or furnished by an S corporation to or for the benefit of its two-percent shareholder-employees for services rendered are treated in the same manner as guaranteed payments for income tax purposes. The benefit is deductible to the S corporation under Section 162, assuming that the requirements for deductibility under that section are met. A two-percent shareholder also includes the value of the benefit in gross income under Section 61. Thus, unlike the original suggestion of nondeductibility contained in the Senate Report, the S corporation's payment for an employee fringe benefit provided to a two-percent shareholder is deductible, but included in the recipient's income.

OBSERVATION. The conclusion reached by Revenue Ruling 91-26 makes more sense than if the "nondeductible" approach were followed. Revenue Ruling 91-26 places the burden of income taxation on the two-percent shareholder as the *recipient* of the benefits. On the other hand, the "nondeductible" approach allocates the cost of the benefit to all of the shareholders of the S corporation, without regard to which of them receives the benefit. Of course, in the case of an S corporation that is owned by a sole shareholder-employee, differing tax treatment leads to the same result, that is, the recipient of the benefit is taxed as an employee, but would have been taxed as a shareholder if the cost were nondeductible. In cases involving more than one shareholder-employee, the approach set forth in Revenue Ruling 91-26 offers a fair method of allocating the tax cost of the employee fringe benefit. The fairness of the result is independent of the fact that a two-percent shareholder rule exists in the first place. Congressional wisdom dictates that a two-percent shareholder of an S corporation is to be treated differently than a shareholder-employee of a C corporation with respect to the receipt of certain employee fringe benefits.

A two-percent shareholder-employee may deduct a percentage of medical insurance premiums expended for the shareholder, his spouse and dependents under Section 162(l).[5] For 1996, 30% of medical insurance premiums may be deducted. In 1997, 40% may be deducted; in 1998 through 2002, 45%; in 2003, 50%; in 2004, 60%; in 2005, 70%; and in 2006 and subsequent years, 80%. The Section 162(l) deduction is available to an individual who is an employee within the meaning of Section 401(c)(1), which treats certain self-employed individuals as employees. A self-employed individual is one who has "earned income," which means net earnings from self-employment as defined in Section 1402(a). Among other items, guaranteed payments to a partner for services are included in net earnings from self-employment under Section 1402(a). In addition, Section 162(l)(5) provides the following:

(5) TREATMENT OF CERTAIN S CORPORATION SHAREHOLDERS. — This subsection shall apply in the case of any individual treated as a partner under section 1372(a), except that —

(A) for purposes of this subsection, such individual's wages (as defined in section 3121) from the S corporation shall be treated as such individual's earned income (within the meaning of section 401(c)(1)), and

(B) there shall be such adjustments in the application of this subsection as the Secretary may by regulations prescribe.

Revenue Ruling 91-26 states that the wages (as defined in Section 3121) of a two-percent shareholder-employee are treated as earned income within the meaning of Section 401(c)(1). Thus, a two-percent shareholder-employee may have a limited personal deduction for the cost of medical care insurance paid by the S corporation and charged against his income.

Accident and health benefits provided for a two-percent shareholder are not includable as wages for FICA and FUTA purposes because they are exempt under the applicable statutory rules.[6] Code sections 3121(a)(2) and 3306(b)(2) provide that any payment made on account of sickness or accident, disability, or medical or hospitalization expenses thereof, are specifically exempt from classification as "wages."

Since Revenue Ruling 91-26 represents a clarification of issues which had been somewhat confused prior to its issuance, the Service indicated that it would provide administrative relief for tax returns filed prior to 1991.[7]

Nonowner employees or shareholder-employees owning less than two percent of the stock of an S corporation are not affected by Revenue Ruling 91-26. The income tax exclusions permitted for employee fringe benefits remain available to such employees and the corporation's premium payments remain deductible.

EMPLOYEE FRINGE BENEFIT PLANNING FOR TWO-PERCENT SHAREHOLDERS

Of the Section 1372 employee fringe benefits affected by Revenue Ruling 91-26, life underwriters and other professionals involved in insurance planning are most likely to be concerned with its effect on medical and health insurance, disability income coverage and group term life insurance. The following summarizes the effect of the ruling on each type of coverage, assuming that the Service's position in the ruling can be extended to the other employee fringe benefits not expressly addressed in the ruling.

Medical and Health Insurance

Two important nontax factors must be considered for these types of coverage:

1. it is essential, rather than discretionary, even if structured with higher deductibles and other features designed to limit costs; and

2.   the cost of coverage has escalated greatly in recent years, with a corresponding effect on payroll for all covered employees, in addition to two-percent shareholder-employees.

As discussed above, Section 162(l) provides a limited deduction to a shareholder-employee. Planning in this area may be confined to the structure of coverage from a cost-benefit standpoint, rather than as a matter of tax analysis. The inclusion of the benefit in the two-percent shareholder-employee's income may be a critical factor for incorporated professionals and smaller C corporations that are contemplating an S corporation election.

Disability Income Policies

An S corporation may establish an accident and health plan for the exclusive benefit of its two-percent shareholder-employees (and for other key employees, as well). An accident and health plan may be discriminatory so that benefits are provided only for selected employees, such as senior management and key employees. Coverage may be designed to benefit shareholder-employees, subject to the requirement that the benefits are provided as a function of the employment relationship and not because of shareholder status.[8]

In any event, an S corporation may provide disability income policies for its two-percent shareholder-employees as a benefit within an accident and health plan. Premium payments for disability income policies are considered to be contributions by an employer to an accident and health plan under Section 106. As such, disability income coverage falls within the ambit of benefits covered by Revenue Ruling 91-26.

A shareholder-employee of a C corporation is generally in a position to choose between using the corporation to pay for a disability income premium or to pay the premium from personal funds. If a C corporation pays the premium, it is a deductible expense and not includable as income to the covered employee. However, in the event that the insured employee suffers a disability, the benefit is taxable to the employee, except to the extent of a tax credit for the permanently and totally disabled under Code section 22(a). On the other hand, if the employee pays the premium out of personal funds, no tax benefit is derived when the premium is paid, but the disability benefit can be received tax free under Section 104. In general, the employee covered by a disability income policy can enjoy a tax benefit at the time when the premium is paid or when the benefit is received. Most individuals expect to remain healthy rather than to become disabled, and therefore, opt to enjoy the favorable tax treatment when the premium is paid, rather than when the benefit is received. In the case of an S corporation, the two-percent shareholder-employee does not have the luxury of choice with regard to the timing of the tax benefit. The premium is taxable as compensation in any event. Presumably, the disability income benefit is tax free whether the S corporation pays the premium directly or the individual pays the premium from after-tax income. It may be preferable for the two-percent shareholder-employee to be overly cautious and pay the premium from after-tax income. Such direct payment should eliminate any potential confusion over whether the premium was paid by the employer or the employee and clearly preserves the employee's right to receive a tax-free benefit. (This practice may amount to administrative simplicity, given that the tax-free benefit should be available under either method of payment, as a matter of tax law.)

Group Term Life Insurance

Under Section 79, an employee receiving the benefit of group term life insurance under a policy carried by the employer is able to exclude the cost of the first $50,000 of death benefit from his or her gross income. Additional amounts of protection provided by the employer are subject to taxation at Table I rates, rather than according to the actual premium.[9] These tax benefits are available to "key employees" of a C corporation, provided that the plan is nondiscriminatory.[10]

Following the same pattern of income taxation described in Revenue Ruling 91-26, the two-percent shareholder-employee of an S corporation is taxed on the full amount of the group term life premium paid by the corporation. In effect, the two-percent shareholder-employee is taxed in the same manner as for a personally owned term insurance policy. The premium is included in the insured's income under Section 61 and is deductible to the S corporation under Section 162.

Since the introduction of more stringent nondiscrimination rules under Section 79, an increasing number of group term "carve-out" or replacement plans have been marketed to both larger and smaller corporations. In the C corporation marketplace, many plans have been pared to a uniform level of coverage or a maximum benefit level of $50,000. The employee fringe benefit restrictions have tended to result in lesser amounts of group term coverage purchased by S corporations for two-percent shareholder-employees. In many instances, the two-percent shareholder-employee may use a bonus or dividend distribution to buy a personally owned policy that offers better protection and economy in the long run than group term coverage.

Employee Fringe Benefits Within Cafeteria Plans

An S corporation may establish a cafeteria plan for the benefit of its employees, pursuant to the terms of Section 125. A "cafeteria plan" is a written plan under which all participants are employees and the participants may choose among two or more benefits consisting of cash and "qualified benefits."[11]

Cafeteria plans are referred to within the discussion of the two-percent shareholder rules because certain benefits permitted under cafeteria plans, such as group term coverage under Section 79 or disability income premiums paid by an employer (excluded under Section 106), for example, may be provided within a cafeteria plan.

For purposes of participating in a cafeteria plan, a two-percent shareholder-employee should be classified as an employee as a threshold question of inclusion.[12] However, the income tax treatment afforded a cafeteria plan participant is determined by separate reference to the requirements of the Code section governing a particular benefit. Assume, for example, that a shareholder-employee of a C corporation receives group term life insurance coverage provided under a nondiscriminatory Section 79 plan. The employee would be entitled to the tax benefits permitted under Section 79: the first $50,000 of coverage is nontaxable and premiums for additional coverage are taxed at Table I rates. If the shareholder-employee owns more than two percent of the stock of an S corporation, he will be taxed on the full premium because of Section 1372. In general, and for cafeteria plan purposes in particular, the shareholder-employee is treated as an employee, assuming that employee status is otherwise warranted. Nonetheless, the shareholder-employee is treated as a partner with respect to the Section 79 benefit, without regard to whether it is furnished inside or outside of a cafeteria plan. A two-percent shareholder-employee should not be permitted to "bootstrap" himself out of the reach of Section 1372 because an employee fringe benefit is furnished within a cafeteria plan.

Split Dollar Plans

Revenue Ruling 91-26 did not directly address split dollar plans. It has been cited in a private letter ruling that addresses the tax treatment of split dollar plans established for the benefit of S corporation shareholder-employees.

In Letter Ruling 9248019, "X," an S corporation, informed the Service that it intended to establish a split dollar plan for the benefit of certain key employees and their spouses. The terms of the plan provided that premiums for the life insurance policies on the participants would be paid on a contributory basis. This meant that X would pay the entire premium, minus the term insurance cost of the death benefit for the employees' personal beneficiaries.

The corporation requested a ruling by the Service that its proposed split dollar plan would not create more than one class of stock within the meaning of Code section 1361(b)(1)(D). In submitting its ruling request, the corporation specified that the purpose of the split dollar arrangement was to provide a fringe benefit for its employees, and that it was "...not a vehicle to circumvent the one class of stock requirement."

The Service agreed that the corporation's payment of premiums under the split dollar plan would be a fringe benefit for its employees and not a vehicle for the circumvention of the one class of stock requirement. In support of its conclusion, the Service cited Revenue Ruling 91-26 and indicated that the payments of accident and health insurance premiums on behalf of two-percent shareholder-employees were not distributions for purposes of the single class of stock requirement.

Otherwise, Letter Ruling 9248019 did not elaborate on a number of issues that might have been more fully addressed. This includes the fact that Revenue Ruling 91-26 dealt expressly with shareholder-employees and Letter Ruling 9248019 referred to life insurance coverage provided for key employees and their spouses. Furthermore, while Revenue Ruling 91-26 was cited with approval, no mention was made of whether split dollar plans or other types of fringe benefits are otherwise subject to Revenue Ruling 91-26.

OTHER BENEFIT AND COMPENSATION PLANNING ISSUES

It has often been said that a closely held corporation functions as the financial alter ego of its owners; the corporation is the source of an owner's wealth and income. Naturally, it is also the source of the additional benefits that are generally provided to executives of larger corporations and to shareholder-employees of smaller corporations. As the first section of this chapter indicates, Congress has seen fit to limit the tax benefits available to two-percent shareholder-employees of S corporations who receive certain employee fringe benefits. Other types of life insurance related benefits such as "bonus plans" (see Chapter 2) and split dollar plans (see Chapter 4) are not subject to the two-percent shareholder rule of Section 1372.

In addition to employee fringe benefits covered under Section 1372, S corporation shareholder-employees are interested in accumulating funds for retirement, as well as providing competitive benefit programs for employees. The balance of this chapter describes how both qualified and nonqualified retirement plans, incentive compensation plans and other programs fit into the overall compensation planning of S corporation shareholder-employees.

QUALIFIED PENSION AND PROFIT SHARING PLANS

The owner of an S corporation is apt to have the business sponsor a qualified pension and/or profit-sharing plan, including a Section 401(k) plan, for many of the same reasons that would apply if it were a C corporation. The advantages of tax deductible contributions and tax deferred earnings are attractive to both S and C corporations. The need to provide retirement benefits to both key employees and rank-and-file employees is a fact of economic life in many industries. At the same time, the nondiscrimination rules that govern all major aspects of qualified plans have made them increasingly complicated and expensive for businesses to maintain. While qualified plans are likely to be subject to continuing amendment and tinkering by Congress and the IRS, it appears that they are here to stay and most S corporations will continue to sponsor some form of qualified pension or profit-sharing plan. Volumes can be and have been written on particular aspects of qualified plans. The treatment of qualified retirement plans in this chapter will be confined to those subjects that are particularly relevant to the S corporation owner or key employee. In general, the Tax Equity and Fiscal Responsibility Act of

1982 (TEFRA) put qualified plans for corporations and unincorporated businesses on an equal footing, subject to certain exceptions, such as the prohibition against plan loans to an owner-employee. For the most part, since 1984, a shareholder-employee of an S corporation has been able to participate in a qualified pension or profit sharing plan on the same basis as his counterpart in a C corporation. One difference worth noting is a restriction on plan loans similar to that applicable to owner-employees of unincorporated businesses. An employee who owns five percent or more of the outstanding shares of an S corporation (a "five-percent owner") is not permitted to borrow from a qualified pension or profit sharing plan of the corporation. A loan by a qualified plan to a five-percent owner is a prohibited transaction.[13]

A shareholder-employee of an S corporation must take into account many of the same additional restrictions applicable to C corporation shareholder-employees. Specifically, the possible application of the top-heavy rules under Section 416; the penalty tax applicable to the receipt of benefits provided for a "five-percent owner" in excess of the plan formula;[14] and the limit on compensation that may be taken into account for purposes of the nondiscrimination rules,[15] among other items, may further limit the benefits available to shareholder-employees and highly compensated employees of S corporations.

An exhaustive analysis of the provisions of the Code, cases, rulings or other IRS pronouncements that affect shareholder-employees or key employees participating in qualified plans sponsored by S corporations, is beyond the scope of this chapter. The trend of recent legislation and administrative actions has tended to impose additional restrictions or qualifications on shareholder-employees and key personnel who partici-pate in qualified plans sponsored by either C or S corporations. In many instances, particular definitions, such as "compensation," for example, must be interpreted within the context of a specific test pertaining to the features of a plan. For instance, Section 414(q) provides a definition of a "highly compensated employee."[16] That definition (as amended in 1996) refers to "compensation," which Section 414(q)(4) specifically defines as follows:

(7) COMPENSATION. — For purposes of this subsection —

(A) IN GENERAL. — The term "compensation" means compensation within the meaning of section 415(c)(3).[17]

However, Section 414, which provides "Definitions and Special Rules" generally applicable within the qualified plan area, also specifically defines "compensation" beyond its meaning within the context of defining a "highly compensated employee." Section 414(s), as amended in 1996, states:

(s) COMPENSATION. — For purposes of any applicable provision —

(1) IN GENERAL. — Except as provided in this subsection, the term "compensation" has the meaning given such term by section 415(c)(3).

(2) EMPLOYER MAY ELECT *NOT* TO TREAT CERTAIN DEFERRALS AS COMPENSATION. — An employer may elect *not* to include as compensation any amount which is contributed by the employer pursuant to a salary reduction agreement and which is not includable in the gross income of an employee under section 125, 402(e)(3), 402(h), or 403(b).[18]

(3) ALTERNATIVE DETERMINATION OF COMPENSATION. — The Secretary shall by regulation provide for alternative methods of determining compensation which may be used by an employer, except that such regulations shall provide that an employer may not use an alternative method if the use of such method discriminates in favor of highly compensated employees (within the meaning of subsection (q)).

(4) APPLICABLE PROVISION. — For purposes of this subsection, the term "applicable provision" means any provision which specifically refers to this subsection.

Thus, both definitions refer to Section 415(c)(3), but vary beyond that reference as to whether other forms of compensation, such as elective deferrals, can be included in an overall definition. The final regulations published under Section 414(s) indicate that its definition of compensation is generally applicable for purposes of applying the rules contained in Sections 401 through 419A. At the same time, it does not apply to sections that specifically define compensation in a different manner. In addition to the compensation definition related to a "highly compensated employee," the Section 414(s) definition of compensation does not apply to the limitations on contributions and benefits under Section 415, nor to the limitation on the deduction of contributions under Sections 404(a) and (b).[19]

In the case of a shareholder-employee of an S corporation, the importance of defining compensation lies in whether dividends received as a shareholder should be considered for various purposes of measuring compensation within the qualified plan area. In other words, is the compensation of an S corporation shareholder-employee confined to some measure of compensation for services rendered or is it expanded to a broader definition? It is worth noting that, as mentioned above in this chapter, the S corporation shareholder-employee may be classified differently than his C corporation counterpart and may be regarded as a self-employed individual, a partner, or may be subject to a particular rule, for purposes of particular benefit planning situations.

It seems clear that "compensation" to an S corporation shareholder-employee should not include dividends received as a shareholder within any of the qualified plan definitions of compensation. To begin with, final regulations published pursuant to Section 414(s) indicate that compensation generally means compensation received by an employee from an employer.[20] The regulations also permit more specific alternative definitions of compensation to be utilized. Apart from the reference to compensation received by an employee, the regulations deal with the meaning of compensation in regard to a self-employed individual. For purposes of self-employed individuals, compensation is defined as "earned income," as provided in Section 401(c)(1). Furthermore, both the general definition under Section 414(s) and the definition for purposes of a highly compensated employee refer to Section 415(c)(3), which reinforces the distinction between compensation received from an employer and earned income of self-employed individuals, as follows:

(3) PARTICIPANT'S COMPENSATION. — For purposes of paragraph (1) —

(A) IN GENERAL. — The term "participant's compensation" means the compensation of the participant from the employer for the year.

(B) SPECIAL RULE FOR SELF-EMPLOYED INDIVIDU- ALS. — In the case of an employee within the meaning of section 401(c)(1), subparagraph (A) shall be applied by substituting "the participant's earned income (within the meaning of section 401(c)(2) but determined without regard to any exclusion under section 911)" for "compensation of the participant from the employer."

* * * * * *

(D) CERTAIN DEFERRALS INCLUDED. — The term "participant's compensation" shall include —

(i) any elective deferral (as defined in section 402(g)(3)), and

(ii) any amount which is contributed or deferred by the employer at the election of the employee and which is not includible in the gross income of the employee by reason of section 125 or 457.

[Subparagraph (D) above is effective for tax years beginning after 1997.]

Alternative definitions of compensation under Section 414(s) regulations also refer to compensation as defined under the Section 415 regulations, which distinguish between "wages, salaries, fees ... and other amounts received for personal services..." and "earned income" under Section 401(c)(2) and its regulations.[21] Another of the alternative definitions of compensation refers to "...wages within the meaning of section 3401(a) ... for which the employer is required to furnish the employee a written statement under sections 6041(d) and 6051(a)(3)" that is, those amounts required to be reported as wages on an employee's form W-2 for income tax purposes.[22]

It should also be noted that the Section 404 limits on the deductibility of contributions by an employer to a qualified plan follow the same line of distinction between compensation paid to employees and self-employed individuals.[23]

COMMENT. Shareholder-employees of S corporations are often able to decide how much money they can receive from the corporation's income in addition to their salaries. For example, suppose that Sam, an S corporation shareholder-employee, receives an annual salary of $100,000. At the end of the year, the corporation may pay a bonus to Sam or may allow its income to be distributed as a dividend to him. If Sam were the shareholder of a C corporation, a dividend would probably not be acceptable and no issue would be presented. However, as the shareholder of an S corporation, Sam may need to consider whether a bonus or a dividend would be desirable. For instance, if an additional bonus of $50,000 could be paid to Sam, an additional $7,500 could be contributed to a defined contribution plan, based upon a contribution level of 15% of compensation. If maximizing qualified plan benefits is Sam's chief concern, he will opt to receive the additional payment as a bonus. In that case, he winds up in the same position as if he were a C corporation shareholder.

However, other factors could be at work in Sam's case. He might be a co-shareholder in a situation in which the other owners expect to receive a distribution of the corporation's earnings. The resolution of how the payment will be made — as compensation or dividend — can vary according to whether:

1.   the shareholder owns a majority or minority interest;

2.   other shareholders are also employed and also receive compensation (and participate in the corporation's qualified plan);

3.   the level of compensation paid to other employees is considered adequate when compared to levels of compensation in a particular industry;

4.   it is preferable to reinvest earnings in excess of a payment sufficient to cover a "tax dividend" to the shareholder;

5.   relationships with banks or other financial institutions might be influenced by a pattern of bonuses or dividends to shareholders; and

6.   other factors.

NONQUALIFIED DEFERRED COMPENSATION PLANNING

In recent years, nonqualified deferred compensation plans have been established by a wide range of C corporations. Part of the impetus for increased interest in nonqualified plans was triggered by the limits imposed on contributions and benefits available from *qualified* pension plans following the enactment of the Tax Equity and Fiscal Responsibility Act of 1982 (TEFRA). Succeeding legislation and various rulings and administrative actions by the IRS have added other restrictions and also made qualified plans more complicated and expensive to administer. The Tax Reform Act of 1986 (TRA '86), for example, suspended further increases in annual contributions and additions permitted under defined contribution plans until benefits under defined benefit plans are increased to a certain level. That particular provision was intended to promote the use of defined benefit plans, rather than defined contribution plans. However, the IRS has whipsawed defined benefit plans by taking a more aggressive position in regard to the funding assumptions permitted for such plans. In addition, tightened nondiscrimination rules in the qualified plan area have had the effect of promoting nonqualified plans, which virtually require that only management and highly compensated personnel be included. Finally, beyond a realization that qualified plans may not provide a sufficient retirement income, broader forces and trends have converged in the process:

1.   more people are retiring at an early age with a greater life expectancy,

2.   Social Security has been perceived as a limited and possibly uncertain income supplement, and

3.   the rate of personal savings in the United States is substantially less than that in many other developed nations.

However, the interest in nonqualified plans as a means of enhancing retirement income was somewhat tempered by the TRA '86 reduction in individual income tax rates. Those rate reductions prompted the thought that future tax rates could only be higher. The increases in individual income tax rates that followed in 1990 and 1993 reinforced the expectation that rates would be raised. Going forward, who can offer solid assurance that rates will decrease in the future? It is safe to say only that the direction of future individual income tax rates will continue to be the product of political crosswinds to raise revenue by increasing rates and to generate votes by cutting rates. A decision to defer additional income is more apt to be motivated by a desire to accumulate investment assets systematically than to project future tax savings. In weighing the merits of receiving current income or deferring income until a future date, an individual employee also takes considerations of financial security into account.

A deferral of the employee's money can be contrasted with an employer contribution to a supplemental income plan which does not affect the employee's current compensation. Supplemental plans have continued to thrive primarily because they allow an efficient and painless accumulation of funds to pay a future stream of income that is seen as an additional benefit.

The flip side of the tax planning coin in the area of nonqualified plans is the employer's perspective. Just as the employee defers income, the employer defers a deduction for future compensation payments. Funds set aside for the future payment of the obligation are nondeductible to the sponsoring corporation. Earnings from funds set aside are also taxable unless nontaxable or tax-deferred investments, such as life insurance or tax-exempt bonds, are utilized. In many situations, the nonqualified plan serves as a management retention tool and the corporation absorbs its expense as a cost of keeping qualified personnel.

Nonqualified Deferred Compensation Plans in S Corporations

When the prospect of a nonqualified deferred compensation plan is raised for an S corporation, the standard view is that a nonqualified plan is unworkable. In many cases, that conclusion may be justified, but a few distinctions should be made in order to illustrate when and how a nonqualified plan fits and does not fit in an S corporation.

First, a distinction should be made between the employee's receipt of benefits and informal funding measures adopted to support the S corporation's future obligation to pay income. Whether or not current income is actually reduced (as in a "true deferral" plan), the promise of future benefits by the employer generally involves a deferral of current income by the employee. In order to avoid current income taxation, the employee must neither be in *constructive receipt* of income nor can the employee receive an *economic benefit* from the plan. The doctrine of constructive receipt should not apply as long as the employee's rights under the plan are forfeitable. However, the IRS has ruled that, even if the employee's rights are nonforfeitable, no constructive receipt of income should result *if*:

1.   the deferred compensation agreement between employer and employee is entered into before compensation is earned, and

2.   the employer's promise to pay is not secured in any way.[24]

In order for the employer's promise to be unsecured, the agreement cannot be formally funded, that is, funds cannot be segregated for the benefit of the employee and protected from the employer's general creditors. While the agreement must be unfunded, it is permissible for the employer to adopt informal funding measures. An informal funding measure involves an investment of funds by the employer to meet its future obligation under the plan without conferring any rights in the investment upon the employee. Corporate owned life insurance policies are frequently purchased by C corporations under an informal funding program.

However, not all plans feature informal funding measures. It is possible for a plan to be established without any informal funding and benefits will be provided on a "pay as you go" basis. In such a case, the employee is wholly dependent upon the employer's ability to maintain assets or generate income sufficient to sustain the promised future benefits. It should be recognized that an S corporation is capable of providing a "pay as you go" plan that will enable either a shareholder-employee or a nonowner employee to defer income. That distinction is worth noting because it calls attention to the fact that the limited appeal of nonqualified plans in the S corporation marketplace is associated as much with financial measures as with income tax treatment. Nonetheless, it is common for an employer to adopt some measure of informal funding. Certainly, from the life underwriter's standpoint, there is little to discuss with a corporate prospect or client if no informal funding will be adopted.

Costs and Benefits: Shareholder v. Employee

In the C corporation marketplace, the sponsoring corporation absorbs the cost of informal funding for a nonqualified deferred compensation plan. In contrast, the shareholders of an S corporation bear the expense of an investment by the corporation out of the income taxable to them. Thus, a C corporation can set aside funds for its sole shareholder-employee and the employee can defer income because the corporation constitutes a separate taxable entity.[25] In the same situation, funds set aside out of the taxable income of the S corporation would be deferred from income for services rendered as an employee, but taxable nevertheless to the shareholder *as a shareholder*. In other words, the investment of funds for the future benefit of an employee is chargeable to the shareholders if made out of the S corporation's taxable income. The direct charge to the S corporation shareholder is the flip side of the passthrough system of taxation. No separate taxable entity is available to bear the cost of informal funding measures. The shareholder is left in a position of supporting the cost of the plan. However, when some of the other limitations of an S corporation are considered, the possibility of a nonqualified plan of deferred compensation should not be automatically ruled out. A minority shareholder owning a small percentage of stock, say 5 or 10 percent, is subject to the two-percent shareholder limitation in regard to the employee fringe benefits discussed earlier in this chapter. Amounts invested out of taxable income to support informal funding for a deferred compensation plan on the minority shareholder's behalf are effectively subsidized by the other shareholders (and a corresponding portion of the cost is assumed by the minority interest holder).

In certain circumstances, a nonqualified plan may be established for a minority shareholder-employee or a nonowner key employee. Beyond the usual reservations that inhibit stock transfers of a few shares to C corporation employees, the potential perils of equity transfers within an S corporation must be taken into account. First, but not foremost, the 75 shareholder limit must not be exceeded in order to maintain the S corporation election. More importantly, the prospect that a shareholder might make a spiteful or negligent transfer of shares to an ineligible shareholder also presents a risk (albeit a risk that can be generally avoided through a shareholders' agreement). Balancing the proper mix of employee and shareholder compensation can also become complicated when several shareholders are involved. It should be remembered that, even if nonvoting shares are utilized, such shares are fully entitled to dividend income to the same extent as voting shares. Depending upon the nature of the business, the outlook of its owners and the "chemistry" of their relationships, the owners of an S corporation may be reluctant to enable key employees to acquire access to corporate information by virtue of a small percentage ownership of stock. Again, the same reasons for caution in transferring equity interests that pertain to the C corporation environment are fully at work in the S corporation setting.

Thus, a nonqualified plan of deferred compensation may be a feasible method of offering incentive compensation to S corporation employees. The fact that the expense is directly borne by the shareholders demands that participants be selected and benefits be designed appropriately in regard to the corporation's financial resources. As in many other S corporation planning situations, the expense charged to the corporation is directly experienced by the shareholders. Nonetheless, if the expense is perceived as a sensible alternative to the transfer of an equity interest, the cost of a shareholder subsidy may be acceptable, and even desirable, as a method of retaining key personnel without diluting ownership.

On the other hand, if the owners of an S corporation are so inclined, a nonqualified plan can be designed as an incentive compensation plan that will permit transfers of equity interests to be made at a future date. A "phantom stock" or "shadow stock" plan may be established for key employees of an S corporation. These types of plans can provide a financial incentive for employees with the economic reward tied to the performance of the corporation. At the same time, the employees need not invest nor must they bear the risk of loss. The phantom stock plan is often designed to grant employees "units" that reflect the financial experience of the corporation. As certain financial targets are met in regard to the asset values or earnings of the corporation, the employees are credited with units that are convertible into shares of stock.

The IRS has ruled that such units granted under a phantom stock plan are not considered to be stock for purposes of determining whether a second class of stock exists in regard to the one class of stock requirement under Section 1361(b)(1).[26] In other rulings, an S corporation's nonqualified deferred compensation plan permitted employees to elect to defer amounts, rather than receive a current bonus. The deferred amounts would be converted into performance units credited to the employees' accounts under the plan. The Service has ruled that the units do not constitute a second class of stock.[27]

The final regulations under Section 1361 pertaining to the one class of stock requirement also address various aspects of fringe benefit and compensation planning. In general, the positions adopted by the Service in the regulations are directed to whether a principal purpose of a given arrangement is to circumvent the one class of stock requirement. For instance, the regulations provide the following example.[28]

EXAMPLE 4. *Agreement to pay fringe benefits.* (i) S, a corporation, is required under binding agreements to pay accident and health insurance premiums on behalf of certain of its employees who are also shareholders. Different premium amounts are paid by S for each employee-shareholder. The facts and circumstances do not reflect that a principal purpose of the agreements is to circumvent the one class of stock requirement of section 1361(b)(1)(D) and this paragraph (l).

(ii) Under paragraph (l)(2)(i) of this section, the agreements are not governing provisions. Accordingly, S is not treated as having more than one class of stock by reason of the agreements. In addition, S is not treated as having more than one class of stock by reason of the payment of fringe benefits.

The regulations under Section 1361 also state that deferred compensation plans do not constitute a second class of stock if certain conditions are satisfied. Specifically, an instrument, obligation or arrangement is not outstanding stock if it:

1.   Does not convey the right to vote;

2.   Is an unfunded and unsecured promise to pay money or property in the future;

3.   Is issued to an individual who is an employee in connection with the performance of services for the corporation or to an

individual who is an independent contractor in connection with the performance of services for the corporation (and is not excessive by reference to the services performed); and

4.   Is issued pursuant to a plan with respect to which the employee or independent contractor is not taxed currently on income.[29]

Furthermore, an S corporation cannot utilize an Employee Stock Ownership Plan (ESOP) to transfer stock to employees. The requirements of Section 1361(b)(1) pertaining to eligible shareholders prevent the possibility that S corporation stock may be owned by an ESOP.

The time span over which a deferred compensation plan may be informally funded, and then discharged through the payment of retirement benefits, should also be carefully considered. For example, beyond the other factors mentioned above, the business continuation plan of an S or a C corporation is inevitably related to the terms of a nonqualified plan. Specifically, when the employee's benefit is unsecured, he or she must feel confident that the corporation will be able to support a future stream of income payments that may be made over an extended period in the future. Naturally, a business which does not have the prospect of continuing as an entity after the death of current owners would not be a likely candidate for a nonqualified plan, apart from the income tax and benefit planning aspects.

In any event, our focus in this chapter is on the unfunded plan. If, contrary to the sentiment often expressed, an S corporation may entertain the prospect of a nonqualified plan, how are life insurance policies used as an informal funding mechanism?

Life Insurance as Informal Funding

A corporate owned life insurance policy may be used as informal funding for the nonqualified deferred compensation plan of an S corporation in generally the same manner as for a C corporation. The income tax consequences of corporate policy ownership to the shareholders follow the pattern described in Chapter 3 with regard to the payment of premiums, effect upon a shareholder's stock basis and the receipt of proceeds.

Prior to TRA '86, many C corporations utilized "financed" life insurance as an informal funding device to meet obligations expected under nonqualified plans. Premiums were paid for four of the first seven policy years and a minimum deposit format assumed thereafter in which loans against the policy cash value were incurred to pay premiums and tax deductible interest. Since that time, the reduction in corporate tax rates and changes in the rules governing the tax deductibility of interest expense have dampened enthusiasm for the use of highly-leveraged life insurance policies. In the same time span, many C corporations that had purchased such leveraged policies have elected to become S corporations.

It is worth noting that interest expense payments made for loans incurred against business owned policies purchased prior to June 21, 1986, remain income tax deductible, provided that the policy was tax qualified under the four-out-of-seven annual premiums test (or one of the other exceptions permitted under Section 264(c)). Policies purchased by a business after June 20, 1986, are subject to the limitation contained in Section 264(a)(4), which states that no deduction shall be allowed for:

> (4) Except as provided in subsection (d), any interest paid or accrued on any indebtedness with respect to 1 or more life insurance policies owned by the taxpayer covering the life of any individual or any endowment or annuity contracts owned by the taxpayer covering any individual, who —

> (A) is an officer or employee of, or

> (B) is financially interested in,

any trade or business carried on by the taxpayer.

Subsection (d) provides that this rule does not apply to interest paid on policies covering "...a key person to the extent that the aggregate amount of such indebtedness ... does not exceed $50,000."

If the taxpayer described in the quoted provision is a C corporation, the interest is deductible by the corporation, and the $50,000 loan limitation applies unless the policy is "grandfathered" because it was purchased prior to June 21, 1986. If an S corporation owns the policy, interest should be deductible in the same manner. The character of interest expense incurred by an S corporation is determined at the corporate level. Unlike investment interest expense, for example, which is a separately stated item and which must be carried over to the shareholder's individual tax return for separate qualification as a deductible item, interest expense from policy loans should be treated as a nonseparately stated item. Therefore, it should be deductible within the $50,000 loan limitation, unless it is "grandfathered" because purchased prior to June 21, 1986. (If purchased by a C corporation prior to June 21, 1986, grandfathered treatment should still apply even if the S corporation election was made subsequent to June 20, 1986; the S election does not affect the date when the policy was purchased.)

Apart from the tax planning consequences of financed policies, the use of life insurance as an informal funding device for deferred compensation plans operates generally according to the same principles as for C corporations. Again, the nondeductible premium expense is charged to the shareholders directly, rather than to the corporate entity. Other areas of plan design for S corporations are likely to be similar to plans put into effect for C corporations of comparable size and participation by management. The use of the following techniques that are familiar to the C corporation environment are apt to be employed by S corporations when corporate owned policies are purchased to provide informal funding:

1.   vanishing premium arrangements;

2.   cost recovery techniques, based upon the receipt of death proceeds to offset the cost (although this may be limited by the number of participants for an S corporation);

3.   post-retirement borrowing, withdrawals or surrenders of cash value; and

4.   the use of actuarial assumptions and projections to determine a target benefit or overall cost for a group of participants over an extended period of time.

Death proceeds received by an S corporation are not threatened by the potential application of the corporate alternative minimum tax, which is often a consideration for small to medium sized C corporations.

Upon the death of the participant, the S corporation receives the insurance proceeds income tax free under Section 101(a). The receipt of proceeds has the effect on the stock basis of the shareholders described in Chapter 3 in the discussion of corporate owned insurance. In addition, just as with a C corporation, the payments by the S corporation of deferred compensation to the beneficiaries of a deceased participant are deductible for income tax purposes. Thus, during the years when benefits are paid to the participant's beneficiaries, the corporate income otherwise taxable to the shareholders is reduced by the deductible compensation payments. Thus, the deferred compensation plan also works as a "deferred deduction" plan. In addition to taking differences in stock ownership into account, age differences among shareholders and plan participants should be considered to assess fairly how the costs and benefits of informal funding and subsequent payout might be allocated.

COMPENSATION OR DIVIDEND: CHARACTERIZATION AND ALLOCATION

Issues

In the course of estate or business continuation planning, the shareholder of an S corporation may transfer shares to one or more family members. The allocation of shares may be directly related to participation in the business or it may reflect a division of ownership that is independent of operating responsibility. All shares, whether voting or nonvoting, are equally entitled to receive dividends or other distributions from the S corporation.

The allocation or characterization of income received by related parties from an S corporation should accurately reflect whether they are actively employed, passive investors or some blend of each role (e.g., investors who receive consulting income). In planning S corporation compensation, benefits and distributions, the following planning implications should be recognized.

1. In a closely held C corporation, the usual compensation planning strategy is to avoid having dividends paid to shareholders. Amounts in excess of salary and benefits that are available to be paid to a shareholder-employee are most likely to be paid as a bonus. Avoiding the payment of a dividend is directly related to the fact that dividends are nondeductible to

the corporation and paid from the corporation's taxable income. The shareholder-employee of an S corporation is taxed at the same federal income tax rate whether a payment is deemed to be compensation or a dividend. On the other hand, a shareholder-employee of an S corporation may prefer to receive a dividend, rather than compensation, if his or her salary is less than the FICA tax wage base ($62,700 in 1996). Income for services, as compared to shareholder income, should reflect the value of services performed in order to avoid IRS challenge.

2.   As discussed in this chapter, amounts paid to shareholder-employees as compensation have a direct bearing on the design of various employee benefit programs and the benefits made available under them.

3.   Section 1366(e) provides a weapon to the IRS to ensure that shareholders receive reasonable compensation. It states:

> (e) TREATMENT OF FAMILY GROUP. — If an individual who is a member of the family (within the meaning of section 704(e)(3)) of one or more shareholders of an S corporation renders services for the corporation or furnishes capital to the corporation without receiving reasonable compensation therefor, the Secretary shall make such adjustments in the items taken into account by such individual and such shareholders as may be necessary in order to reflect the value of such services or capital.

4.   Considerations related to the single class of stock requirement pervade many aspects of S corporation shareholder distributions and employee compensation. However, the final regulations under Section 1361 make it clear that excessive compensation paid to a shareholder-employee, even if nondeductible, does not cause an employment agreement to create a second class of stock. That conclusion is warranted, provided that the facts and circumstances do not indicate that a principal purpose of the employment agreement is to circumvent the one class of stock requirement.[30]

5. In addition to the income tax implications of amounts paid as compensation or shareholder income, it is important for the S corporation adviser to be mindful of the division of labor and respective investment of each shareholder, when the S corporation is owned by more than one person. The shareholders' expectations in regard to the profits and distributions to be received from the corporation must be balanced against their own cash compensation and benefits, within the overall compensation and benefits funded by the corporation's income. A fundamental fact of S corporation life that has been expressed throughout this book is that shareholders are taxed on S corporation income, whether or not it is distributed to them. An S corporation may have an ongoing policy, or an occasional need, for profits to be reinvested in its business operation. In such a case, it is preferable to have a distribution made to the shareholders that will be sufficient to cover the tax liability attributable to their portion of shareholder income, that is, the so-called tax dividend.

However, tax dividend payments are possible only when the S corporation has sufficient cash for distribution. In addition, an expectation that profits will be reinvested should be clearly communicated to minority shareholders in order to avoid frustration and misunderstanding. Any program designed to share ownership with employees should offer an incentive that will yield better job performance. If distributions will be limited and the value of ownership, in the eyes of the controlling shareholders, is the prospect of a long-term buyout or other distant "payday," that view should be made clear to those who acquire a relatively small ownership interest. It is more likely than not that those employees receiving a few shares will perceive it as payment in lieu of compensation. If a transfer of shares does not provide an incentive over time because a lack of distributions curb an employee's interest in his or her "investment," the payment of bonuses or benefits to recognize performance may be a better solution for the S corporation, its owners and its employees.

FOOTNOTE REFERENCES

1. Congressional Committee Reports to P.L. 97-354, Subchapter S Revision Act of 1982 (SSRA).
2. Congressional Committee Reports to P.L. 97-354, Subchapter S Revision Act of 1982 (SSRA).

3. Rev. Rul. 91-26, 1991-1 CB 184.

4. Revenue Ruling 91-26 specifically deals with accident and health insurance premiums. Thus, for example, it does not address the income tax consequences of group term life insurance provided to a two-percent shareholder-employee under a Section 79 plan. However, in regard to the analysis of the ruling's second issue, the overriding purpose of the discussion is to deal with the meaning of how an S corporation is treated as a partnership and a two-percent shareholder-employee is treated as a partner. The interpretation of those two aspects is critical to the conclusion of the ruling. In the author's opinion, a strong presumption can be made that the analysis in the ruling applies to all of the employee fringe benefits covered by Section 1372, that is, those itemized in the Senate Report accompanying the SSRA. It is difficult to imagine that any of the other benefits not explicitly addressed by the ruling would be accorded a different income tax treatment given the Service's focus on the two premises of "as a partnership" and "as a partner".

5. Section 1 of the Self-Employed Health Insurance Act of 1995, P.L. 104-7; Section 311(b) of the Health Insurance Portability and Accountability Act of 1996..

6. IRS Announcement 92-16, 1992-5 IRB 53.

7. In Revenue Ruling 91-26, the Service stated that "For S corporation tax years beginning before January 1, 1991, the Service will not challenge the treatment of accident and health insurance premiums paid by S corporations for two-percent shareholder-employees in accordance with the instructions to the Form 1120S and Schedule K-1 to the Form 1120S. These instructions provide that such fringe benefits are nondeductible by the S corporations and cannot be treated as deductible or excludable employee fringe benefits (except for benefits allowed partners, such as section 162(l))."

8. Amounts received under an accident and health plan must be for the benefit of employees. IRC Sec. 105(e). Stockholder-employees must be covered as employees, rather than as stockholders in order for the tax treatment described in Sections 104 and 105 to apply. See *Alan B. Larkin v. Comm.*, 48 TC 629 (1967), aff'd 394 F.2d 494 (1st Cir. 1968); *Samuel Levine v. Comm.*, 50 TC 422 (1968); *Edw. and Mary Smithback v. Comm.*, TC Memo 1969-136; *Est. of John J. Leidy v. Comm.*, 77-1 USTC 86,190 (4th Cir. 1977).

9. IRC Sec. 79(c) and Reg. §1.79-3.

10. Section 79(d)(6) states that "key employee" is defined under Section 416(i)(1).

11. IRC Sec. 125(d)(1)(A) and (B). "Qualified benefits" are defined in Section 125(f).

12. However, Proposed Regulation §1.125-1, A-4 provides that the term "employee" does not include self-employed individuals. While a partner in a partnership is a self-employed individual, it is not clear whether a two-percent shareholder-employee is treated as a partner or an employee under Section 125. In addition, if treated as an employee for cafeteria plan purposes, a shareholder-employee's stock ownership, apart from the shareholder-employee's actual compensation, could possibly be a factor with respect to the discrimination requirements of Section 125, in that Section 125(e)(1)(B) indicates that a shareholder owning more than five-percent of the voting power or value of all classes of stock of the employer is a "highly compensated participant."

13. See the paragraph that follows Section 4975(d)(15). In pertinent part, it states that "... a shareholder-employee (as defined in section 1379, as in effect on the day before the date of the enactment of the Subchapter S Revision Act of 1982) ... shall be deemed to be an owner-employee." Under the definition contained in former Section 1379, therefore, a five-percent shareholder is deemed to be an owner-employee.

14. IRC Sec. 72(m)(5)(A).

15. $150,000 in 1996, scheduled to increase in the future under Code section 401(a)(17)(B).

16. For purposes of determining whether an employee is a "highly compensated employee," it is worth pointing out that employees of both S and C corporations who are "five-percent owners" of stock are automatically considered to be highly compensated employees (without regard to actual compensation). A "five-percent owner" is defined by reference to Section 416(i), which states that it is a person who owns more than five percent of the outstanding stock or total combined voting power of all stock of a corporation, and that the constructive ownership rules of Section 318 are considered in determining ownership. Compensation paid to a family member (as defined in Section 414(q)(6)(B)) of a five-percent owner was previously treated as if it were paid to a five-percent owner; however, this rule has been eliminated for tax years beginning after December 31, 1996.

17. Code section 414(q)(4), as amended by the Small Job Protection Act of 1996, effective for plan years beginning after December 31, 1997. Prior to amendment (and for plan years beginning before January 1, 1998) the definition specified that the determination of compensation should be made:

(i) without regard to sections 125, 402(e)(3), and 402(h)(1)(B), and

(ii) in the case of employer contributions made pursuant to a salary reduction agreement, without regard to section 403(b).

18. The italicized portions of this paragraph were added by the Small Business Job Protection Act of 1996 and are effective for tax years beginning after 1997. For tax years beginning before 1998, this paragraph read as follows:

(2) EMPLOYER MAY ELECT TO TREAT CERTAIN DEFERRALS AS COMPENSATION. — An employer may elect to include as compensation any amount which is contributed by the employer pursuant to a salary reduction agreement and which is not includable in the gross income of an employee under section 125, 402(e)(3), 402(h), or 403(b).

19. Reg. §1.414(s)-1(a).

20. Reg. §1.414(s)-1; Reg. §1.414(s)-2(d).

21. Reg. §1.415-2(d)(2); Reg. §1.414(s)-1.

22. Reg. §1.414(s)-2(d)(11).

23. IRC Sec. 404(a) generally, and IRC Sec. 404(a)(8), in particular.

24. Rev. Rul. 60-31, 1960-1 CB 174; Rev. Rul. 70-435, 1970-2 CB 100. See also *Comm. v. Oates*, 207 F.2d 711 (7th Cir. 1953), acq.; *Comm. v. Olmstead Inc. Life Agency*, 304 F.2d 16 (8th Cir. 1962); *Ray S. Robinson v. Comm.*, 44 TC 20 (1965), acq.; *Howard Veit v. Comm.*, 8 TC 809, acq.

25. While both C and S corporations are legal entities distinct from their shareholders, the Service will not currently rule on the tax consequences of a nonqualified deferred compensation arrangement with respect to a controlling shareholder-employee eligible to participate in the arrangement. Rev. Proc. 93-3, 1993-1 CB 370, 375.

26. See Let. Rul. 8834085; GCM 39750. Units are not considered to be stock under state law and do not carry the right to vote, to receive dividends, to approve or reject the sale of corporate assets or to receive current or liquidating distributions. Also, see the following rulings, all of which reach a positive result pertaining to the one class of stock requirement for a variety of incentive compensation plans: Let. Ruls. 9233005, 9308022, 9317009, 9317021, 9406017, 9406018, 9406019 and 9406020.

27. See, for example, Let. Ruls. 9032027, 9109025, 9119041.

28. Reg. §1.1361(l)(2)(v), Ex. 4.

29. Reg. §1.1361-1(b)(4).

30. Reg. §1.1361-1(l)(2)(v), Ex. 3.

Appendix A

INTERNAL REVENUE CODE SECTIONS PERTAINING TO S CORPORATIONS

[Note: All Internal Revenue Code sections have been revised to reflect the changes made by the Small Business Job Protection Act of 1996, which was signed by President Clinton on August 20, 1996. Unless otherwise indicated, all sections are effective for tax years beginning after December 31, 1996.]

CODE SECTION 1361

S Corporation Defined

(a) S CORPORATION DEFINED.—

(1) IN GENERAL.—For purposes of this title, the term "S corporation" means, with respect to any taxable year, a small business corporation for which an election under section 1362(a) is in effect for such year.

(2) C CORPORATION.—For purposes of this title, the term "C corporation" means, with respect to any taxable year, a corporation which is not an S corporation for such year.

(b) SMALL BUSINESS CORPORATION.—

(1) IN GENERAL.—For purposes of this subchapter, the term "small business corporation" means a domestic corporation which is not an ineligible corporation and which does not—

(A) have more than 75 shareholders,

(B) have as a shareholder a person (other than an estate, a trust described in subsection (c)(2), or an organization described in subsection (c)(7)) who is not an individual,

(C) have a nonresident alien as a shareholder, and

(D) have more than 1 class of stuck.

(2) INELIGIBLE CORPORATION DEFINED.—For purposes of paragraph (1), the term "ineligible corporation" means any corporation which is—

(A) a financial institution which uses the reserve method of accounting for bad debts described in section 585,

(B) an insurance company subject to tax under subchapter L,

(C) a corporation to which an election under section 936 applies, or

(D) a DISC or former DISC.

(3) TREATMENT OF CERTAIN WHOLLY OWNED SUBSID-IARIES.—

(A) IN GENERAL.—For purposes of this title—

(i) a corporation which is a qualified subchapter S subsidiary shall not be treated as a separate corporation, and

(ii) all assets, liabilities, and items of income, deduction, and credit of a qualified subchapter S subsidiary shall be treated as assets, liabilities, and such items (as the case may be) of the S corporation.

(B) QUALIFIED SUBCHAPTER S SUBSIDIARY.—For purposes of this paragraph, the term "qualified subchapter S subsidiary" means any domestic corporation which is not an ineligible corporation (as defined in paragraph(2)), if—

(i) 100 percent of the stock of such corporation is held by the S corporation

(ii) the S corporation elects to treat such corporation as a qualified subchapter S subsidiary.

(C) TREATMENT OF TERMINATIONS OF QUALIFIED SUBCHAPTER S SUBSIDIARY STATUS.—For purposes of this title, if any corporation which was a qualified subchapter S subsidiary ceases to meet the requirements of subparagraph (B), such corporation shall be treated as a new corporation acquiring all of its assets (and assuming all of its liabilities) immediately before such cessation from the S corporation in exchange for its stock.

(D) ELECTION AFTER TERMINATION.—If a corporation's status as a qualified subchapter S subsidiary terminates, such corporation (and any successor corporation) shall not be eligible to make—

(i) an election under subparagraph (B)(ii) to be treated as a qualified subchapter S subsidiary, or

(ii) an election under section 1362(a) to be treated as an S corporation,

before its 5th taxable year which begins after the 1st taxable year for which such termination was effective, unless the Secretary consents to such election.

(c) SPECIAL RULES FOR APPLYING SUBSECTION (b).—

(1) HUSBAND AND WIFE TREATED AS 1 SHAREHOLDER.— For purposes of subsection (b)(1)(A), a husband and wife (and their estates) shall be treated as 1 shareholder.

(2) CERTAIN TRUSTS PERMITTED AS SHAREHOLDERS.—

(A) IN GENERAL.—For purposes of subsection (b)(1)(B), the following trusts may be shareholders:

(i) A trust all of which is treated (under subpart E of part 1 of subchapter J of this chapter) as owned by an individual who is a citizen or resident of the United States.

(ii) A trust which was described in clause (i) immediately before the death of the deemed owner and which continues in existence after such death, but only for the 2-year period beginning on the day of the deemed owner's death.

(iii) A trust with respect to stock transferred to it pursuant to the terms of a will, but only for the 2-year period beginning on the day on which such stock is transferred to it.

(iv) A trust created primarily to exercise the voting power of stock transferred to it.

(v) An electing small business trust

This subparagraph shall not apply to any foreign trust.

(B) TREATMENT AS SHAREHOLDERS.—For purposes of subsection (b)(1)

(i) In the case of a trust described in clause (i) of subparagraph (A), the deemed owner shall be treated as the shareholder.

(ii) In the case of a trust described in clause (ii) of subparagraph (A), the estate of the deemed owner shall be treated as the shareholder.

(iii) In the case of a trust described in clause (iii) of subparagraph (A), the estate of the testator shall be treated as the shareholder.

(iv) In the case of a trust described in clause (iv) of subparagraph (A), each beneficiary of the trust shall be treated as a shareholder.

(v) In the case of a trust described in clause (v) of subparagraph (A), each potential current beneficiary of such trust shall be treated as a shareholder; except that, if for any period there is no potential current beneficiary of such trust, such trust shall be treated as the shareholder during such period.

(3) ESTATE OF INDIVIDUAL IN BANKRUPTCY MAY BE SHAREHOLDER.—For purposes of subsection (b)(1)(B), the term "estate" includes the estate of an individual in a case under title 11 of the United States Code.

(4) DIFFERENCES IN COMMON STOCK VOTING RIGHTS DISREGARDED.—For purposes of subsection (b)(1)(D), a corporation shall not be treated as having more than 1 class of stock solely because there are differences in voting rights among the shares of common stock.

(5) STRAIGHT DEBT SAFE HARBOR.—

(A) IN GENERAL.—For purposes of subsection (b)(1)(D), straight debt shall not be treated as a second class of stock.

(B) STRAIGHT DEBT DEFINED.—For purposes of this paragraph, the term "straight debt" means any written unconditional promise to pay on demand or on a specified date a sum certain in money if—

(i) the interest rate (and interest payment dates) are not contingent on profits, the borrower's discretion, or similar factors,

(ii) there is no convertibility (directly or indirectly) into stock, and

(iii) the creditor is an individual (other than a nonresident alien), an estate, a trust described in paragraph (2), or a person which is actively and regularly engaged in the business of lending money.

(C) REGULATIONS.—The Secretary shall prescribe such regulations as may be necessary or appropriate to provide for the proper treatment of straight debt under this subchapter and for the coordination of such treatment with other provisions of this title.

(6) OWNERSHIP OF STOCK IN CERTAIN INACTIVE CORPORATIONS.—For purposes of subsection (b)(2)(A), a corporation shall not be treated as a member of an affiliated group during any period within a taxable year by reason of the ownership of stock in another corporation if such other corporation—

(A) has not begun business at any time on or before the close of such period, and

(B) does not have gross income for such period.

[Note: Code section 1361(c)(6), above, was deleted by the Small Business Job Protection Act of 1996, effective for tax years beginning after December 31, 1996. The same Act added Code section 1361(c)(7), which is effective for tax years beginning after December 31, 1997.]

(7) CERTAIN EXEMPT ORGANIZATIONS PERMITTED AS SHAREHOLDERS.—for purposes of subsection (b)(1)(B), an organization which is—

(A) described in section 401(a) or 501(c)(3), and

(B) exempt from taxation under section 501(a)

may be a shareholder in an S corporation.

(d) SPECIAL RULE FOR QUALIFIED SUBCHAPTER S TRUST.—

(1) IN GENERAL.—In the case of a qualified subchapter S trust with respect to which a beneficiary makes an election under paragraph (2)—

(A) such trust shall be treated as a trust described in subsection (c)(2)(A)(i), and

(B) for purposes of section 678(a), the beneficiary of such trust shall be treated as the owner of that portion of the trust which consists of stock in an S corporation with respect to which the election under paragraph (2) is made.

(2) ELECTION.—

(A) IN GENERAL.—A beneficiary of a qualified subchapter S trust (or his legal representative) may elect to have this subsection apply.

(B) MANNER AND TIME OF ELECTION.—

(i) SEPARATE ELECTION WITH RESPECT TO EACH CORPORATION.—An election under this paragraph shall be made separately with respect to each corporation the stock of which is held by the trust.

(ii) ELECTIONS WITH RESPECT TO SUCCESSIVE INCOME BENEFICIARIES.—If there is an election under this paragraph with respect to any beneficiary, an election under this paragraph shall be treated as made by each successive beneficiary unless such beneficiary affirmatively refuses to consent to such election.

(iii) TIME, MANNER AND FORM OF ELECTION.— Any election, or refusal, under this paragraph shall be made in such manner and form, and at such time, as the Secretary may prescribe.

(C) ELECTION IRREVOCABLE.—An election under this paragraph, once made, may be revoked only with the consent of the Secretary.

(D) GRACE PERIOD.—An election under this paragraph shall be effective up to 15 days and 2 months before the date of the election.

(3) QUALIFIED SUBCHAPTER S TRUST.—For purposes of this subsection, the term "qualified subchapter S trust" means a trust—

(A) the terms of which require that—

(i) during the life of the current income beneficiary there shall be only 1 income beneficiary of the trust,

(ii) any corpus distributed during the life of the current income beneficiary may be distributed only to such beneficiary,

(iii) the income interest of the current income beneficiary in the trust shall terminate on the earlier of such beneficiary's death or the termination of the trust, and

(iv) upon the termination of the trust during the life of the current income beneficiary, the trust shall distribute all of its assets to such beneficiary, and

(B) all of the income (within the meaning of section 643(b)) of which is distributed (or required to be distributed) currently to 1 individual who is a citizen or resident of the United States.

A substantially separate and independent share of a trust within the meaning of 663(c) shall be treated as a separate trust for purposes of this subsection and subsection (c).

(4) TRUST CEASING TO BE QUALIFIED.—

(A) FAILURE TO MEET REQUIREMENTS OF PARAGRAPH (3)(A).—If a qualified subchapter S trust ceases to meet any requirement of paragraph (3)(A), the provisions of this subsection shall not apply to such trust as of the date it ceases to meet such requirement.

(B) FAILURE TO MEET REQUIREMENTS OF PARAGRAPH (3)(B).—If any qualified subchapter S trust ceases to meet any requirement of paragraph (3)(B) but continues to meet the requirements of paragraph (3)(A), the provisions of this subsection shall not apply to such trust as of the first day of the first taxable year beginning after the first taxable year for which it failed to meet the requirements of paragraph (3)(B).

(e) ELECTING SMALL BUSINESS TRUST DEFINED—

(1) ELECTING SMALL BUSINESS TRUST.—For purposes of this section—

(A) IN GENERAL.—Except as provided in subparagraph (B), the term "electing small business trust" means any trust if—

(i) such trust does not have as a beneficiary any person other than (I) an individual, (II) an estate, or (III) an organization described in paragraph (2), (3), (4), or (5) of section 170(c),

(ii) no interest in such trust was acquired by purchase, and

(iii) an election under this subsection applies to such trust.

(B) CERTAIN TRUSTS NOT ELIGIBLE.—The term "electing small business trust" shall not include—

(i) any qualified subchapter S trust (as defined in subsection (d)(3)) if an election under subsection (d)(2) applies to any corporation the stock of which is held by such trust, and

(ii) any trust exempt from tax under this subtitle.

(C) PURCHASE.—For purposes of subparagraph (A), the term "purchase" means any acquisition if the basis of the property acquired is determined under section 1012.

(2) POTENTIAL CURRENT BENEFICIARY.—For purposes of this section, the term "potential current beneficiary" means, with respect to any period, any person who at any time during such period is entitled to, or at the discretion of any person may receive, a distribution from the principal or income of the trust. If the trust disposes of all of the stock which it holds in an S corporation, then, with respect to such corporation, the term "potential current beneficiary" does not include any person who first met the requirements of the preceding sentence during the 60-day period ending on the date of such disposition.

(3) ELECTION.—An election under this subsection shall be made by the trustee. Any such election shall apply to the taxable year of the trust for which made and all subsequent taxable years of such trust unless revoked with the consent of the Secretary.

(4) CROSS REFERENCE.—For special treatment of electing small business trusts, see section 641(d).

CODE SECTION 1362

Election; Revocation; Termination

(a) ELECTION.—

(1) IN GENERAL.—Except as provided in subsection (g), a small business corporation may elect, in accordance with the provisions of this section, to be an S corporation.

(2) ALL SHAREHOLDERS MUST CONSENT TO ELECTION.—
An election under this subsection shall be valid only if all persons who are
shareholders in such corporation on the day on which such election is
made consent to such election.

(b) WHEN MADE.—

(1) IN GENERAL.—An election under subsection (a) may be made
by a small business corporation for any taxable year—

(A) at any time during the preceding taxable year, or

(B) at any time during the taxable year and on or before the 15th
day of the 3rd month of the taxable year.

(2) CERTAIN ELECTIONS MADE DURING 1ST 2-1/2 MONTHS
TREATED AS MADE FOR NEXT TAXABLE YEAR.—If—

(A) an election under subsection (a) is made for any taxable year
during such year and on or before the 15th day of the 3rd month of such
year, but

(B) either—

(i) on 1 or more days in such taxable year before the day
on which the election was made the corporation did not meet
the requirements of subsection (b) of section 1361, or

(ii) 1 or more of the persons who held stock in the
corporation during such taxable year and before the election
was made did not consent to the election,

then such election shall be treated as made for the following taxable year.

(3) ELECTION MADE AFTER 1ST 2-1/2 MONTHS TREATED
AS MADE FOR FOLLOWING TAXABLE YEAR.—If—

(A) a small business corporation makes an election under subsection (a) for any taxable year, and

(B) such election is made after the 15th day of the 3rd month of the taxable year and on or before the 15th day of the 3rd month of the following taxable year,

then such election shall be treated as made for the following taxable year.

(4) TAXABLE YEARS OF 2-1/2 MONTHS OR LESS.—For purposes of this subsection, an election for a taxable year made not later than 2 months and 15 days after the first day of the taxable year shall be treated as timely made during such year.

(5) AUTHORITY TO TREAT LATE ELECTIONS, ETC., AS TIMELY.—If—

(A) an election under subsection (a) is made for any taxable year (determined without regard to paragraph (3)) after the date prescribed by this subsection for making such election for such taxable year or no such election is made for any taxable year, and

(B) the Secretary determines that there was reasonable cause for the failure to timely make such election,

the Secretary may treat such an election as timely made for such taxable year (and paragraph (3) shall not apply).

(c) YEARS FOR WHICH EFFECTIVE.—An election under subsection (a) shall be effective for the taxable year of the corporation for which it is made and for all succeeding taxable years of the corporation, until such election is terminated under subsection (d).

(d) TERMINATION.—

(1) BY REVOCATION.—

(A) IN GENERAL.—An election under subsection (a) may be terminated by revocation.

(B) MORE THAN ONE-HALF OF SHARES MUST CONSENT TO REVOCATION.—

An election may be revoked only if shareholders holding more than one-half of the shares of stock of the corporation on the day on which the revocation is made consent to the revocation.

(C) WHEN EFFECTIVE.—Except as provided in subparagraph (D)—

(i) a revocation made during the taxable year and on or before the 15th day of the 3rd month thereof shall be effective on the 1st day of such taxable year, and

(ii) a revocation made during the taxable year but after such 15th day shall be effective on the 1st day of the following taxable year.

(D) REVOCATION MAY SPECIFY PROSPECTIVE DATE.— If the revocation specifies a date for revocation which is on or after the day on which the revocation is made, the revocation shall be effective on and after the date so specified.

(2) BY CORPORATION CEASING TO BE SMALL BUSINESS CORPORATION.—

(A) IN GENERAL.—An election under subsection (a) shall be terminated whenever (at any time on or after the 1st day of the 1st taxable year for which the corporation is an S corporation) such corporation ceases to be a small business corporation.

(B) WHEN EFFECTIVE.—Any termination under this paragraph shall be effective on and after the date of cessation.

(3) WHERE PASSIVE INVESTMENT INCOME EXCEEDS 25 PERCENT OF GROSS RECEIPTS FOR 3 CONSECUTIVE TAXABLE YEARS AND CORPORATION HAS SUBCHAPTER C EARNINGS AND PROFITS.—

(A) TERMINATION—

(i) IN GENERAL.—An election under subsection (a) shall be terminated whenever the corporation—

(I) has accumulated earnings and profits at the close of each of 3 consecutive taxable years, and

(II) has gross receipts for each of such taxable years more than 25 percent of which are passive investment income.

(ii) WHEN EFFECTIVE.—Any termination under this paragraph shall be effective on and after the first day of the first taxable year beginning after the third consecutive taxable year referred to in clause (i).

(iii) YEARS TAKEN INTO ACCOUNT.—A prior taxable year shall not be taken into account under clause (i) unless—

(I) such taxable year began after December 31, 1981, and

(II) the corporation was an S corporation for such taxable year.

(B) GROSS RECEIPTS FROM SALES OF CAPITAL ASSETS (OTHER THAN STOCK AND SECURITIES).—For purposes of this paragraph, in the case of dispositions of capital assets (other than stock and securities), gross receipts from such dispositions shall be taken into account only to the extent of the capital gain net income therefrom.

(C) PASSIVE INVESTMENT INCOME DEFINED.—For purposes of this paragraph—

(i) IN GENERAL.—Except as otherwise provided in this subparagraph, the term "passive investment income" means gross receipts derived from royalties, rents, dividends, interest, annuities, and sales or exchanges of stock or securities (gross receipts from such sales or exchanges being taken into account for purposes of this paragraph only to the extent of gains therefrom).

(ii) EXCEPTION FOR INTEREST ON NOTES FROM SALES OF INVENTORY.—The term "passive investment income" shall not include interest on any obligation acquired in the ordinary course of the corporation's trade or business from its sale of property described in section 1221(1).

(iii) TREATMENT OF CERTAIN LENDING OR FINANCE COMPANIES.—If the S corporation meets the requirements of section 542(c)(6) for the taxable year, the term "passive investment income" shall not include gross receipts for the taxable year which are derived directly from the active and regular conduct of a lending or finance business (as defined in section 542(d)(1)).

(iv) TREATMENT OF CERTAIN LIQUIDA-TIONS.—Gross receipts derived from sales or exchanges of stock or securities shall not include amounts received by an S corporation which are treated under section 331 (relating to corporate liquidations) as payments in exchange for stock where the S corporation owned more than 50 percent of each class of stock of the liquidating corporation.

(D) SPECIAL RULE FOR OPTIONS AND COMMODITY DEALINGS.—

(i) IN GENERAL.—In the case of any options dealer or commodities dealer, passive investment income shall be determined by not taking into account any gain or loss (in the normal course of the taxpayer's activity of dealing in or trading section 1256 contracts) from any section 1256 contract or property related to such a contract.

(ii) DEFINITIONS.—For purposes of this subparagraph—

(I) OPTIONS DEALER.—The term "options dealer" has the meaning given such term by section 1256(g)(8).

(II) COMMODITIES DEALER.—The term "commodities dealer" means a person who is actively engaged in trading section 1256 contracts and is registered with a domestic board of trade which is designated as a contract market by the Commodities Futures Trading Commission.

(III) SECTION 1256 CONTRACT.—The term "section 1256 contract" has the meaning given to such term by section 1256(b).

(E) TREATMENT OF CERTAIN DIVIDENDS.—If an S corporation holds stock in a C corporation meeting the requirements of section 1504(a)(2), the term "passive investment income" shall not include dividends from such C corporation to the extent such dividends are attributable to the earnings and profits of such C corporation derived from the active conduct of a trade or business.

(e) TREATMENT OF S TERMINATION YEAR.—

(1) IN GENERAL.—In the case of an S termination year, for purposes of this title—

(A) S SHORT YEAR.—The portion of such year ending before the 1st day for which the termination is effective shall be treated as a short taxable year for which the corporation is an S corporation.

(B) C SHORT YEAR.—The portion of such year beginning on such 1st day shall be treated as a short taxable year for which the corporation is a C corporation.

(2) PRO RATA ALLOCATION.—Except as provided in paragraph (3) and subparagraphs (C) and (D) of paragraph (6), the determination of which items are to be taken into account for each of the short taxable years referred to in paragraph (1) shall be made—

(A) first by determining for the S termination year—

(i) the amount of each of the items of income, loss, deduction, or credit described in section 1366(a)(1)(A), and

(ii) the amount of the nonseparately computed income or loss, and

(B) then by assigning an equal portion of each amount determined under subparagraph (A) to each day of the S termination year.

(3) ELECTION TO HAVE ITEMS ASSIGNED TO EACH SHORT TAXABLE YEAR UNDER NORMAL TAX ACCOUNTING RULES.—

(A) IN GENERAL.—A corporation may elect to have paragraph (2) not apply.

(B) SHAREHOLDERS MUST CONSENT TO ELECTION.— An election under this subsection shall be valid only if all persons who are shareholders in the corporation at any time during the S short year and all persons who are shareholders in the corporation on the first day of the C short year consent to such election.

(4) S TERMINATION YEAR.—For purposes of this subsection, the term "S termination year" means any taxable year of a corporation (determined without regard to this subsection) in which a termination of an election made under subsection (a) takes effect (other than on the 1st day thereof).

(5) TAX FOR C SHORT YEAR DETERMINED ON ANNUAL-IZED BASIS.—

(A) IN GENERAL.—The taxable income for the short year described in subparagraph (B) of paragraph (1) shall be placed on an annual basis by multiplying the taxable income for such short year by the number of days in the S termination year and by dividing the result by the number of days in the short year. The tax shall be the same part of the tax computed on the annual basis as the number of days in such short year is of the number of days in the S termination year.

(B) SECTION 443(d)(2) TO APPLY.—Subsection (d) of section 443 shall apply to the short taxable year described in subparagraph (B) of paragraph (1).

(6) OTHER SPECIAL RULES.—For purposes of this title—

(A) SHORT YEARS TREATED AS 1 YEAR FOR CARRYOVER PURPOSES.—The short taxable year described in subparagraph (A) of paragraph (1) shall not be taken into account for purposes of determining the number of taxable years to which any item may be carried back or carried forward by the corporation.

(B) DUE DATE FOR S YEAR.—The due date for filing the return for the short taxable year described in subparagraph (A) of paragraph (1) shall be the same as the due date for filing the return for the short taxable year described in subparagraph (B) of paragraph (1) (including extensions thereof).

(C) PARAGRAPH (2) NOT TO APPLY TO ITEMS RESULTING FROM SECTION 338.— Paragraph (2) shall not apply with respect to any item resulting from the application of section 338.

(D) PRO RATA ALLOCATION FOR S TERMINATION YEAR NOT TO APPLY IF 50-PERCENT CHANGE IN OWNERSHIP.— Paragraph (2) shall not apply to an S termination year if there is a sale or exchange of 50 percent or more of the stock in such corporation during such year.

(f) INADVERTENT INVALID ELECTIONS OR TERMINATIONS.— If—

(1) an election under subsection (a) by any corporation—

(A) was not effective for the taxable year for which made (determined without regard to subsection (b)(2)) by reason of a failure to meet the requirements of section 1361(b) or to obtain shareholder consents, or

(B) was terminated under paragraph (2) or (3) of subsection (d),

(2) the Secretary determines that the circumstances resulting in such ineffectiveness or termination were inadvertent,

(3) no later than a reasonable period of time after discovery of the circumstances resulting in such ineffectiveness or termination, steps were taken—

(A) so that the corporation is a small business corporation, or

(B) to acquire the required shareholder consents, and

(4) the corporation, and each person who was a shareholder in the corporation at any time during the period specified pursuant to this

subsection, agrees to make such adjustments (consistent with the treatment of the corporation as an S corporation) as may be required by the Secretary with respect to such period,

then, notwithstanding the circumstances resulting in such ineffectiveness or termination, such corporation shall be treated as an S corporation during the period specified by the Secretary.

(g) ELECTION AFTER TERMINATION.—If a small business corporation has made an election under subsection (a) and if such election has been terminated under subsection (d), such corporation (and any successor corporation) shall not be eligible to make an election under subsection (a) for any taxable year before its 5th taxable year which begins after the 1st taxable year for which such termination is effective, unless the Secretary consents to such election.

CODE SECTION 1363

Effect Of Election On Corporation

(a) GENERAL RULE.—Except as otherwise provided in this subchapter, an S corporation shall not be subject to the taxes imposed by this chapter.

(b) COMPUTATION OF CORPORATION'S TAXABLE INCOME.— The taxable income of an S corporation shall be computed in the same manner as in the case of an individual, except that—

(1) the items described in section 1366(a)(1)(A) shall be separately stated,

(2) the deductions referred to in section 703(a)(2) shall not be allowed to the corporation,

(3) section 248 shall apply, and

(4) section 291 shall apply if the S corporation (or any predecessor) was a C corporation for any of the 3 immediately preceding taxable years.

(c) ELECTIONS OF THE S CORPORATION.—

(1) IN GENERAL.—Except as provided in paragraph (2), any election affecting the computation of items derived from an S corporation shall be made by the corporation.

(2) EXCEPTIONS.—In the case of an S corporation, elections under the following provisions shall be made by each shareholder separately—

(A) section 617 (relating to deduction and recapture of certain mining exploration expenditures), and

(B) section 901 (relating to taxes of foreign countries and possessions of the United States).

(d) RECAPTURE OF LIFO BENEFITS.—

(1) IN GENERAL.—If—

(A) an S corporation was a C corporation for the last taxable year before the first taxable year for which the election under section 1362(a) was effective, and

(B) the corporation inventoried goods under the LIFO method for such last taxable year,

the LIFO recapture amount shall be included in the gross income of the corporation for such last taxable year (and appropriate adjustments to the basis of inventory shall be made to take into account the amount included in gross income under this paragraph).

(2) ADDITIONAL TAX PAYABLE IN INSTALLMENTS.—

(A) IN GENERAL.—Any increase in the tax imposed by this chapter by reason of this subsection shall be payable in 4 equal installments.

(B) DATE FOR PAYMENT OF INSTALLMENTS.—The first installment under subparagraph (A) shall be paid on or before the due date (determined without regard to extensions) for the return of the tax imposed by this chapter for the last taxable year for which the corporation was a C corporation and the 3 succeeding installments shall be paid on or before the due date (as so determined) for the corporation's return for the 3 succeeding taxable years.

(C) NO INTEREST FOR PERIOD OF EXTENSION.—Notwithstanding section 6601(b) for purposes of section 6601, the date prescribed for the payment of each installment under this paragraph shall be determined under this paragraph.

(3) LIFO RECAPTURE AMOUNT.—For purposes of this subsection, the term "LIFO recapture amount" means the amount (if any) by which—

(A) the inventory amount of the inventory asset under the first-in, first-out method authorized by section 71, exceeds

(B) the inventory amount of such assets under the LIFO method.

For purposes of the preceding sentence, inventory amounts shall be determined as of the close of the last taxable year referred to in paragraph (1).

(4) OTHER DEFINITIONS.—For purposes of this subsection—

(A) LIFO METHOD.—The term "LIFO method" means the method authorized by section 472.

(B) INVENTORY ASSETS.—The term "inventory assets" means stock in trade of the corporation, or other property of a kind which would properly be included in the inventory of the corporation if on hand at the close of the taxable year.

(C) METHOD OF DETERMINING INVENTORY AMOUNT.—The inventory amount of assets under a method authorized by section 471 shall be determined—

(i) if the corporation uses the retail method of valuing inventories under section 472, by using such method, or

(ii) if clause (i) does not apply, by using cost or market, whichever is lower.

(D) NOT TREATED AS MEMBER OF AFFILIATED GROUP.—Except as provided in regulations, the corporation referred to in paragraph (1) shall not be treated as a member of an affiliated group with respect to the amount included in gross income under paragraph (1).

CODE SECTION 1366

Pass-Thru Of Items To Shareholders

(a) DETERMINATION OF SHAREHOLDER'S TAX LIABILITY.—

(1) IN GENERAL.—In determining the tax under this chapter of a shareholder for the shareholder's taxable year in which the taxable year of the S corporation ends (or for the final taxable year of a shareholder who dies, or of a trust or estate which terminates, before the end of the corporation's taxable year), there shall be taken into account the shareholder's pro rata share of the corporation's—

(A) items of income (including tax-exempt income), loss, deduction, or credit the separate treatment of which could affect the liability for tax of any shareholder, and

(B) nonseparately computed income or loss.

For purposes of the preceding sentence, the items referred to in subparagraph (A) shall include amounts described in paragraph (4) or (6) of section 702(a).

(2) NONSEPARATELY COMPUTED INCOME OR LOSS DEFINED.—For purposes of this subchapter, the term "nonseparately computed income or loss" means gross income minus the deductions allowed to the corporation under this chapter, determined by excluding all items described in paragraph (1)(A).

(b) CHARACTER PASSED THRU.—The character of any item included in a shareholder's pro rata share under paragraph (1) of subsection (a) shall be determined as if such item were realized directly from the source from which realized by the corporation, or incurred in the same manner as incurred by the corporation.

(c) GROSS INCOME OF SHAREHOLDER.—In any case where it is necessary to determine the gross income of a shareholder for purposes of this title, such gross income shall include the shareholder's pro rata share of the gross income of the corporation.

(d) SPECIAL RULES FOR LOSSES AND DEDUCTIONS.—

(1) CANNOT EXCEED SHAREHOLDER'S BASIS IN STOCK AND DEBT.—The aggregate amount of losses and deductions taken into account by a shareholder under subsection (a) for any taxable year shall not exceed the sum of—

(A) the adjusted basis of the shareholder's stock in the S corporation (determined with regard to paragraphs (1) and (2)(A) of section 1367(a) for the taxable year), and

(B) the shareholder's adjusted basis of any indebtedness of the S corporation to the shareholder (determined without regard to any adjustment under paragraph (2) of section 1367(b) for the taxable year).

(2) INDEFINITE CARRYOVER OF DISALLOWED LOSSES AND DEDUCTIONS.—Any loss or deduction which is disallowed for any taxable year by reason of paragraph (1) shall be treated as incurred by the corporation in the succeeding taxable year with respect to that shareholder.

(3) CARRYOVER OF DISALLOWED LOSSES AND DEDUCTIONS TO POST-TERMINATION TRANSITION PERIOD.—

(A) IN GENERAL.—If for the last taxable year of a corporation for which it was an S corporation a loss or deduction was disallowed by reason of paragraph (1), such loss or deduction shall be treated as incurred by the shareholder on the last day of any post-termination transition period.

(B) CANNOT EXCEED SHAREHOLDER'S BASIS IN STOCK.—The aggregate amount of losses and deductions taken into account by a shareholder under subparagraph (A) shall not exceed the adjusted basis of the shareholder's stock in the corporation (determined at the close of the last day of the post-termination transition period and without regard to this paragraph).

(C) ADJUSTMENT IN BASIS OF STOCK.—The shareholder's basis in the stock of the corporation shall be reduced by the amount allowed as a deduction by reason of this paragraph.

(D) AT-RISK LIMITATIONS.—To the extent that any increase in adjusted basis described in subparagraph (B) would have increased the shareholder's amount at risk under section 465 if such increase had occurred on the day preceding the commencement of the post-termination period, rules similar to the rules described in subparagraphs (A) through (C) shall apply to any losses disallowed by reason of section 465(a).

(e) TREATMENT OF FAMILY GROUP.—If an individual who is a member of the family (within the meaning of section 704(e)(3)) of one or more shareholders of an S corporation renders services for the corporation or furnishes capital to the corporation without receiving reasonable compensation therefor, the Secretary shall make such adjustments in the items taken into account by such individual and such shareholders as may be necessary in order to reflect the value of such services or capital.

(f) SPECIAL RULES.—

(1) SUBSECTION (a) NOT TO APPLY TO CREDIT ALLOW-ABLE UNDER SECTION 34.— Subsection (a) shall not apply with respect to any credit allowable under section 34 (relating to certain uses of gasoline and special fuels).

(2) TREATMENT OF TAX IMPOSED ON BUILT-IN GAINS.—If any tax is imposed under section 1374 for any taxable year on an S corporation, for purposes of subsection (a), the amount so imposed shall be treated as a loss sustained by the S corporation during such taxable year. The character of such loss shall be determined by allocating the loss proportionately among the recognized built-in gains giving rise to such tax.

(3) REDUCTION IN PASS-THRU FOR TAX IMPOSED ON EX-CESS NET PASSIVE INCOME.—If any tax is imposed under section 1375 for any taxable year on an S corporation, for purposes of subsection (a), each item of passive investment income shall be reduced by an amount which bears the same ratio to the amount of such tax as—

(A) the amount of such item, bears to

(B) the total passive investment income for the taxable year.

CODE SECTION 1367

Adjustments To Basis Of Stock Of Shareholders, Etc.

(a) GENERAL RULE.—

(1) INCREASES IN BASIS.—The basis of each shareholder's stock in an S corporation shall be increased for any period by the sum of the following items determined with respect to that shareholder for such period:

(A) the items of income described in subparagraph (A) of section 1366(a)(1),

(B) any nonseparately computed income determined under subparagraph (B) of section 1366(a)(1), and

(C) the excess of the deduction for depletion over the basis of the property subject to depletion.

(2) DECREASES IN BASIS.—The basis of each shareholder's stock in an S corporation shall be decreased for any period (but not below zero) by the sum of the following items determined with respect to the shareholder for such period:

(A) distributions by the corporation which were not includible in the income of the shareholder by reason of section 1368,

(B) the items of loss and deduction described in subparagraph (A) of section 1366(a)(1),

(C) any nonseparately computed loss determined under subparagraph (B) of section 1366(a)(1),

(D) any expense of the corporation not deductible in computing its taxable income and not properly chargeable to capital account, and

(E) the amount of the shareholder's deduction for depletion for any oil and gas property held by the S corporation to the extent such deduction does not exceed the proportionate share of the adjusted basis of such property allocated to such shareholder under section 613A(c)(11)(B).

WORKING WITH S CORPORATIONS
A Practitioner's Guide to Estate, Business, and
Compensation Planning for S Corporations

1997 SUPPLEMENT COVERING
THE TAXPAYER RELIEF ACT OF 1997 (TRA '97)

General

The Taxpayer Relief Act of 1997 (TRA '97), P.L. 105-34, was signed into law on August 5, 1997. This fairly extensive piece of legislation changed several items discussed in this publication as generally summarized below.

One change, a gradual increase in the amount of the gift and estate tax unified credit, affects more than one chapter in this publication. For this reason, this change is noted here in full with a short reference to the unified credit provision in the individual chapters below.

Following TRA '97 the amount of the estate and gift tax unified credit will increase gradually beginning in 1998 according to the following schedule:

Year	Unified Credit Equivalent
1998	$625,000
1999	$650,000
2000 and 2001	$675,000
2002 and 2003	$700,000
2004	$850,000
2005	$950,000
after 2005	$1,000,000

This provision is applicable to estates of decedents dying and gifts made after December 31, 1997. IRC Secs. 2010(a), 2010(c), 2505(a); TRA '97 Sec. 501(a).

Chapter 1, Overview of the S Corporation

Page 4

Personal service corporations are taxed at a rate of 35%. IRC Sec. 11(b)(2).

Page 8

TRA '97 redesignated subsection (c)(7) of Code section 1361 as subsection (c)(6). The language of this subsection, which permits certain tax exempt organizations to be S corporation shareholders, was not altered. This change is effective for tax years beginning after December 31, 1997. IRC Sec. 1361(c)(6). TRA '97 Sec. 1601(c)(4)(B).

Chapter 3, Corporate Owned Life Insurance

Page 44

TRA '97 amended Code section 264(a)(1) which is set forth in the middle of page 44. Although the specific language of this code section has been altered, the general rule of nondeductibility for premiums paid on corporate-owned insurance remains. After amendment, Code section 264(a)(1) reads:

(a) GENERAL RULE — No deduction shall be allowed for —

(1) Premiums on any life insurance policy, or endowment or annuity contract, if the taxpayer is directly or indirectly a beneficiary under the policy or contract.

This change is applicable to contracts issued after June 8, 1997. IRC Sec. 264(a)(1); TRA '97 Sec. 1084(a)(1).

Page 68

Effective for tax years ending after May 6, 1997, TRA '97 changed the taxation of capital gains so that a fairly complex formula is now used to calculate the tax on capital gains. This change would alter the outcome of the numerical example appearing at the top of this page. Generally, the maximum capital gains rate on adjusted net capital gain will be 10% for taxpayers in the 15% marginal rate and 20% for taxpayers in higher marginal rates. Certain types of gain are excluded from these lower rates. Thus, instead of an outcome of 38.9% in the example on this page, using a 20% capital gains rate would give an answer of 25% ($1.00 - $.20 = $.80; $.20 ÷ $.80 = 25%). IRC Sec. 1(h); TRA '97 Sec. 311.

Chapter 4, Split Dollar Plans

Pages 104-105

The annual gift tax exclusion amount, currently $10,000, will be adjusted for inflation after 1998. IRC Sec. 2503(b); TRA '97 Sec. 501(c).

Page 107

The gift and estate tax unified credit is now scheduled to increase gradually beginning in 1998 according to the schedule shown above under the "General" heading.

Page 108, footnote 17

Personal service corporations are taxed at a rate of 35%. IRC Sec. 11(b)(2).

Chapter 5, Business Continuation Planning

Page 113

The annual gift tax exclusion amount, currently $10,000, will be adjusted for inflation after 1998. IRC Sec. 2503(b); TRA '97 Sec. 501(c).

The gift and estate tax unified credit is now scheduled to increase gradually beginning in 1998 according to the schedule shown above under the "General" heading.

Page 114

For gifts made after August 5, 1997, a gift for which the statute of limitations period has passed cannot be revalued for estate tax purposes provided the gift is adequately disclosed on the gift tax return. IRC Secs. 2001(f), 6501(c)(9); TRA '97 Sec. 506.

Page 136

The corporate alternative minimum tax (AMT) will no longer be applicable to small corporations which, generally, are those with less than $5,000,000 in gross receipts. This change applies to tax years beginning after December 31, 1997. IRC Sec. 55(e); TRA '97 Sec. 401(a).

Page 137

Effective for tax years ending after May 6, 1997, TRA '97 changed the taxation of capital gains so that a fairly complex formula is now used to calculate the tax on capital gains. Generally, the maximum capital gains rate on adjusted net capital gain will be 10% for taxpayers in the 15% marginal rate and 20% for taxpayers in higher marginal rates. Certain types of gain are excluded from these lower rates. IRC Sec. 1(h); TRA '97 Sec. 311.

Chapter 6, Estate Planning Considerations

Page 168

TRA '97 amended Code section 1361(b) which is set forth in the middle of page 168. Following this change the reference to "subsection (c)(7)" should now read "subsection (c)(6)." The language of this subsection, which permits certain tax exempt organizations to be S corporation shareholders, was not actually altered; former subsection (c)(7) was merely redesignated as (c)(6). This change is effective for tax years beginning after December 31, 1997. IRC Sec. 1361(c)(6). TRA '97 Sec. 1601(c)(4)(B).

3

Pages 176-177

Code section 1361(e), which is set forth beginning in the middle of page 176, was amended by TRA '97. A new paragraph was added under "(B) CERTAIN TRUSTS NOT ELIGIBLE" which states, "(iii) any charitable remainder annuity trust or charitable remainder unitrust (as defined in section 664(d))." In effect this amendment adds these two types of charitable trusts to the list of trusts that are not eligible to elect to be treated as "electing small business trusts" under Code section 1361(c)(2). This change is effective for tax years beginning after December 31, 1997. IRC Sec. 1361(e)(1)(B). TRA '97 Sec. 1601(c)(1).

Pages 181-182

In the example about Norm and Vera beginning on page 181, the fact that the gift and estate tax unified credit is now scheduled to increase gradually beginning in 1998 according to the schedule shown above under the "General" heading should be considered.

Page 194

The gift and estate tax unified credit is now scheduled to increase gradually beginning in 1998 according to the schedule shown above under the "General" heading.

Page 198

The gift and estate tax unified credit is now scheduled to increase gradually beginning in 1998 according to the schedule shown above under the "General" heading.

Pages 201-202, 205

The fact that the gift and estate tax unified credit is now scheduled to increase gradually beginning in 1998 according to the schedule shown above under the "General" heading should be taken into account in reading the example concerning The Big Company which begins in the middle of page 201.

Page 220

In the discussion under the heading of "Electing Small Business Trust" it should be noted that TRA '97 amended Code section 1361(e) to add charitable remainder annuity trusts and charitable remainder unitrusts to the list of trusts that are not eligible to elect to be treated as "electing small business trusts." This change is effective for tax years beginning after December 31, 1997. IRC Sec. 1361(e)(1)(B). TRA '97 Sec. 1601(c)(1).

Chapter 7, Benefit Planning for Shareholders of S Corporations

Page 232

TRA '97 increased the percentage of health insurance premiums that may be deducted by self-employed persons, including more-than-two-percent shareholders in S corporations, according to the following schedule:

Tax Years Beginning in	Applicable Percentage
1998 and 1999	45%
2000 and 2001	50%
2002	60%
2003	80%
2004	80%
2005	80%
2006	90%
2007 and thereafter	100%

This new provision is effective for taxable years beginning after December 31, 1996.

Page 240

Code section 414(q)(7), which is set forth at the top of page 240, was redesignated as Code section 414(q)(9) by TRA '97. However, the actual language of this subsection did not change. This provision is effective for tax years beginning after December 31, 1996. IRC Sec. 414(q); TRA '97 Sec. 1601(d)(7).

Page 250

The first full paragraph on page 250 states that an Employee Stock Ownership Plan (ESOP) cannot be used by an S corporation. This is no longer true since qualified retirement plans and organizations exempt from tax under Code section 501(c)(3) are now permitted to be shareholders in S corporations.

This provision is effective for tax years beginning after December 31, 1997. IRC Sec. 1361(c)(7)[6] as added by Sec. 1316(a)(2) of the Small Business Job Protection Act of 1996 and redesignated as IRC Sec. 1361(c)(6) by Sec. 1601(c)(4)(B) of TRA '97.

Pages 251-252

Code section 264(a)(4), which is set forth in the middle of page 251, has been amended by TRA '97 and now reads as follows:

(a) GENERAL RULE. — No deduction shall be allowed for —

      (1) Premiums on any life insurance policy, or endowment or annuity contract, if the taxpayer is directly or indirectly a beneficiary under the policy or contract. ...

      (4) Except as provided in subsection (d), any interest paid or accrued on any indebtedness with respect to 1 or more life insurance policies owned by the taxpayer covering the life of any individual, or any endowment or annuity contracts owned by the taxpayer covering any individual.

Although the exception from the general disallowance rule for policies on key employees mentioned on page 251 remains unchanged, TRA '97 added Code section 264(f) which generally provides that no deduction will be allowed for the part of the taxpayer's interest expense which is "allocable to unborrowed policy cash values."

This portion which is "allocable to unborrowed policy cash values" is an amount which bears the same ratio to the interest expense as the taxpayer's average unborrowed policy cash values of life insurance policies and annuity and endowment contracts issued after June 8, 1997 bears to the sum of: (1) in the case of assets which are life policies or annuity or endowment contracts, the average unborrowed policy cash values; and (2) in the case of assets of the taxpayer which do not fall into this category, the average adjusted bases of such assets.

"Unborrowed policy cash value" is defined as the excess of the cash surrender value of a policy or contract (determined without regard to surrender charges) over the amount of the loan with respect to the policy or contract.

The changes made by TRA '97 include an exception to the general rule of nondeductibility of interest expense allocable to unborrowed policy cash values. The exception applies to policies and contracts owned by entities if the policy covers only one individual who, at the time first covered by the policy, is: (1) a 20-percent owner of the entity; or (2) an individual who is an officer, director or employee of the trade or business.

This provision is applicable to contracts issued after June 8, 1997. IRC Secs. 264(a), 264(f); TRA '97 Sec. 1084.

Page 256, footnote 13

      As part of the TRA '97 amendments to Code section 4975, the material quoted in this footnote was deleted. This change is effective for tax years beginning after December 31, 1997. IRC Sec. 4975(d); TRA '97 Sec. 1506(b)(1)(B).

Appendix

Pages 260-267

Code section 1361, which is reproduced on these pages, was amended by TRA '97. Following are portions of subsections (b), (c), and (e) with the changes made by TRA '97 in italics.

(b) SMALL BUSINESS CORPORATIONS —

(1) IN GENERAL — For purposes of this subchapter, the term "small business corporation" means a domestic corporation which is not an ineligible corporation and which does not — ....

(B) have as a shareholder a person (other than an estate, a trust described in subsection (c)(2), or an organization described in *subsection (c)(6)* who is not an individual ...

(3) TREATMENT OF CERTAIN WHOLLY OWNED SUBSIDIARIES. —

(A) IN GENERAL. — *Except as provided in regulations prescribed by the Secretary, for purposes of this title—*

[These amendments were made by TRA '97 sections 1601(c)(3) and 1691(c)(4)(C) and are effective for tax years beginning after December 31, 1996.]

(c) SPECIAL RULES FOR APPLYING SUBSECTION (b). — ...

(6) CERTAIN EXEMPT ORGANIZATIONS PERMITTED AS SHAREHOLDERS. — ...

[This amendment was made by TRA '97 section 1601(c)(4)(B) and is effective for tax years beginning after December 31, 1997.]

(e) ELECTING SMALL BUSINESS TRUST DEFINED. — ...

(B) CERTAIN TRUSTS NOT ELIGIBLE. — The term "electing small business trust" shall not include — ...

(iii) any charitable remainder annuity trust or charitable remainder unitrust (as defined in section 664(d) ...

[This amendment was made by TRA '97 section 1601(c)(1) and is effective for tax years beginning after December 31, 1996.]

Pages 290-295

Code section 1374, which is reproduced on these pages, was amended by TRA '97. Following are portions of subsection (d) with the changes made by TRA '97 in italics.

(d) DEFINITIONS AND SPECIAL RULES. — For purposes of this section — ...

(7) RECOGNITION PERIOD. — The term "recognition period" means the 10-year period beginning with the 1st day of the 1st taxable year for which the corporation was an S corporation. *For purposes of applying this section to any amount includible in income by reason of section 593(e), the preceding sentence shall be applied without regard to the phrase "10-year".*

[This amendment was made by TRA '97 section 1601(f)(5)(B) and is effective for tax years beginning after December 31, 1995.]

(b) SPECIAL RULES.—

(1) INCOME ITEMS.—An amount which is required to be included in the gross income of a shareholder and shown on his return shall be taken into account under subparagraph (A) or (B) of subsection (a)(1) only to the extent such amount is included in the shareholder's gross income on his return, increased or decreased by any adjustment of such amount in a redetermination of the shareholder's tax liability.

(2) ADJUSTMENTS IN BASIS OF INDEBTEDNESS.—

(A) REDUCTION OF BASIS.—If for any taxable year the amounts specified in subparagraph (B), (C), (D), and (E) of subsection (a)(2) exceed the amount which reduces the shareholder's basis to zero, such excess shall be applied to reduce (but not below zero) the shareholder's basis in any indebtedness of the S corporation to the shareholder.

(B) RESTORATION OF BASIS.—If for any taxable year beginning after December 31, 1982, there is a reduction under subparagraph (A) in the shareholder's basis in the indebtedness of an S corporation to a shareholder, any net increase (after the application of paragraphs (1) and (2) of subsection (a)) for any subsequent taxable year shall be applied to restore such reduction in basis before any of it may be used to increase the shareholder's basis in the stock of the S corporation.

(3) COORDINATION WITH SECTIONS 165(g) AND 166(d).— This section and section 1366 shall be applied before the application of sections 165(g) and 166(d) to any taxable year of the shareholder or the corporation in which the security or debt becomes worthless.

(4) ADJUSTMENTS IN CASE OF INHERITED STOCK.—

(A) IN GENERAL.—If any person acquires stock in an S corporation by reason of the death of a decedent or by bequest, devise, or inheritance, section 691 shall be applied with respect to any item of income of the S corporation in the same manner as if the decedent had held directly his pro rata share of such item.

(B) ADJUSTMENTS TO BASIS.—The basis determined under section 1014 of any stock in an S corporation shall be reduced by the portion of the value of the stock which is attributable to items constituting income in respect of the decedent.

[Note: the provisions of subsection (4) above apply in the case of decedents dying after August 20, 1996.]

CODE SECTION 1368

Distributions

(a) GENERAL RULE.—A distribution of property made by an S corporation with respect to its stock to which (but for this subsection) section 301(c) would apply shall be treated in the manner provided in subsection (b) or (c), whichever applies.

(b) S CORPORATION HAVING NO EARNINGS AND PROFITS.—In the case of a distribution described in subsection (a) by an S corporation which has no accumulated earnings and profits—

(1) AMOUNT APPLIED AGAINST BASIS.—The distribution shall not be included in gross income to the extent that it does not exceed the adjusted basis of the stock.

(2) AMOUNT IN EXCESS OF BASIS.—If the amount of the distribution exceeds the adjusted basis of the stock, such excess shall be treated as gain from the sale or exchange of property.

(c) S CORPORATION HAVING EARNINGS AND PROFITS.—In the case of a distribution described in subsection (a) by an S corporation which has accumulated earnings and profits—

(1) ACCUMULATED ADJUSTMENTS ACCOUNT.—That portion of the distribution which does not exceed the accumulated adjustments account shall be treated in the manner provided by subsection (b).

(2) DIVIDEND.—That portion of the distribution which remains after the application of paragraph (1) shall be treated as a dividend to the extent it does not exceed the accumulated earnings and profits of the S corporation.

(3) TREATMENT OF REMAINDER.—Any portion of the distribution remaining after the application of paragraph (2) of this subsection shall be treated in the manner provided by subsection (b).

Except to the extent provided in regulations, if the distributions during the taxable year exceed the amount in the accumulated adjustments account at the close of the taxable year, for purposes of this subsection, the balance of such account shall be allocated among such distributions in proportion to their respective sizes.

(d) CERTAIN ADJUSTMENTS TAKEN INTO ACCOUNT.—Subsections (b) and (c) shall be applied by taking into account (to the extent proper)—

(1) the adjustments to the basis of the shareholder's stock described in section 1367, and

(2) the adjustments to the accumulated adjustments account which are required by subsection (e)(1).

In the case of any distribution made during any taxable year, the adjusted basis of the stock shall be determined with regard to the adjustments provided in paragraph (1) of section 1367(a) for the taxable year.

(e) DEFINITIONS AND SPECIAL RULES.—For purposes of this section—

(1) ACCUMULATED ADJUSTMENTS ACCOUNT.—

(A) IN GENERAL.—Except as otherwise provided in this paragraph, the term "accumulated adjustments account" means an account of the S corporation which is adjusted for the S period in a manner similar to the adjustments under section 1367 (except that no adjustment shall be made for income (and related expenses) which is exempt from tax under this title and the phrase "(but not below zero)" shall be disregarded in section 1367(a)(2)) and no adjustment shall be made for Federal taxes attributable to any taxable year in which the corporation was a C corporation.

(B) AMOUNT OF ADJUSTMENT IN THE CASE OF RE-DEMPTIONS.—In the case of any redemption which is treated as an exchange under section 302(a) or 303(a), the adjustment in the accumulated adjustments account shall be an amount which bears the same ratio to the balance in such account as the number of shares redeemed in such redemption bears to the number of shares of stock in the corporation immediately before such redemption.

(C) NET LOSS FOR YEAR DISREGARDED.—

(i) IN GENERAL.—In applying this section to distributions made during any taxable year, the amount in the accumulated adjustments account as of the close of such taxable year shall be determined without regard to any net negative adjustment for such taxable year.

(ii) NET NEGATIVE ADJUSTMENT.—For purposes of clause (i), the term "net negative adjustment" means, with respect to any taxable year, the excess (if any) of—

(I) the reductions in the account for the taxable year (other than for distributions), over

(II) the increases in such account for such taxable year.

(2) S PERIOD.—The term "S period" means the most recent continuous period during which the corporation has been an S corporation. Such period shall not include any taxable year beginning before January 1, 1983.

(3) ELECTION TO DISTRIBUTE EARNINGS FIRST.—

(A) IN GENERAL.—An S corporation may, with the consent of all of its affected shareholders, elect to have paragraph (1) of subsection (c) not apply to all distributions made during the taxable year for which the election is made.

(B) AFFECTED SHAREHOLDER.—For purposes of subparagraph (A) the term "affected shareholder" means any shareholder to whom a distribution is made by the S corporation during the taxable year.

CODE SECTION 1371

Coordination With Subchapter C

(a) APPLICATION OF SUBCHAPTER C RULES.—Except as otherwise provided in this title, and except to the extent inconsistent with this subchapter, subchapter C shall apply to an S corporation and its shareholders.

(1) IN GENERAL.—Except as otherwise provided in this title, and except to the extent inconsistent with this subchapter, subchapter C shall apply to an S corporation and its shareholders.

(2) S CORPORATION AS SHAREHOLDER TREATED LIKE INDIVIDUAL.—For purposes of subchapter C, an S corporation in its capacity as a shareholder of another corporation shall be treated as an individual.

(b) NO CARRYOVER BETWEEN C YEAR AND S YEAR.—

(1) FROM C YEAR TO S YEAR.—No carryforward, and no carryback, arising for a taxable year for which a corporation is a C corporation may be carried to a taxable year for which such corporation is an S corporation.

(2) NO CARRYOVER FROM S YEAR.—No carryforward, and no carryback, shall arise at the corporate level for a taxable year for which a corporation is an S corporation.

(3) TREATMENT OF S YEAR AS ELAPSED YEAR.—Nothing in paragraphs (1) and (2) shall prevent treating a taxable year for which a corporation is an S corporation as a taxable year for purposes of determining the number of taxable years to which an item may be carried back or carried forward.

(c) EARNINGS AND PROFITS.—

(1) IN GENERAL.—Except as provided in paragraphs (2) and (3) and subsection (d)(3), no adjustment shall be made to the earnings and profits of an S corporation.

(2) ADJUSTMENTS FOR REDEMPTIONS, LIQUIDATIONS, REORGANIZATIONS, DIVISIVES, ETC.—In the case of any transaction involving the application of subchapter C to any S corporation, proper adjustment to any accumulated earnings and profits of the corporation shall be made.

(3) ADJUSTMENTS IN CASE OF DISTRIBUTIONS TREATED AS DIVIDENDS UNDER SECTION 1368(c)(2).—Paragraph (1) shall not apply with respect to that portion of a distribution which is treated as a dividend under section 1368(c)(2).

(d) COORDINATION WITH INVESTMENT CREDIT RECAPTURE.—

(1) NO RECAPTURE BY REASON OF ELECTION.—Any election under section 1362 shall be treated as a mere change in the form of conducting a trade or business for purposes of the second sentence of section 50(a)(4).

(2) CORPORATION CONTINUES TO BE LIABLE.—Notwithstanding an election under section 1362, an S corporation shall continue to be liable for any increase in tax under section 49(b) or 50(a) attributable to credits allowed for taxable years for which such corporation was not an S corporation.

(3) ADJUSTMENT TO EARNINGS AND PROFITS FOR AMOUNT OF RECAPTURE.—Paragraph (1) of subsection (c) shall not apply to any increase in tax under section 49(b) or 50(a) for which the S corporation is liable.

(e) CASH DISTRIBUTIONS DURING POST-TERMINATION TRANSITION PERIOD.—

(1) IN GENERAL.—Any distribution of money by a corporation with respect to its stock during a post-termination transition period shall be applied against and reduce the adjusted basis of the stock, to the extent that the amount of the distribution does not exceed the accumulated adjustments account (within the meaning of section 1368(e)).

(2) ELECTION TO DISTRIBUTE EARNINGS FIRST—An S corporation may elect to have paragraph (1) not apply to all distributions made during a post-termination transition period described in section

1377(b)(1)(A). Such election shall not be effective unless all shareholders of the S corporation to whom distributions are made by the S corporation during such post-termination transition period consent to such election.

CODE SECTION 1372

Partnership Rules To Apply For Fringe Benefit Purposes

(a) GENERAL RULE.—For purposes of applying the provisions of this subtitle which relate to employee fringe benefits—

(1) the S corporation shall be treated as a partnership, and

(2) any 2-percent shareholder of the S corporation shall be treated as a partner of such partnership.

(b) 2-PERCENT SHAREHOLDER DEFINED.—For purposes of this section, the term "2-percent shareholder" means any person who owns (or is considered as owning within the meaning of section 318) on any day during the taxable year of the S corporation more than 2 percent of the outstanding stock of such corporation or stock possessing more than 2 percent of the total combined voting power of all stock of such corporation.

CODE SECTION 1373

Foreign Income

(a) S CORPORATION TREATED AS PARTNERSHIP, ETC.—For purposes of subparts A and F of part III, and part V, of subchapter N (relating to income from sources without the United States)—

(1) an S corporation shall be treated as a partnership, and

(2) the shareholders of such corporation shall be treated as partners of such partnership.

(b) RECAPTURE OF OVERALL FOREIGN LOSS.—For purposes of section 904(f) (relating to recapture of overall foreign loss), the making or termination of an election to be treated as an S corporation shall be treated as a disposition of the business.

CODE SECTION 1374

Tax Imposed On Certain Built-In Gains

Caution: Code Sec. 1374, below, as amended by P.L. 99-514, P.L. 100-647 and P.L. 101-239, generally applies to tax years beginning after December 31, 1986, but only in cases where the first tax year for which the corporation has elected S Corporation status is after December 31, 1986. See ¶33,603.01 et seq. for the present rules and special transitional rules.

(a) GENERAL RULE.—If for any taxable year beginning in the recognition period an S corporation has a net recognized built-in gain, there is hereby imposed a tax (computed under subsection (b)) on the income of such corporation for such taxable year.

(b) AMOUNT OF TAX

(1) IN GENERAL.—The amount of the tax imposed by subsection (a) shall be computed by applying the highest rate of tax specified in section 11(b) to the net recognized built-in gain of the S corporation for the taxable year.

(2) NET OPERATING LOSS CARRYFORWARDS FROM C YEAR ALLOWED.—Notwithstanding section 1371(b)(1), any net operating loss carryforward arising in a taxable year for which the corporation was a C corporation shall be allowed for purposes of this section as a deduction against the net recognized built-in gain of the S corporation for the taxable year. For purposes of determining the amount of any such loss which may be carried to subsequent taxable years, the amount of the net recognized built-in gain shall be treated as taxable income. Rules similar to the rules of the preceding sentences of this paragraph shall apply in the case of a capital loss carryforward arising in a taxable year for which the corporation was a C corporation.

(3) CREDITS.—

(A) IN GENERAL.—Except as provided in subparagraph (B), no credit shall be allowable under part IV if subchapter A of this chapter (other than under section 31) against the tax imposed by subsection (a).

(B) BUSINESS CREDIT CARRYFORWARDS FROM C YEARS ALLOWED.—Notwithstanding section 1371(b)(1), any business credit carryforward under section 39 arising in a taxable year for which the corporation was a C corporation shall be allowed as a credit against the tax imposed by subsection (a) in the same manner as if it were imposed by section 11. A similar rule shall apply in the case of the minimum tax credit under section 53 to the extent attributable to taxable years for which the corporation was a C corporation.

(4) COORDINATION WITH SECTION 1201(a).—For purposes of section 1201(a)—

(A) the tax imposed by subsection (a) shall be treated as if it were imposed by section 11, and

(B) the amount of the net recognized built-in gain shall be treated as the taxable income.

(c) LIMITATIONS.—

(1) CORPORATIONS WHICH WERE ALWAYS S CORPORA-TIONS.—Subsection (a) shall not apply to any corporation if an election under section 1362(a) has been in effect with respect to such corporation for each of its taxable years. Except as provided in regulations, an S corporation and any predecessor corporation shall be treated as 1 corporation for purposes of the preceding sentence.

(2) LIMITATION ON AMOUNT OF RECOGNIZED BUILT-IN GAINS.—The amount of the net recognized built-in gain taken into account under this section for any taxable year shall not exceed the excess (if any) of—

(A) the net unrealized built-in gain, over

(B) the net recognized built-in gain for prior taxable years beginning in the recognition period.

(d) DEFINITIONS AND SPECIAL RULES.—For purposes of this section—

(1) NET UNREALIZED BUILT-IN GAIN—The term "net unrealized built-in gain" means the amount (if any) by which—

(A) the fair market value of the assets of the S corporation as of the beginning of its 1st taxable year for which an election under section 1362(a) is in effect, exceeds

(B) the aggregate adjusted bases of such assets at such time.

(2) NET RECOGNIZED BUILT-IN GAIN.—

(A) IN GENERAL.—The term "net recognized built-in gain" means, with respect to any taxable year in the recognition period, the lesser of—

(i) the amount which would be taxable income of the S corporation for such taxable year if only recognized built-in gains and recognized built-in losses were taken into account, or

(ii) such corporation's taxable income for such taxable year (determined as provided in section 1375(b)(1)(B)).

(B) CARRYOVER.—If, for any taxable year, the amount referred to in clause (i) of subparagraph (A) exceeds the amount referred to in clause (ii) of subparagraph (A), such excess shall be treated as a recognized built-in gain in the succeeding taxable year. The preceding sentence shall apply only in the case of a corporation treated as an S corporation by reason of an election made on or after March 31 1988.

(3) RECOGNIZED BUILT-IN GAIN.—The term "recognized built-in gain" means any gain recognized during the recognition period on the disposition of any asset except to the extent that the S corporation establishes that—

(A) such asset was not held by the S corporation as of the beginning of the 1st taxable year for which it was an S corporation, or

(B) such gain exceeds the excess (if any) of—

(i) the fair market value of such asset as of the beginning of such 1st taxable year, over

(ii) the adjusted basis of the asset as of such time.

(4) RECOGNIZED BUILT-IN LOSSES.—The term "recognized built-in loss" means any loss recognized during the recognition period on the disposition of any asset to the extent that the S corporation establishes that—

(A) such asset was held by the S corporation as of the beginning of the 1st taxable year referred to in paragraph (3), and

(B) such loss does not exceed the excess of—

(i) the adjusted basis of such asset as of the beginning of such 1st taxable year, over

(ii) the fair market value of such asset as of such time.

(5) TREATMENT OF CERTAIN BUILT-IN ITEMS.—

(A) INCOME ITEMS.—Any item of income which is properly taken into account during the recognition period but which is attributable to periods before the 1st taxable year for which the corporation was an S corporation shall be treated as a recognized built-in gain for the taxable year in which it is properly taken into account.

(B) DEDUCTION ITEMS.—Any amount which is allowable as a deduction during the recognition period (determined without regard to any carryover) but which is attributable to periods before the 1st taxable year referred to in subparagraph (A) shall be treated as a recognized built-in loss for the taxable year for which it is allowable as a deduction.

(C) ADJUSTMENT TO NET UNREALIZED BUILT-IN GAIN.—The amount of the net unrealized built-in gain shall be properly adjusted for amounts which would be treated as recognized built-in gains or losses under this paragraph if such amounts were properly taken into account (or allowable as a deduction) during the recognition period.

(6) TREATMENT OF CERTAIN PROPERTY.—If the adjusted basis of any asset is determined (in whole or in part) by reference to the adjusted basis of any other asset held by S corporation as of the beginning of the 1st taxable year referred to in paragraph (3)—

(A) such asset shall be treated as held by the S corporation as of the beginning of such 1st taxable year, and

(B) any determination under paragraph (3)(B) or (4)(B) with respect to such asset shall be made by reference to the fair market value and adjusted basis of such other asset as of the beginning of such 1st taxable year.

(7) RECOGNITION PERIOD.—The term "recognition period" means the 10-year period beginning with the 1st day of the 1st taxable year for which the corporation was an S corporation.

(8) TREATMENT OF TRANSFER OF ASSETS FROM C CORPORATION TO S CORPORATION.—

(A) IN GENERAL.—Except to the extent provided in regulations, if—

(i) an S corporation acquires any asset, and

(ii) the S corporation's basis in such asset is determined (in whole or in part) by reference to the basis of such asset (or any other property) in the hands of a C corporation,

then a tax is hereby imposed on any net recognized built-in gain attributable to any such assets for any taxable year beginning in the recognition period. The amount of such tax shall be determined under the rules of this section as modified by subparagraph (B).

(B) MODIFICATIONS.—For purposes of this paragraph, the modifications of this subparagraph are as follows:

(i) IN GENERAL.—The preceding paragraphs of this subsection shall be applied by taking into account the day on which the assets were acquired by the S corporation in lieu of the beginning of the 1st taxable year for which the corporation was an S corporation.

(ii) SUBSECTION (c)(1) NOT TO APPLY.—Subsection (c)(1) shall not apply.

(9) REFERENCE TO 1ST TAXABLE YEAR.—Any reference in this section to the 1st taxable year for which the corporation was an S corporation shall be treated as a reference to the 1st taxable year for which the corporation was an S corporation pursuant to its most recent election under section 1362.

(e) REGULATIONS.—The Secretary shall prescribe such regulations as may be necessary to carry out the purposes of this section including regulations providing for the appropriate treatment of successor corporations.

CODE SECTION 1375

Tax Imposed When Passive Investment Income Of Corporation Having Accumulated Earnings and Profits Exceeds 25 Percent Of Gross Receipts

(a) GENERAL RULE.—If for the taxable year an S corporation has—

(1) accumulated earnings and profits at the close of such taxable year, and

(2) gross receipts more than 25 percent of which are passive investment income,

then there is hereby imposed a tax on the income of such corporation for such taxable year. Such tax shall be computed by multiplying the excess net passive income by the highest rate of tax specified in section 11(b).

(b) DEFINITIONS.—For purposes of this section—

(1) EXCESS NET PASSIVE INCOME.—

(A) IN GENERAL.—Except as provided in subparagraph (B), the term "excess net passive income" means an amount which bears the same ratio to the net passive income for the taxable year as—

(i) the amount by which the passive investment income for the taxable year exceeds 25 percent of the gross receipts for the taxable year, bears to

(ii) the passive investment income for the taxable year.

(B) LIMITATION.—The amount of the excess net passive income for any taxable year shall not exceed the amount of the corporation's taxable income for such taxable year as determined under section 63(a)—

(i) without regard to the deductions allowed by part VIII of subchapter B (other than the deduction allowed by section 248, relating to organization expenditures), and

(ii) without regard to the deduction under section 172.

(2) NET PASSIVE INCOME.—The term "net passive income" means—

(A) passive investment income, reduced by

(B) the deductions allowable under this chapter which are directly connected with the production of such income (other than deductions allowable under section 172 and part VIII of subchapter B).

(3) PASSIVE INVESTMENT INCOME, ETC.—The terms "passive investment income" and "gross receipts" have the same respective meanings as when used in paragraph (3) of section 1362(d).

(4) COORDINATION WITH SECTION 1374.—Notwithstanding paragraph (3), the amount of passive investment income shall be determined by not taking into account any recognized built-in gain or loss of the S corporation for any taxable year in the recognition period. Terms used in the preceding sentence shall have the same respective meanings as when used in section 1374.

(c) CREDITS NOT ALLOWABLE.—No credit shall be allowed under part IV of subchapter A of this chapter (other than section 34) against the tax imposed by subsection (a).

(d) WAIVER OF TAX IN CERTAIN CASES.—If the S corporation establishes to the satisfaction of the Secretary that—

(1) it determined in good faith that it had no subchapter C earnings and profits at the close of a taxable year, and

(2) during a reasonable period of time after it was determined that it did have subchapter C earnings and profits at the close of such taxable year such earnings and profits were distributed,

the Secretary may waive the tax imposed by subsection (a) for such taxable year.

CODE SECTION 1377

Definitions And Special Rule

(a) PRO RATA SHARE.—For purposes of this subchapter—

(1) IN GENERAL.—Except as provided in paragraph (2), each shareholder's pro rata share of any item for any taxable year shall be the sum of the amounts determined with respect to the shareholder—

(A) by assigning an equal portion of such item to each day of the taxable year, and

(B) then by dividing that portion pro rata among the shares outstanding on such day.

(2) ELECTION TO TERMINATE YEAR.—

(A) IN GENERAL.—Under regulations prescribed by the Secretary, if any shareholder terminates the shareholder's interest in the corporation during the taxable year and all affected shareholders and the corporation agree to the application of this paragraph, paragraph (1) shall be applied to the affected shareholders as if the taxable year consisted of 2 taxable years the first of which ends on the date of the termination.

(B) AFFECTED SHAREHOLDERS.—For purposes of subparagraph (A), the term "affected shareholders" means the shareholder whose interest is terminated and all shareholders to whom such shareholder has transferred shares during the taxable year. If such shareholder has transferred shares to the corporation, the term "affected shareholders" shall include all persons who are shareholders during the taxable year.

(b) POST-TERMINATION TRANSITION PERIOD.—

(1) IN GENERAL.—For purposes of this subchapter, the term "post-termination transition period" means—

(A) the period beginning on the day after the last day of the corporation's last taxable year as an S corporation and ending on the later of—

(i) the day which is 1 year after such last day, or

(ii) the due date for filing the return for such last year as an S corporation (including extensions),

(B) the 120-day period beginning on the date of any determination pursuant an audit of the taxpayer which follows the termination of the corporation's election and which adjusts a subchapter S item of income, loss, or deduction of the corporation arising during the S period (as defined in section 1368(e)(2)), and

(C) the 120-day period beginning on the date of a determination that the corporation's election under section 1362(a) had terminated for a previous taxable year.

(2) DETERMINATION DEFINED.—For purposes of paragraph (1), the term "determination" means—

(A) a determination as defined in section 1313(a), or

(B) an agreement between the corporation and the Secretary that the corporation failed to qualify as an S corporation.

(c) MANNER OF MAKING ELECTIONS, ETC.—Any election under this subchapter, and any revocation under section 1362(d)(1), shall be made in such manner as the Secretary shall by regulations prescribe.

CODE SECTION 1378

Taxable Year Of S Corporation

(a) GENERAL RULE.—For purposes of this subtitle, the taxable year of an S corporation shall be a permitted year.

(b) PERMITTED YEAR DEFINED.—For purposes of this section, the term "permitted year" means a taxable year which—

(1) is a year ending December 31, or

(2) is any other accounting period for which the corporation establishes a business purpose to the satisfaction of the Secretary.

For purposes of paragraph (2), any deferral of income to shareholders shall not be treated as a business purpose.

CODE SECTION 1379

Transitional Rules On Enactment

(a) OLD ELECTIONS.—Any election made under section 1372(a) (as in effect before the enactment of the Subchapter S Revision Act of 1982) shall be treated as an election made under section 1362.

(b) REFERENCES TO PRIOR LAW INCLUDED.—Any references in this title to a provision of this subchapter shall, to the extent not inconsistent with the purposes of this subchapter, include a reference to the corresponding provision as in effect before the enactment of the Subchapter S Revision Act of 1982.

(c) DISTRIBUTIONS OF UNDISTRIBUTED TAXABLE INCOME.— If a corporation was an electing small business corporation for the last preenactment year, subsections (f) and (d) of section 1375 (as in effect before the enactment of the Subchapter S Revision Act of 1982) shall continue to apply with respect to distributions of undistributed taxable income for any taxable year beginning before January 1, 1983.

(d) CARRYFORWARDS—If a corporation was an electing small business corporation for the last preenactment year and is an S corporation for the 1st postenactment year, any carryforward to the 1st postenactment year which arose in a taxable year for which the corporation was an electing small business corporation shall be treated as arising in the 1st postenactment year.

(e) PREENACTMENT AND POSTENACTMENT YEARS DEFINED.—For purposes of this subsection—

(1) LAST PREENACTMENT YEAR.—The term "last preenactment year" means the last taxable year of a corporation which begins before January 1, 1983.

(2) 1ST POSTENACTMENT YEAR.—The term "1st postenactment year" means the 1st taxable year of a corporation which begins after December 31, 1982.

Appendix B

INTERNAL REVENUE SERVICE RULINGS PERTAINING TO S CORPORATIONS

REVENUE RULING 91-26
1991-1 CB 184

Section 1372—Partnership Rules To Apply For Fringe Benefit Purposes

(Also Sections 106, 162, 707; 26 CFR 1.106-1, 1.162-7, 1.707-1.)

Employee fringe benefits; S corporations and partnerships. For purposes of the employee fringe benefit provisions of the Code, a 2-percent shareholder who is also an employee of an S corporation is treated like a partner of a partnership. Employee fringe benefits paid or furnished by an S corporation to or for the benefit of its 2-percent shareholder-employees in consideration for services rendered, are treated for income tax purposes like partnership guaranteed payments under section 707(c) of the Code. Rev. Rul. 72-596 revoked.

ISSUES

1. If a partner performs services in the capacity of a partner and the partnership pays accident and health insurance premiums for current year coverage on behalf of such partner without regard to partnership income, what is the Federal income tax treatment of the premium payments?

2. If an S corporation pays accident and health insurance premiums for current year coverage on behalf of a 2-percent shareholder-employee, what is the Federal income tax treatment of the premium payments?

FACTS

Situation 1. AB is a partnership in which individuals A and B are equal partners. During 1989, AB paid accident and health insurance premiums for 1989 coverage on behalf of each partner under AB's accident and health plan.

The premiums paid by AB on behalf of A and B were for services rendered by A and B in their capacities as partners and were payable without regard to partnership income. The premiums paid by AB would qualify as ordinary and necessary business expenses under section 162(a) of the Code if paid by AB on behalf of individuals who were not partners of AB. The value of the premiums to A and B is equal to the cost of the premiums paid on behalf of A and B, respectively.

Situation 2. X corporation made a valid election to be an S corporation under section 1362 of the Code effective for its taxable year beginning January 1, 1989. Three individuals own X's stock in the following portions: C, 51 percent; D, 48 percent, and E, 1 percent. C, D, and E are also employees of X.

During 1989, X paid accident and health insurance premiums for 1989 coverage on behalf of each of its employees under X's accident and health plan. The premiums paid by X would qualify as ordinary and necessary business expenses under section 162(a) of the Code if paid by X on behalf of individuals who were not "2-percent shareholders." The value of the premiums to C, D, and E is equal to the cost of the premiums paid on behalf of C, D, and E, respectively.

LAW AND ANALYSIS

Section 106 of the Code excludes from the gross income of an employee coverage provided by an employer under an accident or health plan.

Section 162(l) of the Code allows as a deduction, in the case of an individual who is an employee within the meaning of section 401(c)(1), an amount equal to 25 percent of the amount paid during the taxable year for insurance that constitutes medical care for the individual and the individual's spouse and dependents. This provision applies to taxable years beginning after December 31, 1986, and before January 1, 1992.

Section 401(c)(1) of the Code treats certain self-employed individuals as employees. Section 401(c)(1)(B) defines a "self-employed individual," with respect to any taxable year, as an individual who has earned income (as defined in section 401(c)(2)) for the taxable year. Section 401(c)(2) defines "earned income" as, in general, the net earnings from self-employment as defined in section 1402(a). Under section 1402(a), the term net earnings from self-employment is defined to include, with certain specified exceptions, a partner's distributive share of income or loss described in section 702(a)(8) from any trade or business carried on by a partnership in which the individual is a partner. Guaranteed payments to a partner for services also are included in net earnings from self-employment. In addition, section 162(l)(5)(A) provides that, for purposes of section 162(l), if a shareholder owns more than 2 percent of the outstanding stock of an S corporation, the shareholder's wages (as defined in section 3121) from the S corporation are treated as "earned income" within the meaning of section 401(c)(1).

Situation 1

Section 707(c) of the Code provides that payments to a partner for services, to the extent the payments are determined without regard to the income for the partnership, are considered as made to one who is not a member of the partnership, but only for purposes of section 61(a) (relating to gross income) and, subject to section 263 (prohibiting deductions for capital expenditures), for purposes of section 162(a) (relating to trade or business expenses). These payments are termed "guaranteed payments."

Section 1.707-1(c) of the Income Tax Regulations provides that for a guaranteed payment under section 707(c) of the Code to be deductible by the partnership, it must meet the same tests under section 162(a) as it would if the payment had been made to a person who was not a member of the partnership. Generally, for purposes of Code provisions other than sections 61(a) and 162(a), guaranteed payments are treated as a partner's distributive share of ordinary income. The regulation states, by way of an illustration, that a partner who receives guaranteed payments is not entitled to exclude them from gross income as disability payments under section 105(d) (as in effect prior to its repeal by section 122(b) of the Social Security Amendments of 1983, Pub. L. No. 98-21, 1983-2 C.B. 309, 315). The regulation also provides that a partner who receives guaranteed payments is not, by virtue of the payments regarded as an employee of the partnership for purposes of withholding of tax at source, deferred compensation plans, and other purposes.

Amounts paid in cash or in kind by a partnership, without regard to its income, to or for the benefit of its partners, for services rendered in their capacities as partners, are guaranteed payments under section 707(c) of the Code. A partnership is entitled to deduct such cash amounts, or the cost to the partnership of such in-kind benefits, under section 162(a), if the requirements of that section are satisfied (taking into account the rules of section 263). Under section 61(a), the cash amount or the value of the benefit is included in the income of the recipient-partner. The cash amount or value of the benefit is not excludible from the partner's gross income under the general fringe benefit rules (except to the extent the Code provision allowing exclusion of a fringe benefit specifically provides that it applies to partners) because the benefit is treated as a distributive share of partnership income under section 1.707-1(c) of the regulations for purposes of all Code sections other than sections 61(a) and 162(a), and a partner is treated as self-employed to the extent of his or her distributive share of income. Section 1402(a). *See also* Rev. Rul. 69-184, 1969-1 C.B. 256 (employment taxes); *cf.* section 401(c), which recognizes that partners are self-employed individuals but treats them as employees for certain limited purposes.

Therefore, AB may deduct under section 162(a) of the Code (subject to section 263) the cost of the accident and health insurance premiums paid on behalf of A and B. A and B may not exclude the cost of the premiums from their gross income under section 106, but must include the cost of the premiums in gross income under section 61(a). Provided all the requirements of section 162(l) are met, however, A and B may deduct the cost of the premiums to the extent provided by section 162(l).

A partnership may account for accident and health insurance premiums paid on behalf of a partner as a reduction in distributions to the partner. Under these circumstances, the premiums are not deductible by the partnership, so distributive shares of partnership income and deduction (and other payment items) are not affected by payment of the premiums. A partner may deduct the cost of the premiums paid on that partner's behalf to the extent allowed under section 162(l).

Situation 2.

Section 1372 of the Code provides that, for purposes of applying the income tax provisions of the Code relating to employee fringe benefits, an

S corporation shall be treated as a partnership, and any person who is a "2-percent shareholder" of the S corporation shall be treated like a partner of a partnership. Section 1372(b) defines a "2-percent shareholder" as any person who owns (or is considered as owning within the meaning of section 318) on any day during the taxable year of the S corporation more than 2 percent of the outstanding stock of the corporation or stock possessing more than 2 percent of the total combined voting power of all stock in the corporation.

Under section 1372 of the Code, for purposes of applying the provisions of the Code relating to employee fringe benefits, a 2-percent shareholder who is also an employee of an S corporation is treated like a partner of a partnership. Employee fringe benefits paid or furnished by an S corporation to or for the benefit of its 2-percent shareholder-employees in consideration for services rendered, therefore, are treated for income tax purposes like partnership guaranteed payments under section 707(c). An S corporation is entitled to deduct the cost of such employee fringe benefits under section 162(a) if the requirements of that section are satisfied (taking into account the rules of section 263). Like a partner, a 2-percent shareholder is required to include the value of such benefits in gross income under section 61(a) and is not entitled to exclude such benefits from gross income under provisions of the Code permitting the exclusion of employee fringe benefits (except to the extent the Code provision allowing exclusion of a fringe benefit specifically provides that it applies to partners).

Therefore, X may deduct under section 162(a) of the Code the cost of the accident and health insurance premiums paid on behalf of C, D, and E. C and D may not exclude the cost of the premiums from their gross income under section 106, but must include the cost of the premiums in gross income under section 61(a). Provided all the requirements of section 162(l) are met, however, C and D may deduct the cost of the premiums to the extent provided by section 162(l). E (who does not own more than 2 percent of X's stock) may exclude from gross income under section 106 the cost of the premiums paid by X on E's behalf.

Unlike a partnership, an S corporation may not account for accident and health insurance premiums paid on behalf of a shareholder-employee as a reduction in distributions to the shareholder-employee because the shareholder-employee's pro rata share of S corporation income would not be subject to employment taxes.

HOLDINGS

1. Accident and health insurance premiums paid by a partnership on behalf of a partner are guaranteed payments under section 707(c) of the Code if the premiums are paid for services rendered in the capacity of partner and to the extent the premiums are determined without regard to partnership income. As guaranteed payments, the premiums are deductible by the partnership under section 162 (subject to the capitalization rules of section 263) and includable in the recipient-partner's gross income under section 61. The premiums are not excludable from the recipient-partner's gross income under section 106; however, provided all the requirements of section 162(l) are met, the partner may deduct the cost of the premiums to the extent provided by section 162(l).

A partnership must report the cost of accident and health insurance premiums that are guaranteed payments on its U.S. Partnership Return of Income (Form 1065) and the Schedule K-1s. A partnership is not required to file a Form 1099 or a Wage and Tax Statement (Form W-2) for accident and health insurance premiums that are guaranteed payments.

2. Under section 1372 of the Code, accident and health insurance premiums paid by an S corporation on behalf of a 2-percent shareholder-employee as consideration for services rendered are treated like guaranteed payments under section 707(c) of the Code. Therefore, the premiums are deductible by the corporation under section 162 (subject to the capitalization rules of section 263), and includable in the recipient shareholder-employee's gross income under section 61. The premiums are not excludable from the recipient shareholder-employee's gross income under section 106; however, provided all the requirements of section 162(l) are met, the shareholder-employee may deduct the cost of the premium to the extent provided by section 162(l).

An S corporation may deduct as salary and wages accident and health insurance premiums paid on behalf of its 2-percent shareholder-employees on its U.S. Income Tax Return for an S Corporation. The S corporation is required to file a Wage and Tax Statement (Form W-2) for each 2-percent shareholder-employee. The Form W-2 must include for a 2-percent shareholder-employee the cost of accident and health insurance premiums paid on behalf of the shareholder-employee in the shareholder-employee's wages.

EFFECT ON OTHER REVENUE RULINGS

Rev. Rul. 72-596, 1972-2 C.B. 395, concerns the deductibility under section 162 of the Code of premiums paid by a partnership on behalf of its partners for workmen's compensation insurance. Rev. Rul. 72-596 relies on the general rule that a partner is not an employee and suggests that workmen's compensation premiums are deductible by the partnership only if paid on behalf of an employee.

The partners in Rev. Rul. 72-596 were acting in their capacities as partners and the workmen's compensation premiums were payable without regard to partnership income. Thus, the premiums are guaranteed payments under section 707(c) of the Code, and as such are deductible by the partnership under section 162 (if the requirements of that section are satisfied) and includible in the incomes of the partners under section 61. Rev. Rul. 72-596 is incorrect to the extent it concludes otherwise. Rev. Rul. 72-596 is revoked.

ADMINISTRATIVE RELIEF

For S corporation tax years beginning before January 1, 1991, the Service will not challenge the treatment of accident and health insurance premiums paid by S corporations for 2-percent shareholder-employees in accordance with the instructions to the Form 1120S and Schedule K-1 to the Form 1120S. These instructions provide that such fringe benefits are nondeductible by the S corporation and cannot be treated as deductible or excludable employee fringe benefits (except for benefits allowed partners, such as section 162(l)).

The Service does not consider payments of accident and health insurance premiums by an S corporation on behalf of 2-percent shareholder-employees to be distributions for purposes of the single class of stock requirement of section 1361(b)(1)(D).

DRAFTING INFORMATION

The principal author of this revenue ruling is Christine Ellison of the Office of Assistant Chief Counsel (Passthroughs and Special Industries). For further information regarding this revenue ruling contact Christine Ellison on (202) 377-9667 (not a toll-free call).

REVENUE RULING 92-48
1992-1 CB 301

ISSUE

Can a trust that qualifies as a charitable remainder trust under section 664 of the Internal Revenue Code be the subject of a "qualified subchapter S trust" (QSST) election under section 1361(d)(2)?

FACTS

X is a small business corporation that made a valid election in 1985 to be an S corporation. In 1990, A, an individual who owned shares of stock in X, transferred some of those shares to a valid charitable remainder unitrust, TR, described in section 664(d)(2) of the Code. Under the terms of TR, the trustee is required to pay annually to B, an individual and a citizen of the United States, for life an amount equal to the lesser of (1) the amount of TR's income (determined under section 643(b)) for the taxable year, or (2) 12 percent of the net fair market value of TR's assets valued as of the first day of the taxable year. If the amount of TR's income for the taxable year exceeds the amount determined under (2), then the payment to B is to include the excess income to the extent that the aggregate of the amounts paid in prior years to B was less than 12 percent of the aggregate net fair market value of TR's assets for those years. At B's death, the trustee must distribute all of TR's remaining principal and income, other than any amount due B or B's estate, to Y, an organization described in section 170(c). Upon A's transfer of the X stock to TR, B filed a QSST election with respect to TR under section 1361(d)(2).

LAW AND ANALYSIS

The tax treatment of charitable remainder trusts is governed by subpart C of part I of subchapter J of the Code (sections 661 through 664), whereas the tax treatment of QSSTs is governed by section 1361 and, by cross reference, subpart E of part I of subchapter J (sections 671 through 679). The rules under subpart C can require tax results that are incompatible with those required by the rules under subpart E.

The rules governing the taxation of charitable remainder trusts are contained in section 664 of the Code, a section within subpart C of part I of subchapter J. Section 664(a) states that notwithstanding any other provision of subchapter J, the provisions of section 664 shall, in accordance with the regulations, apply in the case of a charitable remainder trust. In general, under section 664(d), a charitable remainder trust is a trust pursuant to which an annuity or unitrust amount, determined under a specified formula, is payable at least annually for either the life or lives of a named individual or individuals or for a term of years (not to exceed 20 years). Section 664(b) provides rules for characterizing the distributed amounts in the hands of the income beneficiaries (e.g., as ordinary income, capital gain, or distribution of corpus). Under sections 664(d)(1)(B) and 664(d)(2)(B), no amount other than the annuity or unitrust amount may be paid to or for the use of any person other than an organization described in section 170(c). Any amount earned by the trust in excess of the amount distributed to the beneficiaries is accumulated for eventual payment to or for the use of an organization described in section 170(c). The remainder interest in the trust is payable on the termination of the annuity or unitrust payments.

Section 1361(b)(1)(B) of the Code permits only individuals, estates, and trusts described in section 1361(c)(2)(A) to be shareholders of S corporations. Under section 1361(d)(1)(A), a QSST is treated as a trust described in section 1361(c)(2)(A) and therefore is a permissible S corporation shareholder. The rules governing the taxation of QSSTs are provided by section 1361 and, by reference, sections 671 through 679 (subpart E of part I of subchapter J).

Section 1361(d)(3) of the Code defines the term "qualified subchapter S trust." For a trust to meet that definition, all of the income (within the meaning of section 643(b)) of the trust must be distributed (or be required to be distributed) currently to one individual who is a citizen or resident of the United States. In addition, the terms of the trust must require that (i) during the life of the current income beneficiary there is only one income beneficiary of the trust; (ii) any corpus distributed during the life of the current income beneficiary may be distributed only to that beneficiary; (iii) the income interest of the current income beneficiary in the trust terminates on the earlier of such beneficiary's death or the termination of the trust; and (iv) upon the termination of the trust during the life of the current income beneficiary, the trust must distribute all of its assets to the beneficiary.

Under section 1361(d)(2)(A) of the Code, QSST status must be elected by the beneficiary of the trust (or the beneficiary's legal representative). If a QSST election is made, section 1361(d)(1)(B) provides that for purposes of section 678(a), the QSST beneficiary is treated as the owner of that portion of the trust that consists of stock it an S corporation. Section 671 provides that, where it is specified in subpart E of part I of subchapter J of the Code that the grantor or another person is to be treated as the owner of any portion of a trust, the items of trust income, deductions, and credits attributable to that portion are included in computing the taxable income and credits of the grantor or other person. Any remaining portion of the trust is subject to subparts A through D of part I of subchapter J.

Section 678(a) of the Code (which, under certain circumstances, treats a person other than a grantor as the owner of a trust) is within subpart E of part I of subchapter J (sections 671 through 679). Thus, a beneficiary who makes a QSST election agrees, pursuant to section 678(a), to be treated as the owner of the trust to the extent that the trust assets consist of S corporation stock and hence agrees to be taxed under section 671 to that extent.

To the extent that a QSST's assets consist of S corporation stock, the QSST's beneficiary is treated as the owner of a grantor trust under subpart E. This tax result is incompatible with the rule that a charitable remainder trust function exclusively under section 664 of the Code.

Moreover, other rules of subpart E are inconsistent with the rules of section 664, in particular the rules for how beneficiaries are taxed on both distributed and undistributed amounts of trust income.

On a given set of facts, the character and amount of trust income taken into account by the beneficiary could be the same whether the trust was governed by the charitable remainder trust rules or the QSST rules. However, the identity of treatment under such circumstances would be coincidental. The incompatible tax treatment of trust income under subparts C and E of part I of subchapter J precludes the beneficiary of a charitable remainder trust from making a valid QSST election under section 1361 of the Code.

The QSST election filed by B is invalid. Accordingly, as TR is an ineligible shareholder, X's S election is terminated under section 1362(d)(2) of the Code as of the date of A's transfer of the X stock to the trust. The transfer has no effect on the validity of TR's status as a charitable remainder trust.

HOLDING

A trust that qualifies as a charitable remainder trust under section 664 of the Code cannot be the subject of a "qualified subchapter S trust" election under section 1361(d)(2).

If stock of an S corporation is transferred to a charitable remainder trust (other than a trust described in section 1361(c)(2)(A)(iii) of the Code), the corporation's S election is terminated because the charitable remainder trust is not an eligible shareholder. The corporation may be eligible for relief from inadvertent termination of its S election under section 1362(f).

DRAFTING INFORMATION

The principal author of this revenue ruling is David McDonnell of the Office of Assistant Chief Counsel (Passthroughs and Special Industries). For further information regarding this revenue ruling, contact Mr. McDonnell on (202) 377-9470 (not a toll-free call).

REVENUE RULING 92-73
1992-2 CB 224

Section 1361 — S Corporation Defined

ISSUE

Is a trust that qualifies as an individual retirement account under section 408(a) of the Internal Revenue Code a permitted shareholder of an S corporation under section 1361?

LAW

Section 1361(a)(1) of the Code defines an "S corporation" as a small business corporation for which an election under section 1362(a) is in effect.

Section 1361(b)(1) of the Code defines a "small business corporation" as a domestic corporation that is not an ineligible corporation and
that does not (A) have more than 35 shareholders, (B) have as a shareholder a person (other than an estate and other than a trust described in
section 1361(c)(2)) who is not an individual, (C) have a nonresident alien
as a shareholder, or (D) have more than one class of stock.

Section 1361(c)(2)(A)(i) of the Code provides that a trust may be a
shareholder of an S corporation if the entire trust is treated under subpart
E of part I of subchapter J of chapter 1 of the Code as owned by an
individual who is a citizen or resident of the United States. When any
portion of a trust is treated as owned by an individual under subpart of part
I of subchapter J of chapter 1 of the Code, section 671 provides that there
will be included in computing the taxable income and credits of the owner
those items of income, deductions, and credits of the trust that are
attributable to that portion of the trust, to the extent that such items would
be taken into account in computing taxable income or credits of an
individual.

Section 1361(d)(1) of the Code provides that if a beneficiary of a
"qualified subchapter S trust" (QSST) so elects, the trust will be treated as
a trust described in section 1361(c)(2)(A)(i) and thus will be a permitted
shareholder of an S corporation. If the election is made by a beneficiary
of a QSST, section 1361(d)(1)(B) provides that, for purposes of section
678(a), the beneficiary will be treated as the owner of that portion of the
QSST that consists of stock in the S corporation. If the beneficiary of a
QSST is treated for purposes of section 678(a) as the owner of that portion
of the QSST that consists of stock in the S corporation, the income,
deductions, and credits of the S corporation that are allocated to the QSST
are included in computing the beneficiary's taxable income and credits, in
accordance with section 671.

Section 1361(d)(3) of the Code provides that a QSST is a trust the
terms of which require that (i) during the life of the current income
beneficiary, there shall be only one income beneficiary of the trust; (ii) any
corpus distributed during the life of the current income beneficiary may
be distributed only to the beneficiary; (iii) the income interest of the
current income beneficiary in the trust shall terminate on the earlier of the
beneficiary's death or the termination of the trust; and (iv) upon the
termination of the trust during the life of the current income beneficiary,

the trust shall distribute all of its assets to the beneficiary. In addition, for a trust to be a QSST, all of the income of the trust must be distributed (or required to be distributed) currently to one individual who is a citizen or resident of the United States.

Section 408(a) of the Code provides that the term "individual retirement account" means a trust created or organized in the United States for the exclusive benefit of an individual or the individual's beneficiaries, but only if the written governing instrument creating the trust meets the requirements specified in section 408(a).

Section 408(d)(1) of the Code provides, generally, that any amount paid or distributed out of an individual retirement account will be included in the gross income of the payee or distributee, as the case may be, in the manner provided under section 72 (relating to the taxation of annuities).

ANALYSIS

A trust is permitted to be a shareholder of an S corporation only if the trust is described in section 1361(c)(2)(A)(i) of the Code or is a QSST that is treated as a trust described in section 1361(c)(2)(A)(i) because the beneficiary has so elected under section 1361(d). In either case, under subpart E of part I of subchapter J, the beneficiary of the trust is taxed currently on the trust's share of S corporation income, deductions, and credits. By contrast, under section 408(d) of the Code, the beneficiary of a section 408(a) trust is taxed when distributions are made from the trust and is taxed in the manner provided under section 72. A section 408(a) trust cannot also be a trust described in section 1361(c)(2)(A)(i) or a QSST treated as a trust described in section 1361(c)(2)(A)(i) because the rules that apply to a trust described in section 1361(c)(2)(A)(i) or QSST treated as such a trust are incompatible with the rules that apply to a section 408(a) trust. Therefore, a section 408(a) trust cannot satisfy the rules applicable to a trust that is a permitted shareholder of an S corporation.

HOLDING

A trust that qualifies as an individual retirement account under section 408(a) of the Code is not a permitted shareholder of an S corporation under section 1361.

If a shareholder inadvertently causes a termination of an S corporation by transferring stock to a trust that qualifies as an individual retirement account under section 408(a) of the Code, relief may be requested
under section 1362(f) and the regulations thereunder.

DRAFTING INFORMATION

The principal author of this revenue ruling is Daniel M. McCabe of
the Office of Assistant Chief Counsel (Passthroughs and Special Industries). For further information regarding this revenue ruling contact Mr.
McCabe on (202) 622-3495 (not a toll-free call).

REVENUE RULING 93-31
1993-1 CB 186

Section 663 — Complex Trust Exclusions

Section 1361 — S Corporation Defined

ISSUE

Is a substantially separate and independent share of a trust, within the
meaning of section 663(c) of the Internal Revenue Code, a qualified
subchapter S trust (QSST), if there is a remote possibility that the corpus
of the trust will be distributed during the lifetime of the current income
beneficiary to someone other than that beneficiary?

FACTS

X is a small business corporation that made a valid election in 1987
to be an S corporation. During 1993, A, an individual, transferred shares
of stock in X to T, a trust.

The terms of the trust instrument provide that income is payable in
equal shares to B and C. Upon the death of either B or C, one-half of the
remaining trust corpus is to be distributed to whomever that beneficiary
has appointed or, in the absence of an appointee, to that beneficiary's
estate. The trust instrument further provides that, in general, distributions
from T are to be made in substantially the same manner as if separate trusts
had been created. However, the trust instrument also authorizes the trustee

had been created. However, the trust instrument also authorizes the trustee to distribute all or a portion of the trust corpus to B if necessary (after taking account of B's other income) for B's health, education, support or maintenance. B has other income that is so substantial that the possibility of exercise of the power to distribute corpus by the trustee is remote.

LAW AND ANALYSIS

Section 1361(a)(1) of the Code defines the term "S corporation" as a small business corporation for which an election under section 1362(a) is in effect for the taxable year.

Section 1361(b)(1)(B) of the Code provides that a small business corporation cannot have as a shareholder a trust other than a trust described in section 1361(c)(2).

Section 1361(c)(2)(A) of the Code provides that, for purposes of section 1361(b)(1)(B), trusts described in section 1361(c)(2)(A)(i)- (iv) may be shareholders of a small business corporation. In the situation presented, T is not a trust described in section 1361(c)(2)(A)(i)-(iv). However, an election may be made under section 1361(d)(2) to treat a trust not otherwise described in section 1361(c)(2)(A)(i) as though it were described in that section if the trust is a QSST.

For a trust to qualify as a QSST under section 1361(d)(3) of the Code, all of the income (within the meaning of section 643(b)) of the trust must be distributed (or required to be distributed) currently to one individual who is a citizen or resident of the United States. In addition, under section 1361(d)(3)(A), the terms of the trust must require that (i) during the life of the current income beneficiary there may be only one income beneficiary of the trust; (ii) any corpus distributed during the life of the current income beneficiary may be distributed only to that beneficiary; (iii) the income interest of the current income beneficiary in the trust must terminate on the earlier of that beneficiary's death or the termination of the trust; and (iv) upon the termination of the trust during the life of the current income beneficiary, the trust must distribute all of its assets to that beneficiary. Section 1361(d)(3) further provides that a substantially separate and independent share of a trust, within the meaning of section 663(c), is treated as a separate trust for purposes of section 1361(c) and (d).

Section 663(c) of the Code requires that if a single trust has more than one beneficiary, substantially separate and independent shares of different beneficiaries are treated as separate trusts for the sole purpose of determining the amount of distributable net income in the application of sections 661 and 662. The existence of substantially separate and independent shares and the manner of treatment as separate trusts. are determined in accordance with regulations.

Under section 1.663(c)-1(c) of the Income Tax Regulations, the separate share rule may apply even though separate and independent accounts are not maintained for each share on the books of account of the trust, and even though no physical segregation of assets is made or required.

Section 1.663(c)-3(a) of the regulations provides, in part, that the applicability of the separate share rule will generally depend upon whether distributions of the trust are to be made in substantially the same manner as if separate trusts had been created.

Section 1.663(c)-3(b) of the regulations provides, in part, that separate share treatment will not be applied to a trust or portion of a trust subject to a power to distribute corpus to or for one or more beneficiaries within a group or class of beneficiaries, unless payment of corpus to one beneficiary cannot affect the proportionate share of corpus of any shares of the other beneficiaries, or unless substantially proper adjustment must be made (under the governing instrument) so that substantially separate and independent shares exist. However, under section 1.663(c)-3(d), separate share treatment may apply to a trust even if the trust is subject to a power to pay out to a beneficiary of a share of the trust an amount of corpus in excess of the beneficiary's proportionate share of the trust corpus if the possibility of exercise of the power is remote.

In the situation presented, the possibility that B will receive more than B's proportionate share of the trust corpus is ignored for purposes of section 663(c) of the Code because it is remote. As a result, the shares of B and C in T are treated as separate trusts under section 663(c), and therefore also as separate trusts under section 1361(d)(3). Accordingly, each share of T must meet the QSST requirements of section 1361(d)(3) for X to retain its status as a small business corporation after the transfer of shares in X to T.

The cross-reference in section 1361(d)(3) to the separate share rule under section 663(c) does not modify the express statutory requirements of section 1361(d)(3) that must be met for a trust to qualify as a QSST. Therefore, the applicability of the separate share rule under section 662(c) does not override the requirement in section 136l(d)(3)(ii) that, for a trust to be a QSST and thus an eligible shareholder of a small business corporation under sections 1361(d), its terms must provide than there is only one income beneficiary and that any corpus distributed during the life of the current income beneficiary may be distributed only to that beneficiary. Moreover, it is clear that section 1361(d) envisions a trust with a single current income beneficiary. Section 1361(d)(2) provides that the beneficiary must elect to be treated as a QSST and section 1361(d)(1) provides that the beneficiary is taxed on his or her allocable share of the S corporation income. Allowing any trust having beneficiaries with contingent interests to hold stock in an S corporation would create uncertainty, for example, in determining whether and when the contingent beneficiaries should be taxable on S corporation income and who should make the QSST election.

Because the trust instrument in this situation provides for the possibility (however remote) that corpus allocable to C's separate share will be distributed to B, C's share of T does not meet the section 1361(d)(3)(A)(ii) requirement that the terms of a QSST require that any corpus distributed during the life of the current income beneficiary may be distributed only to that beneficiary.

Therefore, A's transfer of stock in X to T caused a termination of X's status as an S corporation.

HOLDING

A substantially separate and independent share of a trust, within the meaning of section 663(c) of the Code, is not a QSST if there is a remote possibility that the corpus of the trust will be distributed during the lifetime of the current income beneficiary to someone other than that beneficiary.

If a shareholder inadvertently causes a termination of an S corporation by transferring stock to a trust that does not meet the definition of a QSST, relief may be requested under section 1362(f) of the Code and the regulations thereunder.

DRAFTING INFORMATION

The principal author of this revenue ruling is J. Scott Hargis of the Office of Assistant Chief Counsel (Passthroughs and Special Industries). For further information regarding this revenue ruling, contact Mr. Hargis on (202) 622-3050 (not a toll-free call).

LETTER RULING 9248019

August 31, 1992

This ruling is in reply to correspondence dated June 4, 1992, and subsequent correspondence, written on behalf of X, requesting a ruling that X's "split-dollar" life insurance agreement will not create more than one class of stock within the meaning of section 1361(b)(1)(D) of the Internal Revenue Code.

X, a corporation that has filed an S election, plans to provide a fringe benefit to key employees and their spouses through a split-dollar life insurance agreement. Under the agreement, X will pay 100% of the premiums on existing insurance policies, purchased and owned by the employees and their spouses individually, less the term insurance cost as determined under Rev. Rul. 64-328, 1964-2 C.B. 11.

X's articles of incorporation provided that "no distinction shall exist between the shares of the corporation or the holders thereof." The State of Y Corporations Code section 202(e) provides that the articles of incorporation define any rights, preferences, privileges, and restrictions granted to or imposed upon the respective classes.

Furthermore, X's submission represents that, because the purpose of this split-dollar arrangement is to provide a fringe benefit to employees, it is not a vehicle for the circumvention of the one class of stock requirement.

Section 1361(a) of the Code provides that the term "S corporation" means, with respect to any tax year, a small business corporation for which an election under section 1362(a) is in effect for the year.

Section 1361(b)(1) of the Code provides that the term "small business corporation" means a domestic corporation which is not an ineligible corporation and meets the requirements specified in sections 1361(b)(1)(A) through (D).

Section 1361(b)(1)(D) provides that S corporations may not possess more than one class of stock.

Section 1.1361-1(1)(2)(i) of the Income Tax Regulations provides the determination of whether all outstanding shares of stock confer identical rights to distribution and liquidation proceeds is made based on the corporate charter, articles of incorporation, bylaws, applicable state law, and binding agreements relating to distribution and liquidation proceeds (collectively, the governing provisions). A commercial contractual agreement, such as a lease, employment agreement, or loan agreement, is not a binding agreement relating to distribution and liquidation proceeds and thus is not a governing provision unless a principal purpose of the agreement is to circumvent the one class of stock requirement of section 1361(b)(1)(D) and this paragraph (1).

Rev. Rul. 64-328 holds that when there is a split-dollar arrangement, in which the employer pays the portion of the premiums equal to the increases in the cash surrender value and the employee pays the balance, if any, of the premiums, and in which, from the proceeds payable upon the employee's death, the employer receives at least an amount equal to the funds it has provided, with the beneficiary receiving the balance, the value of the insurance protection in excess of the premiums paid by the employee must be included in the employee's income.

Rev. Rul. 78-420, 1978-2 C.B. 67, amplifying Rev. Rul. 64-328, holds that in situations that are identical, but for the fact that an employee's spouse is the owner of the policy, a benefit accrues to the employee-spouse similar to the benefit that would accrue were the employee-spouse the owner of the policy.

Rev. Rul. 91-26, 1991-1 C.B. 185, states that the Service does not consider payments of accident and health insurance premiums by an S corporation on behalf of 2-percent shareholder-employees to be distributions for purposes of the single class of stock requirement of section 1361(b)(1)(D) of the Internal Revenue Code.

Like the payment of accident and health insurance premiums described in Rev. Rul. 91-26, X's payment of premiums under the split-dollar life insurance agreement is a fringe benefit to employees, not a vehicle for the circumvention of the one class of stock requirement. Therefore, based solely on the representations made and the information submitted, it is held that X's split-dollar life insurance agreement with its employees and their spouses will not create more than one class of stock within the meaning of section 1361(b)(1)(D) of the Internal Revenue Code.

Except as specifically ruled upon above, no opinion is expressed concerning the federal income tax consequences of the above-described facts under any other provision of the Code. Specifically, no opinion is expressed or implied concerning whether X's S corporation election was a valid election under section 1362 of the Code.

This ruling is directed only to the taxpayer who requested it. Section 6110(j)(3) of the Code provides that it may not be used or cited as precedent.

LETTER RULING 9318007

January 29, 1993

This ruling is in reply to correspondence dated December 29, 1992, and prior correspondence, written on behalf of X, requesting a ruling that X's "split-dollar" life insurance agreement will not create more than one class of stock within the meaning of section 1361(b)(1)(D) of the Internal Revenue Code.

X, a corporation that has filed an S election, plans to enter into a split-dollar life insurance agreement with an irrevocable trust created by one of its shareholders, A. A is the President and Chief Executive Officer of X. X will pay the premiums on the insurance policy. However, at the time X pays the premiums, A, or the irrevocable trust created by A, must reimburse X to the extent the payment confers an economic benefit on A.

Section 1361(a) of the Code provides that the term "S corporation" means, with respect to any tax year, a small business corporation for which an election under section 1362(a) is in effect for the year.

Section 1361(b)(1) of the Code provides that the term "small business corporation" means a domestic corporation which is not an ineligible corporation and meets the requirements specified in section 1361(b)(1)(A) through (D).

Section 1361(b)(1)(D) of the Code provides that S corporations may not possess more than one class of stock. Section 1.1361-1(l)(1) of the Income Tax Regulations provides that, except as provided in section 1.1361-1(l)(4) (relating to instruments, obligations, or arrangements treated as a second class of stock), a corporation is treated as having only one class of stock if all outstanding shares of stock of the corporation confer identical rights to distribution and liquidation proceeds.

Section 1.1361-1(l)(2)(i) of the regulations provides that the determination of whether all outstanding shares of stock confer identical rights to distribution and liquidation proceeds is made based on the corporate charter, articles of incorporation, bylaws, applicable state law, and binding agreements relating to distribution and liquidation proceeds (collectively, the governing provisions). A commercial contractual agreement, such as a lease, employment agreement, or loan agreement, is not a binding agreement relating to distribution and liquidation proceeds and thus is not a governing provision unless a principal purpose of the arrangement is to circumvent the one class of stock requirement of section 1361(b)(1)(D) and section 1.1361-1(l).

Rev. Rul. 79-50, 1979-1 C.B. 138, holds that when there is a split-dollar arrangement in which a corporation pays the portion of the premiums equal to the increases in the cash surrender value and the shareholder pays the balance, if any, of the premiums, and in which, from the proceeds payable upon the shareholder's death, the corporation receives at least an amount equal to the funds it has provided, with the beneficiary receiving the balance, the value of the insurance protection in excess of the premiums paid by the shareholder must be included in the shareholder's income. In addition, this benefit flowing from the corporation to the shareholder is a distribution within the meaning of section 301(a) of the Code made by the corporation to the shareholder with respect to its stock and must be treated in accordance with section 301(c).

Because the arrangement provides that, at the time X pays the premiums, A, or the irrevocable trust established by A, must reimburse X to the extent the payment confers an economic benefit to that shareholder, X's split-dollar arrangement does not alter rights to distribution and liquidation proceeds. Therefore, based solely on the representations made and the information submitted, it is held that X's split-dollar life insurance agreement with the irrevocable trust established by A will not create more than one class of stock within the meaning of section 1361(b)(1)(D) of the Code.

Except as specifically ruled upon above, no opinion is expressed concerning the federal income tax consequences of the above-described facts under any other provision of the Code. Specifically, no opinion is expressed or implied concerning whether X's S corporation election was a valid election under section 1362 of the Code.

This ruling is directed only to the taxpayer who requested it. Section 6110(j)(3) of the Code provides that it may not be used or cited as precedent.

TECHNICAL ADVICE MEMORANDUM 9604001

September 8, 1995

[1] ISSUES

(1) When Subsidiary paid single premiums on two life insurance contracts as described below, what amount was includable each year in Taxpayer's gross income?

(2) If Trust was designated as the owner of the insurance policies, did Taxpayer make a gift subject to the gift tax?

FACTS

[2] Taxpayer is Chairman and C.E.O. of Holding and owns 51 percent of Holding. Holding owns 98 percent of Subsidiary. The corporate minutes of Subsidiary and other information submitted indicate that in 1991 Subsidiary, two insurance companies, and Trust entered into the following transaction: (1) Subsidiary paid a dollars to each of the insurance companies for two paid-up $500,000 life insurance policies on the life of Taxpayer; (2) the insurance companies issued the life insurance

policies to Trust as owner of the policies; (3) Trust entered into "split dollar" agreements with Subsidiary; and (4) Trust assigned the policies to Subsidiary as collateral for Trust's obligation under the split-dollar agreements to repay the a dollars in premiums it paid to each insurance company.

[3] Under the terms of the split-dollar agreements, Trust continues as the owner of the policies and designated beneficiary of the policy proceeds. In addition, the trustees possess all incidents of ownership in the policies. Article 7.b of the agreement provides that Subsidiary has an unqualified right to receive a portion of the death benefits equal to the total amount of the premiums paid. No amount shall be paid from the death benefit proceeds to the beneficiary designated under the policy until the full amount due Subsidiary has been paid. The agreements may be terminated for a number of reasons, including: (a) bankruptcy or cessation of operations of Subsidiary; (b) termination of Taxpayer's employment; and (c) written notice by Trust or by Taxpayer. If the agreements are terminated prior to Taxpayer's death, then Trust must reimburse Subsidiary before the collateral will be returned to Trust. If the policies are canceled or surrendered, Subsidiary is to be reimbursed from the cash surrender proceeds. The insurance documents indicate that, in year four of the policies, their cash surrender value will exceed the amount of premiums paid.

[4] The split-dollar and collateral assignment agreements provide the following additional pertinent information:

(1)   Any dividends on the policies are applied to purchase paid-up additional insurance on the life of Taxpayer.

(2)   The owners of the policies may borrow from the policies or pledge or assign the policies, but only to extent that the cash surrender value of a policy exceeds the amount of the premiums paid by Subsidiary.

LAW AND ANALYSIS — Issue (1):

[5] Section 61(a)(1) of the Internal Revenue Code generally provides that gross income includes compensation for services.

[6] According to section 451(a) of the Code, the amount of any item of gross income shall be included in the gross income for the taxable year in which received by the taxpayer, unless, under the method of accounting used in computing taxable income, such amount is to be properly accounted for as of a different period.

[7] If, in connection with the performance of services, property is transferred to any person other than the person for whom the services were performed, the excess of the fair market value of the property over the amount paid for the property is included in the service provider's gross income in the first taxable year in which the rights of the service provider in the property are transferable or are not subject to a substantial risk of forfeiture. See, generally, section 83(a) of the Code.

[8] According to section 1.83-3(e) of the regulations, the term "property" includes a beneficial interest in assets (including money) which are transferred or set aside from the claims of creditors of the transferor, for example, in a trust or escrow account. In the case of the transfer of a life insurance contact, the term "property" includes only the cash surrender value of the contract.

[9] Property is considered "transferred" for purposes of section 83(a) of the Code when a person acquires a beneficial interest in the property. Evidence that a "transfer" may not have occurred is when the property is required to be returned upon the occurrence of an event that is certain to happen, such as a termination of employment. See section 1.83-3(a)(1) and section 1.83- 3(a)(3).

[10] Section 1.83-1(a)(2) provides that the cost of life insurance protection under a life insurance contract is taxable generally under section 61 of the Code during the period the contract remains substantially nonvested. This of course would also be the case during a period when a service provider receives insurance protection from a life insurance contract that is not "property" because it has not been set aside from the claims of the employer's creditors or is not "transferred" to the employee.

[11] The Service's position in the area of a traditional "split dollar" life insurance arrangement is set out in Rev. Rul. 64-328, 1964-2 C.B. 11, as amplified by Rev. Rul. 66-110, 1966-1 C.B. 12, Rev. Rul. 67-154, 1967-1 C.B. 11, and Rev. Rul. 78-420, 1978-2 C.B 67.

[12] Rev. Rul. 64-328 describes the split-dollar arrangement that was popular at the time the Rev. Rul. was published. An employer and employee typically joined in purchasing an insurance contract, in which there was a substantial investment element, on the life of the employee. The employer provided funds to pay part of the annual premiums to the extent of the increase in the cash surrender value each year, and the employee paid the balance of the annual premiums. In Rev. Rul. 64-328, the employer was entitled to receive, out of the proceeds of the policy, an amount equal to the cash surrender value, or at least a sufficient part thereof to equal the funds it provided for premium payments.

[13] Two systems are discussed in Rev. Rul. 64-328 that were used to secure the repayment of the premiums paid by the employer, the "endorsement system" and the "collateral assignment system." In the endorsement system the employer owns the policy and was responsible for the payment of the annual premiums. The employee was then required to reimburse the employer for the employee's share of the premiums. Under the collateral assignment system, the employee in form owns the policy and pays the entire premium thereon. The employer in form made annual loans, without interest (or below the fair rate of interest), to the employee of amounts equal to the yearly increases in the cash surrender value, but not exceeding the annual premiums. The employee then executed an assignment of the policy to the employer as collateral security for the loans. The loans were generally payable at the termination of employment or the death of the employee.

[14] Under the described split-dollar arrangements, Rev. Rul. 64-328 noted that the practical effect was that, although the employee pays a substantial part of the first premium, after the first year the employee's share of the premium decreases rapidly, and in some cases it even becomes zero after a relatively few years. (In the table set out in the Rev. Rul., at page 14, the employee is not required to make further premiums after three years.) Thus, the Rev. Rul. concludes that the amount to be included in income each year that a split-dollar arrangement is in effect is the annual value of the benefit received by the employee under the arrangement, which is an amount equal to the one-year term cost of the declining life insurance protection to which the employee is entitled from year to year, less the portion, if any, provided by the employee.

[15] In amplifying Rev. Rul 64-328, Rev. Rul. 66-110 concludes that any benefit received from a split-dollar arrangement in addition to the current insurance protection discussed in Rev. Rul. 64-328 is also includable in the employee's gross income. According to Rev. Rul. 66-110, that additional benefit may be a policyholder dividend distributed directly to the employee or it may be paid in the form of additional one-year term insurance, or paid-up life insurance for a period of more than one year.

[16] The collateral assignment split dollar arrangement in this case is different than the one discussed under Rev. Rul. 64-328. Rather than paying annual premiums on the policy, Subsidiary supplied a single premium to the insurance companies large enough so that the earnings would cover the annual premiums attributable to the death protection portion of the policies. However, because the cash value in the policies remained subject to the Subsidiary's general creditors, the conclusion in Rev. Rul. 64-328 should apply because Taxpayer is in the same position as the employee in the revenue ruling after the employer has paid the premiums on the policy for a period of three years. In the revenue ruling, after three years, the earnings on the built up cash surrender value of the policy equaled or exceeded the premium due from the employee. Therefore, the employer was obligated to pay the entire premium with no payment due from the employee. Here, the only factual difference is that Subsidiary attained the fully paid up status by making one premium payment on each policy so that thereafter neither Taxpayer nor Subsidiary was required to make further payments on the policies. We find that difference to be insignificant.

[17] Accordingly, the holdings in Rev. Rul. 64-328 and Rev. Rul 66-110, are applicable to the facts in this case.

[18] The provisions of sections 61 and 83 of the Code do not alter the application of the holdings of the above-cited revenue rulings. (Section 83 was enacted after the Rev. Ruls. were published.) Under section 61 of the Code and section 1.83-1(a)(2) of the regulations, the insurance protection provided to Taxpayer is includable in Taxpayer's gross income. The cash surrender values in the policies are not taxable to Taxpayer under section 83 because they remained subject to the claims of Subsidiary's general creditors and to the claims of Subsidiary as a creditor. Thus they were not "property" "transferred" to an employee. The only income therefore reportable by Taxpayer in the years at issue is the value each year of the

cost-free life insurance protection under section 61. Income will be reportable in later years under section 83 to the extent that the cash surrender values of the policies exceed the premiums paid by Subsidiary because this is the amount that is returnable to Subsidiary.

[19] Having determined that Taxpayer in years at issue received income attributable to cost-free life insurance, the question remains as to its value. Rev. Rul. 64-328 also provides that the table contained in Rev. Rul 55-747, 1955-2 C.B. 228, may be used to compute the one-year term cost per $1,000 of the insurance protection. However, Rev. Rul. 66-110, amplified by Rev. Rul. 67-154, 1967-1 C.B. 11, provides that, in any case where the current published premium rates per $1,000 of insurance protection charged by the same insurer for individual one-year term life insurance available to all standard risks are lower than those set forth in Rev. Rul. 55-747, the lower rates may be used.

[20] Rev. Rul. 67-154 provides that in referring to rates that may be substituted for those in Rev. Rul. 55-747, Rev. Rul. 66-110 contemplates gross premium rates charged by an insurer for initial issue insurance, available to all standard risks. Rev. Rul. 67-154 further provides that dividend option rates are not available to all standard risks since an individual seeking to purchase only a basic policy of term insurance could not obtain it at those rates.

[21] The question of whether Taxpayer has included the proper amount in income under the split-dollar arrangement in this case depends upon whether Taxpayer has used rates that are, in fact, published gross premium rates charged by an insurer for initial issue insurance, current for the years at issue and available to all standard risks. This question is a question of fact to be resolved by the District Director, while keeping in mind these factors:

(1) The rates used must be those of the same insurer and not those of a parent corporation or brother/sister corporation in the same related group of corporations.

(2) The rates used must be for one-year term insurance available for all standard risks. The requirements of Rev. Rul. 66-110 will not be met unless an individual seeking to purchase only a basic policy of initial issue term insurance could obtain it at those rates.

[22] Accordingly, the rates used by Taxpayer may not be applicable to only nonsmokers, they may not be applicable only to policies in excess of a certain dollar amount, they may not be dividend option rates, and they may not be applicable to, for example, only five-year term insurance.

LAW AND ANALYSIS — Issue 2

[23] Rev. Rul. 78-420 further amplified Rev. Rul. 64-328 to conclude, in situation 2, that, when the split dollar arrangement calls for the employee's wife to be the owner of the policy, to select the beneficiary, and to pay a portion of the annual premiums, the employee receives income equal to the value of the insurance protection discussed in Rev. Rul. 64-328. Also, Rev. Rul. 78-420 concludes that the value of the life insurance protection provided by the employer which is included in the income of the taxpayer is deemed to be transferred by the employee to the wife for purposes of section 2511 of the Code, and is subject to the gift tax imposed by section 2501.

[24] Accordingly, in this case, Taxpayer is considered to have made a gift to Trust each year equal to the amount included in his income each year under the split-dollar arrangements with Subsidiary.

[25] CONCLUSIONS

(1) Under the split-dollar arrangements described above, under sections 61 and 83 of the Code, Taxpayer must include in income each year that the arrangement is in force (a) an amount equal to the one- year term cost of declining life insurance and (b) any cash surrender buildup in the policies that exceeds the amount that is returnable to Subsidiary when the arrangement is discontinued. The issue of whether Taxpayer included the proper amount in income each year is a factual question that may be resolved by the District Director in accordance with the guidelines set out above.

(2) Taxpayer has made a gift to Trust for purposes of section 2511 of the Code each year equal to the amount included in his income each year under the split-dollar arrangements wish Subsidiary. This amount is subject to the gift tax under section 2501.

INDEX

Need Additional Copies?

Use this handy postage-paid form to order additional copies of *Working with S Corporations* or its companion publication, *Working with LLCs.* You can also call **1-800-543-0874** and ask for **Operator TM** or **FAX** this form to **1-800-874-1916**.

Single copy $29.95	25 copies, ea. 23.50	250 copies, ea. 21.50
5 copies, ea 26.95	50 copies, ea. 22.95	500 copies, ea. 20.00
10 copies, ea 24.95	100 copies, ea. 22.50	1,000 copies, ea. 19.00

PACKAGE PRICE - both books $49.90 (Save $10.00!)

PAYMENT INFORMATION

*Add shipping & handling charges to all orders as indicated. If your order exceeds total amount listed in chart, call 1-800-543-0874 for shipping & handling charge. Any order of 10 or more or over $250.00 will be billed for shipping by actual weight, plus a handling fee. Unconditional 30 day guarantee.

SHIPPING & HANDLING (Additional)

Order Total	Shipping &Handling
$20.00 -$39.99	$6.00
40.00 - 59.99	7.00
60.00 - 79.99	9.00
80.00 - 109.99	10.00
110.00 - 149.99	12.00
150.00 - 199.99	13.00
200.00 - 249.99	15.50

SALES TAX (Additional)

Sales tax is required for residents of the following states: CA, DC, FL, GA, IL, NJ, NY, OH, PA.

The National Underwriter Co.
Customer Service Dept #2-TM
505 Gest Street
Cincinnati, OH 45203-1716

2-TM

Please send me _____ copies of *Working with S Corporations,* 2nd Edition (#147)

_____ copies of *Working with LLCs* (#241)

❏ Check enclosed*   ❏ Charge my VISA/MC/AmEx (circle one)   ❏ Bill me

Card #_____ *Exp. Date*_____

*Signature*_____

*Name*_____ *Title*_____

*Company*_____

*Street Address*_____

*City*_____ *State* _____ *Zip+4*_____

Business Phone (_____)_____

Make check payable to The National Underwriter Company. Please include the appropriate shipping & handling charges and any applicable sales tax.

Offer expires 12/31/97

2-TM

The National Underwriter Co.
505 Gest Street
Cincinnati, OH 45203-1716

PROOF OF PURCHASE FOR CONTINUING EDUCATION

Working with S Corporations: A Practioner's Guide To Estate,
Business and Compensation Planning for S Corporations
by Dennis C. Reardon, J.D., LL.M, CLU, ChFC
©1996, The National Underwriter Company

YOU MUST RETURN THIS PROOF OF PURCHASE WITH YOUR COMPLETED EXAM.

BUSINESS REPLY MAIL

FIRST CLASS MAIL   PERMIT NO. 68   CINCINNATI, OH

POSTAGE WILL BE PAID BY ADDRESSEE

The National Underwriter Co.
Customer Service Dept. #2-TM
505 Gest Street
Cincinnati, OH 45203-9928